# Wartime Fashion

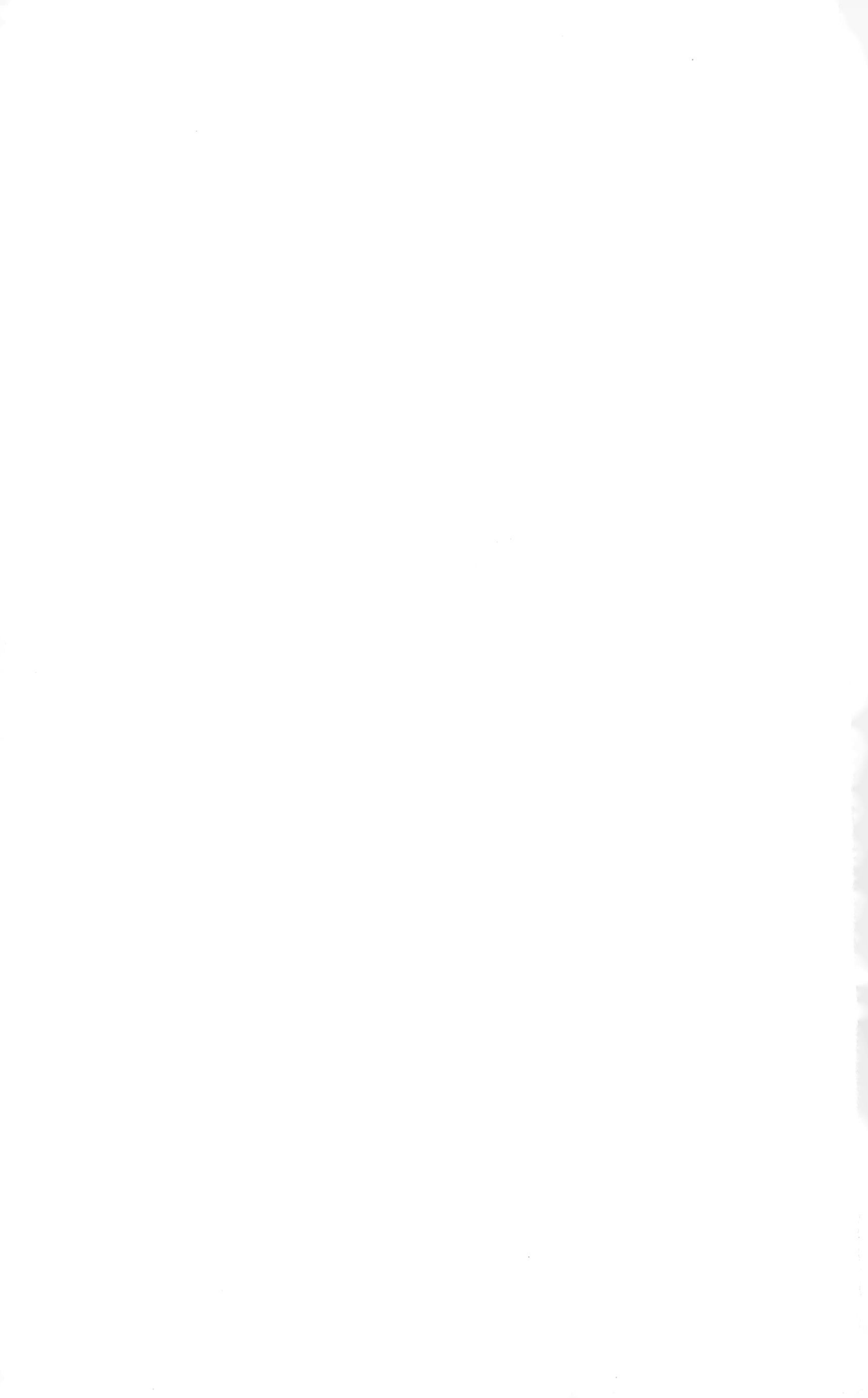

# Wartime Fashion

## From Haute Couture to Homemade, 1939–1945

Geraldine Howell

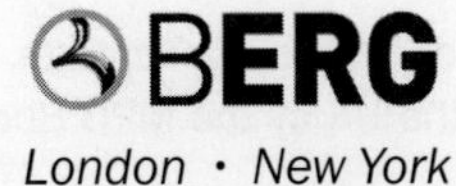

London • New York

English edition
First published in 2012 by
**Berg**
Editorial offices:
50 Bedford Square, London WC1B 3DP, UK
175 Fifth Avenue, New York, NY 10010, USA



Berg is an imprint of Bloomsbury Publishing Plc.

**Library of Congress Cataloging-in-Publication Data**

Howell, Geraldine.
Wartime fashion : from haute couture to homemade,
1939-1945 / Geraldine Howell.
p. cm.
Includes bibliographical references and index.
ISBN 978-0-85785-070-6 (alk. paper) — ISBN 978-0-85785-071-3 (alk. paper) —
ISBN 978-0-85785-429-2 (alk. paper) — ISBN 978-0-85785-428-5 (alk. paper)
1. Clothing and dress—Great Britain—History—20th century. 2. Women's
clothing—Great Britain—History—20th century. 3. Fashion—Great Britain—
History–20th century. 4. Fashion design—Great Britain—History—20th
century. 5. World War, 1939-1945—Great Britain. 6. Great Britain—
History—George VI, 1936-1952. 7. Great Britain—Social life and
customs—20th century. I. Title.
GT738.H69 2012
391'209410904—dc23 2012027467

**British Library Cataloguing-in-Publication Data**

A catalogue record for this book is available from the British Library.

ISBN 978 0 85785 070 6 (Cloth)
978 0 85785 071 3 (Paper)
e-ISBN 978 0 85785 429 2 (epub)
978 0 85785 428 5 (ePDF)

Typeset by Apex CoVantage, LLC.
Printed in the UK by the MPG Books Group

**www.bergpublishers.com**

# Contents

# List of Illustrations

# Acknowledgements

I would like to begin by thanking Madeleine Ginsburg for her early interest in and ideas about writing on the dress history of the Second World War, which helped me to see my way ahead. PhD study took place in the History of Art and Architecture Department at the University of Reading under the rigorous supervision of Dr. Sue Malvern. Her careful guidance and tireless tracking of my work will always be hugely appreciated. She continued to offer support during the transition period from doctorate to book, and her understanding and thoughtfulness have been significant. I would also like to thank Professor Lou Taylor, whose meticulous review of both doctoral submission and subsequent book manuscript has been critically valuable in shaping the final versions of both. Her encouragement is deeply appreciated not least in helping me achieve the greater courage of my convictions. Grateful thanks also to Amy de la Haye for her work reviewing the final manuscript.

In terms of the help received and interest shown in the project by staff at various institutions, I would like to extend my warmest appreciation to: Daniel Milford-Cottam at the Victoria and Albert Museum, who facilitated my work with the Utility Prototype Collection with such enthusiasm and energy; to Sheila Shreeve MBE, Claire Dolman and Catherine Clarke at the Walsall Museum, who gave unstintingly of their time and resources while I worked with both the Hodson Shop Collection and the Museum's complimentary dress and paper archives; and to Kate Loubser of the Worthing Museum for making available her range of Utility and Second World War clothing and for her help and engagement with the study. Thanks must also be extended to all those individuals unknown to me who facilitated my use of archive material at the Imperial War Museum, the Public Records Office, the National Newspaper Library, the British Library and the Mass Observation Archive, University of Sussex.

Finally, I wish to thank Kathryn Earle for her enthusiasm from the beginning; Anna Wright for her advice, experience and lively, enthusiastic communications with me; and Emily Ardizzone, Sophie Hodgson, Laura Larsen and Emily Johnston for all their help in bringing the book to completion. A good team.

# Introduction

The following work provides a comprehensive analysis of Second World War dress practice and appearance in context. It places dress at the forefront of a complex series of cultural chain reactions and uses new archival and primary source evidence to clarify how clothing was made and acquired across the class spectrum both immediately before and during the war, how and why clothing was rationed and the nature of the design philosophies that came to underpin wartime clothing and dress practice. A particular story emerges that reveals the social and economic significance of dress and the development of a clothing strategy that facilitated ways of creating social cohesion and consensus in a time of national crisis. Changing attitudes to dress reflected the changing framework of political and social life in wartime Britain. As different patterns of consumerism developed, so notions of fashion and the fashionable evolved in line with the stringencies of wartime living and design and manufacture reoriented towards the provision of quality clothing at an appropriate price for all. These changes were seen as being integral to the spirit of national unity fostered by the government and pivotal to the sustaining of patriotism and public morale.

From knitting comforts[1] to operating clothing exchanges, applying new grooming routines to putting on service uniform, the need to sustain the essentials of dress and appearance was a part of war intimately understood by all. The purpose and value of clothing as indicators of the quality and type of life experienced across the different sectors of society became increasingly appreciated by government, industry and the public in the context of the greater fairness and democracy demanded by a state of war. The way in which the clothing needs of the entire nation could be met, both through rationing and mechanisms of self-help, required a rethinking of dress philosophy for many and offered a change in terms of comfort and quality for more than a few. Traditional attitudes towards related practices of hygiene, grooming and personal appearance also underwent something of a transformation within some sectors of society, and this, together with changing approaches to the wearing and care of clothing, helped promote and apply new standards for dress and personal presentation.

The need for quality materials and appropriate design became central to clothing policy. Altered approaches to fabric production and the cut, make and finish of garments resulted from a judicious change of emphasis regarding processes of manufacture and design to create quality clothing in sufficient quantity for all. Keynote styles such as the tailored British suit endorsed a sense of national identity and heritage whilst the well-cut and durable clothing required by the government contrived to maintain standards of dress despite the deprivations of wartime living.

While controlling the capacity to buy clothing through a comprehensive system of clothes rationing created unprecedented levels of intervention into the private lives of the public, so also controlling textile and garment production constructed a unique set of economic conditions under which the textile and clothing industries now had to operate. In consequence, the limited supplies and styles of civilian dress brought about a new emphasis on home craft skills and making-do in the name of patriotic thrift. Restricted choice and the need for practical, easy-care clothing encouraged the use of alternative types of dress, particularly for working clothes either in or beyond the home. As ever more women sought paid employment, the clothing and elements of personal appearance associated with the workplace became visual indicators of the evolving roles and responsibilities of women in society and their often more complicated and less predictable lifestyles. The new dress protocols reflected the gendered shifts in attitude by, and about, women, attitudes also seen to be emerging out of the new paradigms for fitness and health that significantly renegotiated existing prejudice against women in terms of their mental and physical capacities.

Wartime fabric and garment manufacture both built on pre-war models of production that had already been established by mass-production retailers on the pre-war high street. A tiered production of Utility cloth and clothing became the central element of the government's strategy for providing fit-for-purpose clothing across the price spectrum, and the Utility programme promoted quality control and the value for money consumers demanded in the context of their severely reduced purchasing power. The introduction of austerity restrictions on the design and construction of all garments manufactured from spring 1942 was the last phase of the government's policy for the economic enhancement and greater efficiency of the clothing industry and resulted in all the variations on chic simplicity that became the signature style for the rest of the war years. Ostentatious or opulent dressing continued to be inappropriate in the context of both the spare lines of wartime dress and the prevalence of the uniformed woman, but the social advantage it had represented in the past remained, if less visible, revealed through the fashion rhetoric and attitudes towards dress of the upper classes. Thus any apparent democratization of dress was always to some extent disingenuous despite the clear improvements experienced in the quality of clothing provision for the poorest sectors of society.

A dress history of this period, therefore, covers a good deal of ground in relation to both the material culture of the textiles and clothing produced and the broader elements of cultural change in Britain which they in turn reveal. Through the detailed narratives of dress and personal appearance, a highly visual story emerges of the relationship between classes, changing perspectives on femininity and altered priorities for living exemplified by thrift and making-do. Many different types of sources from examples of high street Utility wear to the government papers that brought them into being here combine to construct a vivid and comprehensive picture of the place and importance of clothing for women at war. Critical engagement with the dress practice of the period reveals something of the quality of the different lives experienced by ordinary women across the class spectrum and thereby provides a specific dress history discourse that cooperates with and extends received historical understanding of the period.

## READERS' NOTE

Throughout the text, the terms *fashion history* and *dress history* have been applied with care. Popular clothing of often limited longevity, created by a range of both predictable and less predictable cultural forces, is regarded as fashion and gives rise to the fashionable. Dress encompasses a much-wider remit and includes all the clothing worn at a particular time. Fashion is part of dress history while dress history is not necessarily part of fashion. Fashion describes the types of clothing bought by those with some level of expendable income who can afford elements of decorative clothing worn out of choice and for pleasure. Dress refers to all clothing but specifically includes those garments worn both out of necessity, often as a consequence of limited income, and/or practicality.

–1–

# Buying into Fashion: The Social Background

During the 1930s, the desire to possess beautiful clothes had, arguably, never been stronger for two reasons. The first was the expanding variety of retail outlets now providing greater choice in fashionable clothing and the second the arrival on the high street of cheaper clothing ranges catering for more modest incomes. The rich continued to patronize the couture or high-end dressmakers and along with the wealthier middle classes chose quality ready-made[1] clothes from the more exclusive department stores or independent women's fashion shops. Chain stores like Marks and Spencer and variety multiple shops such as Dorothy Perkins created ready-made fashion lines for the budget shopper and flourished on the high street by providing mass-produced versions of Paris fashions or cinema screen styles. For the very poor, the shopping experience was limited to clothing clubs or second-hand options, both of which could prove uneconomical and exploitative. There existed, therefore, a wide disparity between the richest and poorest in terms of clothing, a fact that was rendered less visible than it might otherwise have been by the growing consumerism on the high street. This chapter considers in brief, therefore, those class divisions endemic to 1930s society which created the parameters for commercial production of clothing at whatever level. It introduces some of the key lifestyle indicators that helped construct class identities at that time and which would be affected to a greater or lesser extent by the onset of war. A key concept here is the capacity to spend and to reflect class culture through dress and adornment practices.

The rich set the pace, establishing a dress practice and a way of life that the cinemas and popular magazines of the day promoted, and in this way those lower down the social scale participated, vicariously, in what was to many an otherwise closed world. Dress clearly bespoke class and was a powerful reflection of status. At the same time, ready-made dress increasingly began to operate as a mechanism that might to some degree facilitate the emulation of the upper classes by the lower.

The still-buoyant and influential lifestyle of the rich continued to be responsible for upholding many traditional attitudes to life that had become indelibly associated with being British. The country house milieu with its various sporting pursuits, the London season and presentations at court, Henley,

Ascot or the Varsity balls, all espoused a way of life essentially wealthy but also quintessentially British, and one central to the establishment not merely of fashion but of what could be construed as the fashionable. This lifestyle revealed itself through dress protocols that, while no longer embracing the five or six changes of outfit a day as in Edwardian times, still retained a rigorous devotion to the art of dressing correctly for every occasion. The minutia of this day-to-day application of an often-unwritten code of dress practice unobtrusively maintained class divisions and social hierarchies, even as it underpinned the notion of nationality, heritage and, to an extent, patriotism.

In Britain during the 1930s, the Prince of Wales and his set represented the most exclusive tier of society. Piers Brendon suggests that Edward had 'spent his whole life in the hectic pursuit of pleasure' and that 'his private universe . . . consisted of smart nightspots, louch weekends, high jinks, horseplay, jazz and jigsaw puzzles. It was embellished with gold lighters and jewelled cigarette cases, Art Deco cuff-links and Faberge boxes. Edward sympathised with the poor but associated with the rich.'[2] Images of opulence and wealth were also highly visible during the 'esoteric social ritual known as the Season'. Described as the 'few brief summer weeks when all Society threw itself into a frenzy of carefully organized gaiety',[3] this part of the fashionable year for the wealthy upper classes focused on the debutantes—young seventeen- and eighteen-year-old girls—being presented at court for the first time in a social rite of passage that signified a coming of age and entry into adulthood. It also very much established readiness for the social networking leading to a suitable marriage, an institution still desired by most women.[4] During the Season, the calendar of entertainments organized to follow court presentation brought out lavish displays of wealth through extravagant dress practice, encompassing adornment at the highest level short of state occasions.[5] As De Courcy expressed it, 'snobbery was not so much a common fault as a wholesale acceptance of the idea that society was divided into classes, which might meet, mingle, respect, like and even love each other, but never blend.'[6] Norman Hartnell, describing the early 1930s, affirmed that 'everything revolved around the Courts in summer'. Historical continuity was maintained through the 'presiding deities' of these events, who were the 'dowagers' with 'vivid memories of how things were done in the opulent, colourful reign of Edward the Seventh, but tinged with memories of the dignity and manners associated with his august mother'.[7] The power of the past—in terms of the established traditions of fashionable display, its purposes and protocols—is clear.

The wealthy elite's strict cognizance of wardrobe etiquette and interest in and attention to the fine details of personal appearance promoted a rhetoric of fashion connoisseurship that accompanied the images of clothing and accessories in the glossy magazines. Examples of this type of language describing the exclusive products of the couture and high-end designer houses are readily found in British *Vogue*. In spring 1934, Elsa Schiaparelli designed a short-waisted jacket with small peplum in a highly ruched black taffeta to be worn over a directoire-style dress in 'treebark crepe' with accessorizing 'cellophane scarf'.[8] This description connotes a number of things. The reader had to be familiar with historic lines of dress—in this case the directoire line, long skirted and with a high waist, low décolleté and often puffed sleeves—and have an in-depth knowledge of quality fabrics, here some of the newest fabrics on the market. While most people would probably have heard of taffeta, even if they had never owned anything in it, the concepts of tree bark crepe[9] and cellophane[10] might well have been novel. In similar vein, in 1936 *Vogue* carried an image of another Schiaparelli ensemble created in black bengaline with 'gold and coloured paillettes which arabesque down the front of its short fitted jacket, and black, glycerised ostrich feathers on the Mongolian tribesman's hat'.[11] Bengaline, a light fabric of silk and cotton or silk and wool, inferred some association with Indian silk from Bengal, which in turn could carry overtones of Empire, while the use of African ostrich feathers[12] maintained an air of the exotic and distant. To what extent even the moneyed shopper would have known the precise features of dress of the Mongolian tribesman, history does not relate. In all, the outfit, in rather exaggerated form, alluded to India, Africa and central Asia. Such could be the hyperbole of fashion.

Readers of *Vogue* also included the wealthier members of the middle and upper middle classes, who in their own way, and with some subtlety, played out imitations of the still-fashionable and traditional country house parties and seasonal events adhered to by the wealthy and royal sets. The domestic and perhaps more provincial ideal here can be seen in contrast to the relatively distant, if fascinating, world of the titled and really rich whose way of life was essentially cosmopolitan. Through seasonal travel to the stylish resorts of Europe and farther afield, fashion for the wealthy became more of a global phenomenon, wherein the secret of success lay in the perfect synthesis of the international and, specifically, French, with a certain bespoke Britishness. But for those tethered by working commitments, however professional, to a less leisured way of living, fashion reflected a more consistently British lifestyle, recognizable by and nearer to those lower down the social hierarchy. Here, also, the imagery was attractive and desirable, creating possibilities for emulation by those less well off. The social seasons of the rich and cultured were just as capable of being played out, if less grandly, among the wealthier middle classes from professional, well-educated backgrounds. Economic success predetermined a specific way of life that included a range of sophisticated social and sporting events also requiring knowledge of the dress codes and protocols associated with them.

This lifestyle is well illustrated in Jan Struther's book of short tales entitled *Mrs Miniver*,[13] published in late 1939. The fictional character of Caroline

Miniver represented an upper-middle-class woman[14] whose exploits were designed to 'brighten up the Court Pages of The Times' with stories about 'an ordinary sort of woman who leads an ordinary sort of life'.[15] Struther's readership still comprised the more affluent classes, but the stories were instructive paradigms for codes and patterns of behaviour that identified what it was to be 'ordinary' middle class as opposed to wealthy at that time. The everyday life, cares and concerns of this wife and mother established the priorities as well as the privileges of this lifestyle, indirectly revealing the good taste and style of what E. M. Forster had called the 'top drawer but one'.[16]

The short, meditative stories spanned a period of just over a year from October 1938 to December 1939, placing the tensions of approaching hostilities alongside the changing seasons and seasonal interests of Mrs. Miniver and her family. The titles are a good indication of the social preoccupations of this class and range from 'The New Car' and 'The Eve of the Shoot' through 'The New Engagement Book' and 'In Search of a Charwoman' to 'The Twelfth of August' and 'The Autumn Flit'. Each skilfully delineated particular events that represented a status and class, sustained through particular patterns of consumption and leisure. The stories did not directly set out to highlight issues of fashion. Rather, they revealed benchmarks for a middle-class way of life with its own daily and seasonal rituals such as the correct moment to store summer clothes, the uplifting qualities of fresh-cut flowers, the right type of stationery or the morale-boosting effects of a new dressing gown. Near enough to the lower middle classes to be recognized as representing a secure set of lifestyle values that were often considered attractive if not always possible to emulate, and at the margins of the class above from whom the way of life had originally been derived, what emerges from Struther's work is a sense of a privileged middle-class identity as it was understood from within its own ranks at the time.

The issue of class was, and remains, complex. Stevenson describes it as 'an elusive concept' where 'the boundaries . . . are at best blurred and usually quite difficult to establish definitively'.[17] Any reading of class and the social culture it reflected tended to rely to some degree on 'clothes and speech . . . the obvious badges . . . difficult to gauge accurately at the margins, but clear enough for the great majority of people to be able to assign themselves to "upper", "middle" or "working" class'.[18] Where the middle middle classes ended and the lower middle classes began was therefore not always easy to determine. Certainly the new homeowners who flocked to purchase modest semi-detached housing on the new suburban developments of the 1930s were less well off than their more affluent middle-class counterparts. Yet the choice to move from renting to buying reflected the rise in wages through the decade that facilitated the repayment of mortgages, especially in tandem with tax relief incentives.[19] While there is some evidence to suggest that the new purchasers often lived rather straightened lives—Wilson and Taylor refer to women 'struggling to create a genteel lifestyle'[20]—for those who chose not to spend the additional money in this way, life did become financially more secure. The high street was the beneficiary and responded by producing a much larger range of middle- and lower-priced goods commensurate with the pockets of this more secure upper-working-class and lower-middle-class tier of consumers. The following chapter on the development and rise of volume production clothing will look in more detail at the way in which the needs of these lower-income groups were addressed by particular types of shops and stores and with what success.

With the advent of evacuation in September 1939, the government and public at large would be forced to confront a quite different element of class consciousness and a level of social inequality that had received no constructive acknowledgement for too long. While the wage-earning working class and lower middle classes had a limited degree of economic stability,[21] and might now have access to the better lifestyle represented by cheaper mass-produced goods on the high street, for those on the lowest tier of the social ladder, a world away from the well-appointed lives of the middle and upper classes and without any financial security, life was hard indeed. Lack of decent housing, food and clothing—whether through long-term unemployment, oversized families or sickness—would become, in the early months of war, cause for serious political concern. John Hilton, in his series of Sir Halley Stewart lectures given in 1938, had guessed the existence of four million people 'either just square with nothing in hand or . . . in debt for a larger or smaller amount'[22] and had surveyed three hundred families 'in poverty and distress' who had sought help from charitable organizations and who 'at any given time do not know how to make ends meet and who are, for long spells or for the time being, on the brink or in the abyss of under-nourishment and penury and debt'.[23] While a level of public social assistance was in place, Hilton had called into question whether it was adequate,[24] and he was clearly vindicated in this concern as those teetering on destitution became evident in the first major wave of evacuation during the autumn. A lack of suitable clothing, in particular, began to signal an entrenched level of economic disadvantage that spoke volumes for the type of life experienced in the poorest homes. This level of want and neglect could not be allowed to continue in the face of war. Need must be prioritized over want[25] and better mechanisms put in place to support those wholly untouched by the growing commercial prosperity experienced by other sectors of the working class. As an understanding of demarcation within class thus became clearer, it was essential to ameliorate the greatest gulfs between people if national unity in war was to be achieved. While supplying financial and gift aid was the first line of support and one which continued throughout the war, there was a clear requirement to know more about how people survived at this level of need and how they could be best supported. Gradual reduction in unemployment as the war industries gathered momentum would be key to creating better standards of living while, with regard to clothing, one component of the cost-of-living index—providing better quality textiles and clothing at the lowest price points—became an essential longer-term step necessary for underpinning the fair shares ideology of clothes rationing. While this would clearly benefit the population as a whole, it would prove of especial value to those struggling against exploitation and poor quality at the most needy end of the market. Thus the prospect of shopping for durable fit-for-purpose clothing, which had been a virtual impossibility for the poorest families prior to war, would become increasingly manageable.[26]

This sector of the population would be the only one to have their capacity to buy *improved* rather than curtailed. For most other consumers, wartime economies in textile and clothing manufacture would play a significant part in reorientating lifestyle *away* from the spend culture that had resulted from the growing prosperity of the pre-war years. This had the effect of curbing the more obvious signs of class division reflected in capacity to buy. Exactly how the needs of the poorest were addressed will be returned to in greater detail in Chapter 5, which assesses the social impact of evacuation.

The way in which clothes were made and purchased was about to undergo, therefore, notable changes during the war years, and certainly the consumer trends of the 1930s would, for most, be reversed. During the years immediately before the war, the high street continued to offer an increasing variety of fashion options, from couture to chain store, and it is to these different components of the high street and their clientele that we now turn to investigate how pockets were matched to products to provide fashion for almost all.

–2–

# Shopping for Fashion in the Pre-War Years

Much has been written about the glamorous dress choices available to the wealthy during the 1930s. Examples of clothes representing the more opulent end of the market are easy to find in the glossy magazines of the time and in museums featuring dress, where they are considered collectable in much the same way as other works of art of the period. Less is generally written about the fashions produced for more limited incomes, and examples of these clothes are also far less evident in public collections. Yet during the 1930s, the British high street was offering a much broader range of fashion clothing for middle-, lower-middle- and working-class buyers, providing choice and variety at more modest prices. The main focus of this chapter, therefore, is less on how and where the rich and privileged acquired their clothes and more on the types of clothing now available for less affluent consumers, the shops where these could be bought and the prices paid. In this way, a more accurate picture of the shopping experiences of consumers across the class spectrum can be achieved.

Any review of the clothing industry in Britain during the 1930s has to begin, however, by acknowledging the continuing currency and vibrancy of Parisian couture, which designed clothes and accessories for the wealthiest sector of society dressing for the seasonal and royal events to which they had privileged access. Taylor and Wilson state that Norman Hartnell was charging 'approximately 45 guineas' for dresses in 1939, which gives some idea of the prices couture clothing could command.[1] Given that the repayments on a spacious semi-detached house could come to about twenty-five pounds a year, as revealed by an advertisement for housing in the Barnhurst Park Estate in 1933 where homes were being offered for £395 freehold in weekly payments of 9 shillings (s) 6 pence (d),[2] the relative spending capacity of different elements of the population can be gauged. It is also instructive to compare the prices of these dresses with those from other sectors of the fashion industry quoted later in this chapter. London couture houses also sought to provide classic country clothes redolent of a particularly British way of life that recognized the importance of signature traditional British fabrics. Immediately before the war, the 'good tweed suit' was popular 'for both sexes'[3] and would remain a staple of the British woman's wardrobe throughout the war years. By

1943, Digby Morton was quoting at least twenty-five pounds for this type of suit made bespoke so that at the couture end, prices remained high as well as being subject to purchase tax.[4] While these tailored clothes in quality wools maintained a distinctly British sense of style, in general at this time fashion-orientated clothing was presumed to emerge, in however diluted a form, from the trends inspired by the Parisian designers who revealed their new silhouettes in twice-yearly shows. Their ideas were then interpreted by retailers and manufacturers providing more affordable ready-to wear options, whether from exclusive high-end department stores or the cheaper chain stores and variety multiples. The high street endeavoured to offer Parisian style, no matter how impressionistic, reflecting the power to control and influence dress practice that Paris continued to wield throughout the 1930s.[5]

For the majority of the British public, shopping for clothing on their local high streets meant either buying fabric to make their own clothes or buying ready-made. The making of fashionable clothing without commissioning a designer or independent dressmaker had emerged during the latter half of the nineteenth century in the burgeoning department store. Selling a variety of practical and decorative domestic commodities, these stores also offered quality bespoke fashions that required staffed workrooms employing needlewomen and tailoresses. At quiet times when orders were thin, these workrooms began to design and make clothes in line with current fashions. *The Working Party Report on Light Clothing* of 1947, a report focussed exclusively on the developments in production of children and women's wear, saw this retailing move as the probable 'commencement of the trade in ready-made clothing'[6] and established the important paradigm that, as these clothes might have to remain stock items if they did not sell from the shop floor immediately, their design was to be relatively simple in make and inexpensive. As a result, whether foreseen or not, 'they began to attract custom from the less wealthy classes'.[7] Thus the problem of holding stock that might go out of fashion was addressed partly by recognizing that different sectors of society would be happy with less sophisticated interpretations of fashion lines. Here was the beginning of the acceptance of ready-made fashion garments, bought from shops of repute yet not bespoke.

In the early years of the twentieth century, however, there was still little real business in this area.[8] Middle- and upper-class homes generally had clothes made up by others, although many middle-class women, dependent on income, would still have considered some level of home sewing a prerequisite of their social role. Working-class women made all their family's clothing needs. Manufacturers trading in piece goods ordered suitable fabrics from textile firms that could then be cut into appropriate blocked shapes using modern bandsaw technology. That this was the way clothing was still largely obtained by the less affluent was confirmed by a cost-of-living index of 1904 that revealed 'working class family budgets . . . included a very small allowance for expenditure on women's under-clothing [and] nothing at all for such items as dresses, blouses and pinafores, nothing for children's wear, but a comparatively large amount for piece goods'.[9] In contrast, an index of 1937–1938 would show money spent on piece goods had been reduced by 'nearly 70 per cent [while] that for women and children's clothing had increased by nearly 1000 per cent'.[10] Clearly the industry was about to undergo a dramatic change that would account for this shift.

The triggers that caused the move from handcrafted garments to the products of industrial manufacture were largely connected in the first instance with innovations in the mechanized output of both cloth and clothing. Powered sewing machines, bandsaw cutting and industrial steam irons all contrived in the later years of the nineteenth century to offer opportunities for speedier and more plentiful provision of clothing. These developments all took place in the arena of men's wear, where the need for simple suits, trousers and jackets in limited designs, relatively unaffected by fashion, could be achieved with economy and efficiency using the new technologies.[11] Catering for a working- and lower-middle-class customer with limited means, these first forays into mechanized and increasingly factory-based production offered a cheap alternative to either hand-made or second-hand and therefore prospered.[12] At the same time as there were innovations effecting change at the cheaper and cheap end of the men's wear market, the department stores and other high street drapery retailers, particularly in London, were making their own ways into obtaining ready-made clothing direct from manufacturers. As Chapman records, 'towards the end of the century [nineteenth] the traditional piece goods trade with the drapers declined in favour of the ready-made garment trade, where the great retailers had the advantage of the wholesalers.'[13] Instead of operating via wholesalers in the purchase of cloth, stores such as Harrods and Liberty were instead placing contracts with manufacturers for specific types of quality clothing lines. In initiating a relationship direct with production, the retailer cut out the role and expense of the wholesaler acting as middleman. This provided one of several possible models of business practice for the merchandising of apparel.[14]

As men's wear developed into a growing and profitable ready-made industry, it contrived a further move into the new area of wholesale bespoke—whereby the customer was individually measured for a suit that was then factory made. At the same time, the higher end of the high street began successfully selling elements of women's and children's ready-made clothing to enhance their bespoke provision, opening up the possibility of expansion in ready-to-wear. As Wray points out, however, whereas factory production had triggered the creation of ready-made in men's wear, the same was not true of the industrial production of women's clothing of the type already providing the garments and accessories for high street drapers and department stores.[15] She states that 'much of this early development of ready-made clothing production was based on the employment of home workers, operating treadle machines and making-up garments, cut in central warehouses by wholesale clothiers, on the contract, or "sweating", system. This method of production was facilitated by the ample supply of cheap labour in the form of women working for low piece rates in their own homes on machines hired from their employers.'[16] Only when this system was rendered economically unviable via a combination of minimum wages and working hours and the demise of cheap labour sources[17] was there a 'quickened rate of changeover to factory production'.[18] The greater use of mechanization and factory output of this sector of the clothing industry did not then begin to take shape until the 1920s. By this time, the industrial output of inexpensive and low-cost men's wear was clearly reflecting the success of what Godley calls 'large scale retailers'.[19]

By a comparable stage, women's wear had moved more securely into the factory arena but would not find itself suited to long runs of similar lines—a first premise of mass output—as the market was much more fashion led. On this basis, and with a variety of different markets to fulfil arguably reflecting a broader range of the social scale than mass-produced men's wear was catering for, women's wear continued to be produced in smaller units. These could respond to the demand for fashion-distinct garments that often required greater skill at the individual operator level than did the staple products of the large men's wear organizations. Thus the two industries were established on quite different lines, and they would continue to reflect these fundamental differences until after the Second World War.[20]

This was the way the clothing industry was operating at the beginning of the 1920s. While Leeds dominated the men's wear market, employing largely unskilled female labour in increasingly large mass-production factories,[21] London, and in particular the East End, was established as the centre for the women's wear industries. Manufacturers and workshops here were conveniently placed to take advantage of the many retailing outlets across London, both price conscious and prestigious, while improved motor transport meant that frequent deliveries of smaller fashion ranges could be undertaken quickly and efficiently. The women's light clothing industry continued to operate on this basis for most of the 1920s.

While firms like Burton's, Hepworth's and the Fifty Shilling Tailor (the firm of Henry Price) created large vertical business structures producing garments from their own factories and distributing them through their own shops, the women's wear sector benefited from remaining small and diverse. Output was made more efficient with the advent of further new technologies such as attachments for lockstitch machines that enabled 'frilling, pleating and ruching' to be completed automatically,[22] and the most important element in any business's success was the strength of their network of trading links. Regular and repeat orders through the chain from manufacturer to wholesaler or distributor created some security, particularly where a manufacturer was producing ranges of less fashionable and year-round clothing such as women's underwear lines, classic clothes or children's wear.

To a limited extent, this type of production offset the serious problem that confronted the light clothing women's wear sector, one not applicable to men's wear, which was the seasonal nature of fashion clothing. Autumn and winter orders began to be placed by retailers in May and spring and summer orders in October. These orders were never especially large as neither wholesalers nor retailers wanted to hold on to potentially unsaleable stock. Fashion buyers needed to maintain a shop floor that reflected the latest fashion stories through a variety of garments that were regularly updated. This clearly mitigated against long production runs of similar garments across the seasons, which would have contributed greater security to the industry as a whole. Instead, once the initial lines had been ordered, firms hoped for repeat business and were flexible enough to create variations on styles current for the season. They were likely to experience capacity working periods at the onset of the season but a downturn as the season tailed off. This often resulted in periods of both 'short time working and unemployment'.[23]

The position of women's ready-made factory clothing further consolidated during the 1930s, as we shall see below. The problem of short- or part-time working remained, however, particularly for those firms reliant on smaller fashion orders. Speculative production, often by new producers tempted into the industry at times of seasonal glut, could result in unsold stock and slump, which tended to be offset by fierce price cutting. This in turn led to poorer quality production—in terms of both material and making standards—that did nothing to enhance the reputation of the industry and was further responsible for allowing cheap but very poor quality lines of clothing to filter through to the public marketplace.[24] This was one explanation for some of the poorest quality merchandise available. As Wray points out, 'Shoddy production was particularly prevalent in dressmaking (although it was also found in tailored garments) and the desire to remedy this unsatisfactory state of affairs probably accounts for the very willing co-operation of the light clothing industry with the Board of Trade in connection with the improvement in making and sizing standards for light clothing which resulted from war-time Making of Civilian Clothing (Restrictions) Orders.'[25]

A brief resume of current business practice during the 1920s reveals that there were three common operational models for women's wear production. Small manufactures producing ranges for wholesale to store and sell on were the smallest of the types as wholesalers could not risk stock falling out of style during the process of storage and marketing. By far the more popular method of business was the second practice of individual manufacturers selling direct to distributors. There were two approaches here; either the manufacturers' travellers initiated business links with various high street drapers or stores or the retailers themselves placed orders with manufacturers for specific commodities. All the main high street providers of apparel, from exclusive department stores down to small independent drapers, could operate in this way, and goods were made for all price points. Wray suggests that 'by the 1930s the bulk of the output of fashion outerwear was being distributed direct from manufacturer to retailer'.[26] This model was the most successful despite remaining the victim of seasonal slump unless orders became either regular, sizeable or preferably both. While the gradual demise of home working and smaller sweated outworking units had shifted garment production into the manufacturing factory space, in general the size of these businesses remained small for the reasons we have seen. Factory production was clearly not synonymous with mass production, and by 1939, this was still largely the case. By this time, 86 per cent of the clothing industry as a whole operated in units of up to one hundred people with only the remaining 14 per cent employing over one hundred and only 6 per cent over two hundred.[27]

The last figure is representative of the third model of business practice, which only began during the 1920s but became increasingly important into the 1930s. This was the expansion of large-scale factory production in men's wear *into* women's wear and the development of larger production units from already existing smaller factories. From the outset, there was no necessary correlation between poor or poorer quality and larger-scale production. Longer runs simply favoured less fashion-focussed lines that did not date as quickly, and the choice of cheaper fabrics reflected the developing market for lower-priced clothing that would sell in larger numbers more quickly.[28] John Barran, an established manufacturer of mass-produced men's wear, spurred on by a post-First World War slump, began to use his mass-manufacturing techniques for women's wear in 1927 as other smaller factory units began to extend in the same direction. Across the two decades, a number of household names came into being as named brands emerging from this type of manufacturing; Marlbeck of Leeds and the Co-Operative Wholesale Society in Manchester opened new factories during the 1920s followed by Tootals producing Chesro dresses from Bolton in 1930, Berketex with tailored dresses from London in 1937 and Harella and Windsmoor with their women's wear factories in London during 1939.[29] The tailored suits and smarter lines of dress that 1930s factory production began to provide created increasingly better-quality garments that sold to middle- and upper-middle-class customers, and a good reputation was established particularly for the country-style tweeds and classic clothes that emphasized a distinctively British design signature.[30]

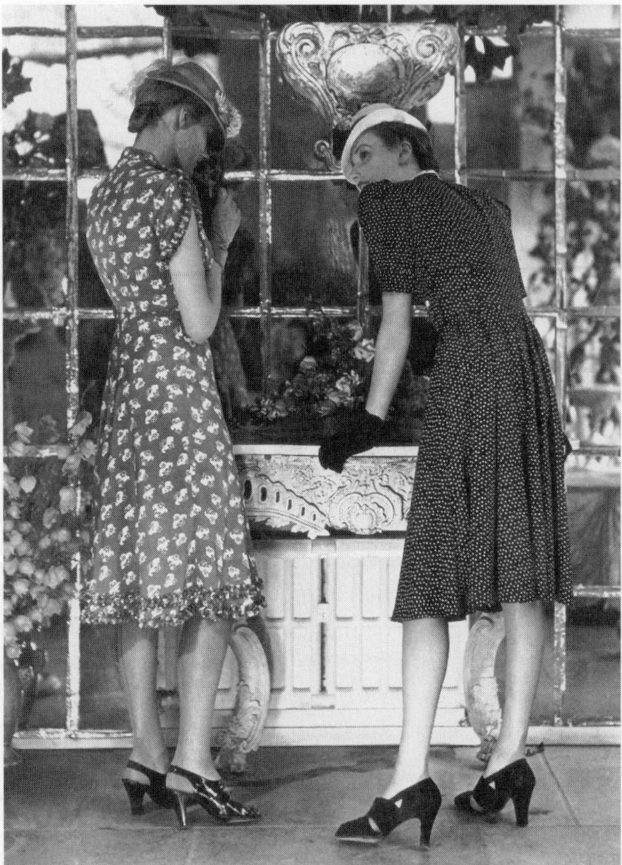

**Figure 1** Summer Dresses, 4 May 1939. Examples of fashions for the summer immediately preceding war. Picture Post/Hulton Archive/Getty Images. © 2004 Getty Images (3060103).

The extent to which manufacturers dealt directly with retailers or chose to use wholesalers is not always clear. The less on-trend fashion lines that were becoming a familiar staple of the more up-market manufacturing companies offered fewer risks for the wholesaler, and much branded material was marketed through the wholesalers' established industry links. This meant the manufacturers needed neither their own marketing operation nor travellers to advertise their ranges and could cut costs on these accordingly.[31] From the retailers' end, there was no desire to diversify back to manufacturing women's wear. The number of fashion lines needed to sustain a profitable shop floor, whether in a small draper's or a large department store, mitigated against this.[32] Variety and stock turnover were key to success here, and retail businesses across the price and size spectrum could only achieve these by recourse to a range of manufacturing and wholesaling outlets.

Two areas that particularly affected this greater take-up of factory production and also the larger scale of certain operations were the types of clothing becoming fashionable and the fabrics available from which to make them. The longer, cleaner lines of women's fashions for the two decades before the Second World War, as opposed to the highly constructed skirts and bodices of Victorian and Edwardian styles, leant themselves to mechanized manufacture. The Board of Trade Working Party was conscious that fabric shortages during the First World War had already created shorter skirts and lighter weights in underclothing,[33] and the simplified pattern blocks and construction methods required to make up the new modern styles were a great impetus to increased factory production. Simplicity did not rule out the subtle variations of design and decorative finish which added variety and choice to a basic silhouette. This process was considerably advanced by the advent of more modern machinery devices to enhance design features and add surface decoration quickly and efficiently, as we have seen. Thus the various tiers of factory production, large-scale through to modest, contrived to create a selection of fashion merchandise for the high street that was more comprehensive and retailed across more price points than had ever been encountered before. This in turn highlighted a now-developing 'dress consciousness'[34] that further boosted high street sales and the general prosperity of the clothing industry in this period.

The other important development in women's clothing output was the increasing use of rayon fabric for light clothing. Wray suggests that initial factory growth during the 1920s had tended to favour tailored clothing,[35] which would have prioritized wool and wool mix fabrics, while the smaller manufacturers creating a full range of garments and accessories required by high street retailers worked with cottons, silks and wools. Dress production now began to follow the tailored classic into factory production, coinciding with a marked expansion in the rayon-weaving industry. Rayon was a much cheaper fabric than silk, and the staple fibre, or short lengths cut from continuous filaments, could be spun into yarns to create a wide variety of different fabrics. It could be used alone or form mixes with both cotton and wool. Rayon yarn had the 'effect of brightening' a woollen fabric, and the branded fabric "Luvisca" blended rayon and cotton together to produce a 'clean, smart fabric' that wore well and 'laundered satisfactorily'.[36] Rayon could be produced, like any fabric, in a range of qualities but in general lacked the warmth of wool and the strength of cotton. It could be obtained from three types of synthetic fibre—viscose, acetate and cuprammonium rayon—and had already produced branded materials such as Courtauld's Fibro, British Celanese's Celafibre and Bamberg's Cuprama. Acetate rayon had to be carefully laundered as it lost lustre if washed in a very hot soap solution and melted under a hot iron.[37] Rayon had also enabled the production of the Trubenized or semi-stiff collar through the use of a cellulose acetate film compacted between two surface fabrics.[38] The great selling feature of rayon was that it had been created to imitate silk but was much cheaper. While it had none of the strength or durability of silk, artificial or art silk nevertheless became increasingly popular, and the rayon industry expanded during the 1930s, out-producing cotton and becoming an 'ally' of wool.[39] Wray cites a 1935 Census of Production Report indicating that nearly five and a half million pounds of rayon were being absorbed into dress and tailoring manufacture as opposed to just over three million pounds of cotton.[40] Initially produced as a cheap silk substitute, Wilson and Taylor note that by the 'late 1930s the quality of rayon fabric had clearly improved and was used by middle and even top-quality ready-to-wear companies'.[41] The growth of the rayon industry also allowed for the continuing importance of both cotton and wool as British exports. Hargreaves and Gowing state that by 1937, of the six most valuable exports, cotton yarns and manufactures had been the most important at sixty-nine million pounds and woollen and worsted yarns and manufactures fifth at thirty-six million pounds.[42] The development of another fibre that could play a major role in providing quality clothing at a reasonable price would significantly open up British options for supplying the civilian and military cloth and clothing required under wartime conditions.[43]

Clothing quality across the industry varied considerably. At the cheapest end was the poor-quality production, both in terms of fabric and make, of the most unstable and often speculatively begun workshops and small factories already discussed. These are likely to have provided the poorest quality merchandise on sale at the club shops that will be explored further in Chapter 5, 'Evacuation'. Serving members of clothing clubs who 'paid' for goods via club cheques, the sale of these unfit-for-purpose commodities represented the very worst end of the clothing trade catering for those on the most reduced means. Here, new might compare unfavourably with certain qualities of second-hand, although both markets reflected the existence of a tier of living at or below the poverty line where maintaining even a most basic level of clothing was a constant struggle. Margery Spring Rice, in her study *Working Class Wives,* published in 1939,[44] accurately revealed the hand-to-mouth existence shared by those on very low wages and the unemployed, both long- and short-term, living on Assistance Board relief. She was able to give some idea of the weekly budgets that many impoverished families had to live on, and this establishes what constituted some of the poorest incomes in Britain at the time.

Of the 1,250 women interviewed for the study, about 220 had 4s or under per head per week to spend on housekeeping, 460 between 4s 1d and 6s,

250 between 6s 1d and 8s, and 144 between 8s 1d and 10s.[45] Out of this, rent, fuel and food had to be found, as well as sundries including clothes, boots and shoes. Taking Mrs. B of Blackburn as an example, some understanding can be reached of the limited access to new clothes experienced by those with severely reduced means. Her unemployed husband received 28s 3d unemployment benefit, or 'dole', a week. Out of this, Mrs. B had to feed herself and her husband, her father living with them, and one three-year-old child (and she was expecting another). She spent approximately 11s a week on food, 2s 6d for gas for lighting and 3s on coal. Her weekly outgoings of 16s 6d meant rent could not have exceeded 11s, and anything less than that would have left her money for such things as the cigarettes which she bought for her husband but little else. This places Mrs. B loosely in the third category of 6–8s a week. She only bought clothing when her husband had seasonal work in the summer and then darned and patched them thereafter. Many interviewees referred to having to mend clothes regularly with little opportunity to buy.[46]

Living with such little or seasonal money may have severely restricted buying new but did not rule it out entirely. While the very cheap club shops and their like offered little in terms of value for money, there were retailers trying to offer a better quality of product at low cost often based on the premise of larger turnover. The most important operator in this field was Marks and Spencer, which had started out catering for just such low-income customers. With humble beginnings as a pedlar 'knocking at doors in the Yorkshire Dales',[47] Michael Marks had known what it was like to have very little money. Setting up his trestle table to sell a small variety of wholesale-bought goods in the open market at Kirkgate, Leeds, in 1884, he worked 'the two days a week to which business was restricted' and spent the rest of his time as a pedlar or possibly trading in the local markets of the West Riding of Yorkshire.[48] He sold cheaply, often supplying goods of the haberdashery type for people who made their clothes largely at home, and within two years had moved to the covered market in Leeds at a very low rent and selling nothing over a penny.[49] Business flourished, and Marks opened more bazaars, all still trading at a penny. By 1901, when the name of his new partner Tom Spencer appeared alongside his as stallholder, Marks was paying a rent of twenty shillings a week for two stalls in Ashton-under-Lyne from which a rough turnover of sales can be calculated. In 1903, the bazaars were trading in a wide variety of merchandise, some of which Briggs suggests 'would have cost more than a penny',[50] but most items remained at this price. Given Rowntree's view from his survey of the poor in York in 1899 that a woman might purchase all her year's clothing requirements for £1 11s, the attraction of a cheap store like Marks and Spencer can be understood.[51] The clothing workers themselves were being paid only 3 1/4d. per hour in 1911 and 8d. per hour by 1918.[52]

Simon Marks took over the business after his father's death in 1907, and in the years prior to the First World War, he continued to turn stalls into profitable high street shops in as central locations as possible. By 1915, the company had 145 branches with 56 in and around London. But war took its toll, and as goods became harder to come by and more expensive, the penny price policy had to be abandoned. Up until this stage, the business had operated on the basis of selling a wide variety of cheap produce through a growing chain of outlets. Marks's buying policy, established from the earliest years, was often to purchase direct 'from manufacturers . . . thus cutting out the profits of the middlemen', with goods coming from 'different parts of Europe, including Germany, Austria and France'.[53] Wartime trading stringencies had lowered profits, but Simon Marks continued to acquire new premises in the post-war years, although retail policy was not as rigid as it had been. By the 1920s, Marks and Spencer's were selling a 'confusing jumble of goods of all kinds varying in price from one penny to three pounds'.[54] At this stage, Marks and Spencer was still associated with a wide range of cheap goods. But after a formative visit to the United States to explore aspects of retailing, Marks introduced a new five shilling maximum price that was carefully calculated to take the brand rather more upmarket. As Chislett points out, he no longer wanted to 'compete directly with Woolworth's, which sold nothing for more than sixpence. Simon's plan was to restyle the store into one which offered quality goods at a very competitive price.[55] In this lay the new ground that Marks and Spencer's was about to break. While ostensibly moving the business up a notch, in cost terms Marks was keen to offer value-for-money commodities which would sell so well that he could maintain the fixed price of nothing more than five shillings for an ever-better product. Profit margins even on the basis of the five shillings price limit would still be small in the existing economic climate, and the need to sell large quantities of goods relatively quickly throughout all the stores was essential. This brought the new volume clothing industries to the fore in deciding on future stock, and clothing lines thus 'took on an unprecedented importance'.[56] Five shillings still limited the company's activities 'to the cheaper quality grades of women's outerwear'[57] by this period yet reflected Marks' belief that in the current economic and technological climate, it would be possible to make 'continuous improvements in quality and value in textiles which . . . was now the fundamental principle according to which Marks and Spencer should operate'.[58] This was the premise upon which the company moved away from the previous 'jumble' of goods and into women's fashion apparel. By 1930–1931, they had 'distributed no fewer than one million dresses'.[59]

What became crucial and central to the business plan to sell low-priced but good-quality garments giving value for money was the method of sourcing and purchasing stock. Prices needed to be kept low, and Marks and Spencer wanted to continue to bypass wholesale trading and deal directly with manufacturers. This was not always easily achieved owing to the powerful hold that the Wholesale Textile Association appeared to maintain over certain manufacturers. Founded in 1912 to 'resist the encroachments of the manufacturers and major retail houses' into the warehousing and retailing business, it had remained a rather 'secretive' organization whose main business at the time of its inception seemed to be 'blacklisting manufacturers who contracted directly with retailers'.[60] Israel Sieff encountered something of this pressure when he approached the manufacturing firm Corah's of Leicester in 1926. On the first three occasions he was turned away, but on the fourth the chairman agreed to see him. Sieff explained that Marks and Spencer's customers wanted 'sound quality at reasonable prices, rather than expensive variety of choice' and that he could offer Corah's regular orders for fewer ranges which would be profitable. The chairman's answer reflects the trading policy of the times: He felt their other customers would be resentful of the competition from a down-market chain store and would take their business elsewhere.[61]

Sieff later met one of Corah's directors keen to do business with a company that required 'a thousand dozen of men's half hose a week'. Despite the climate of the general strike and with trade in general being poor the new chains and their type of merchandise were still viewed with a snobbish hostility that clearly reflected less on the quality of the products themselves and rather more on the entrenched prejudices of other retail sectors. Sieff acknowledged to Corah's production director that 'some manufacturers who do business with us ask me to use the back entrance in case some of their customers see the bazaar man coming in, and take umbrage'.[62] Corah's took the work, thus beginning a mutually profitable association that was to last well into the post-war era. What fundamentally changed these relatively strained relations between retailer and manufacturer was the severe economic depression Britain experienced between 1929 and 1932. During this time, Marks and Spencer's low-price quality promise continued to attract custom, allowing the company to expand and offer manufacturers work in a depleting market. Ever 'responsive to consumer demand',[63] aware of what their customers could afford and the quality that could be offered for that price, stock was carefully negotiated and closer collaboration forged with producers. Marks believed that 'continuity of production, the levelling out of peaks and valleys, was one of the main anxieties of the manufacturers' that efficient business coordination with Marks and Spencer could help achieve.[64] Long runs of fewer lines and regular work could go some way towards resolving the age-old problem of short or seasonal employment in the clothing industry.

Garment and accessory specifications were tightened in accordance with inventories of the volume selling lines, and cloth choice improved on the basis of bulk orders at lower prices. These ideas would be further pursued with the opening of a textiles laboratory in 1935 and a Merchandise Development Department and Design unit in 1936. Sieff believes the company continued to grow most of all because they understood their customer: 'We answered the people's prayer. Their prayer for goods at prices which even in their days of impoverishment they could just about afford to buy. Not all of them, God knows. But what we had to offer was within reach of most of them. To the others, beyond the pale of purchasing power, we held out what we could.'[65] Throughout the 1930s, Marks and Spencer worked to provide reasonable quality at consistently low prices.

Chief competitors in the field were the smaller chain groups British Home Stores and Littlewoods Ltd, who were also selling 'dresses, blouses and skirts in the cheaper lines'.[66] Another growing sector on the high street was that of the variety multiples that tended to specialize in particular areas of fashion clothing. In general there were two divisions in this market, the knitted or soft separates, underwear and hosiery sector, and women's outerwear, which included coats, suits and dresses. During the 1930s, the outerwear shops became ever more popular as they offered 'well-cut and fashionable dresses, skirts, jackets and coats within the range of working-class and lower-middle class incomes'.[67] By 1939, the substantial lead in the field that had once been held by the hosiery and knit sector had been cut considerably, and they now had only marginally more outlets than outerwear.[68] Leading high street names in separates and hosiery included Dorothy Perkins Ltd and Etam Ltd, and for outerwear Richard Shops Ltd.[69] In the same way as the chain stores, the multiples bought stock in considerable quantity and effected cost savings through mass production.

As Wray points out, however, 'it must be emphasised that more than half the supplies of women's outer wear was distributed by small, unit shop, retailers in the 1930s. These included not only local drapers' shops, particularly in small market towns or in suburban districts, but also a growing number of specialist dress or "madam" shops.' These were probably the 'direct successors of the retail bespoke dressmaking establishments whose trading activities were curtailed by the expansion of ready-made clothing'.[70] With the growth of branded goods in a variety of price bands, 'madam' shops were often able to provide familiar names—in underwear, stockings or clothing products, for example—as easily as a department store and with greater local convenience.[71] The smaller retailer reflected the more personal end of the market where service was prioritized and alterations might be undertaken and these shops continued to enjoy a limited prosperity in the years leading up to the war.[72] This type of outlet could trade in garments across the price spectrum depending on location and local clientele.

The wholesalers used by Edith and Flora Hodson in their small Willenhall shop, north of Birmingham, give some indication of the type and price of garments available for a middle- to lower-middle- and salaried working-class shopper from the area. Using long-established wholesale businesses such as Bell and Nicolson Ltd, Wilkinson and Riddell and Larkins,[73] the sisters were able to purchase small amounts of ladies light clothing and underwear along with haberdashery and some children's wear at modest but not cheap prices to which they added their own markup. In 1937, for example, Bell and Nicolson were offering rayon crepe afternoon dresses from 12s 11d and two-piece suits using boucle knits and plain wool for 8s 11d while a year later, Wilkinson and Riddell were advertising a crepe afternoon gown for 8s 11d and a velvet simple afternoon frock for 10s 11d. A wool suit was offered at 12s 11d, and a lightweight angora-mixture wool dress range began at 8s 11d. For spring 1939, Wilkinson and Riddell offered a wool fabric frock at 7s 11d and an art silk frock at 12s 11d. A simple 'special purchase' ladies woollen cloth skirt was priced as cheaply as 1s 7d by April 1939, with other skirt prices going up to between 3s and 7s 11d depending on fabric and design, the highest priced skirt being advertised as an 'exceptionally smart' plaid wool dress skirt. Blousettes started from 3s, ladies slacks 4s and art silk underwear 5s. All wool jumpers at 2s 3d and 3s were short-sleeved and revealed decorative finishes such as cornelly work or embroidery for the price, with one of the range being offered in ladies Celanese. An art silk 'Macclesfield' frock cost 11s 6d, and finally a 'new style material washing frock', which might have alluded to rayon now rather than cotton, was priced at 12s 11d.[74] As Marks and Spencer bought direct from manufacturers, their selling prices were nearer to these wholesale figures at which the Hodson sisters bought. The sisters marked up their garments to sell on using a code that has not yet been broken so actual selling prices are often unknown. The types of wholesalers the sisters used had warehouses all over Britain, with Bell and Nicolson for example having branches in Cardiff, Liverpool, Northampton and Bristol while Wilkinson and Riddell had branches in Leicester, Liverpool, Manchester, Nottingham and Bristol. The prices they sold for remain therefore a good indication of medium-priced clothing with some more price-conscious garments, all aiming for a reasonable quality in terms of design, fabric and cut.

In January 1939, to put these prices in perspective, *Vogue*'s section on 'smart fashion for a limited budget', penned for the more affluent middle and the upper classes, was advertising a seven-and-a-half-guinea 'bargain' suit from Dickens and Jones,[75] while retail bespoke at Jaqumar Jeune-Filles 'for the young girl or married woman' were providing less 'elaborate' dresses at prices kept between fourteen and twenty-five pounds 'because the clothes are simply cut and finished'.[76] When these prices are compared to those for 'inexpensive frocks smartly cut and finished' at 2s 11d advertised in the window of Marks and Spencer in the mid 1930s[77] some idea of the extent of the price differentials operating across the high street in Britain in the middle and later 1930s can be gauged.

Value-for-money ready-to-wear had a salutary effect on other mechanisms of clothes purchasing. As Tebbutt points out, 'these cheap consumer goods steadily undermined the disposal of second-hand clothing which had traditionally been a mainstay of the working class wardrobe. The mill girls would not have second-hand clothes, and the youths in the works would not look at "reach-me-downs."' New production methods 'brought smart, cheap clothing within reach of many more women'.[78] As Cyril Naylor wrote, looking back at the interwar years as an employee of Marks and Spencer, 'in those days when the Lancashire lass doffed her clogs and shawl it was to M and S she came to widen her horizons with the brighter clothes and adornment she deserved'.[79] Poorer quality garments were less and less associated with the chain store product but rather now with a certain type of small factory using 'cheap fabrics, skimped sizing and low overheads'.[80]

For the larger-scale production, there had to be some standardization both of material and design in order, as Worth suggests, to 'ensure standardization of production' across so many different stores and lines.[81] The notion of standardization was becoming contentious in the clothing industry by the later 1930s, particularly in the realm of men's wear, where the largest type of true mass production was being undertaken. Marks had, however, already made clear his philosophy that uniformity could be combined with variety. If 'uniformity makes for economy in production, it is variety which makes the appeal to the purchaser. We aim at standardisation of basic fabrics, but we avoid standardised uniformity in the finished article. . . . The period is long past when low prices meant low quality and bad taste.'[82] Variety of design and detail could still be achieved within, for example, dress or blouse manufacture because the numbers of garments being produced for any one line were large. This kept costs low, which in turn safeguarded the fashion-conscious design elements that secured quick sales and the diversity of stock that regularly appeared on the shop floor. The textile laboratory set up in 1935 and the Merchandise Development Department of 1936 both reflected Simon Mark's desire to actively pursue research into fabric construction and garment quality and to improve quality throughout the production line.[83]

In summary, the high street of the 1930s offered more opportunities to purchase fashion across a range of price points than ever before. A great deal of what could now be bought had been created by some level of factory production, which had, overall, brought prices down even if quality was not always consistent. The growth of high street trading had been encouraged and sustained by a falling cost of living through the 1930s, and regular employment secured spending capacity. As Hilton remarked, by 1938 there had been 'an increase of 12% in the real wages of workpeople generally. By that I mean that because of the lower food and other prices in 1938 as against 1924, the rather higher wages buy 12% more of those things on which the housewife spends the wages than could be bought with the wages in 1924.'[84] Bentley and colleagues confirm that there was an 'increase in salaried workers from just under 600,000 to 750,000 between 1920 and 1938 [and that] the income of wage earners—unless they were amongst the 10–20% who were actually unemployed during the Depression—rose substantially'.[85] At the top end of the ready-made shopping experience were still the more exclusive department stores such as Harrods, Liberty or Selfridges[86] and the higher-end independent retailers represented by such firms as Jaeger and Dereta, who manufactured and distributed their own in-house designs.[87] The multiple fashion shops specializing in hosiery and underwear either manufactured their own lines or sourced from elsewhere while the outerwear retailers bought 'the bulk of their goods . . . direct from manufacturers who produced special ranges and types of goods against large orders'.[88] Both provided variety at modest cost. It was the chain stores, however, that delivered mass fashion at the lowest prices still commensurate with quality and value for money. Bespoke reflected the most luxurious end of the fashion spectrum while a tier of cheap, shoddy goods persisted at its most disreputable end. While wartime policy for clothing provision would reflect some continuities with pre-war production in terms of prioritizing quality clothing at affordable prices, it would significantly affect these two extremes, severely curtailing the luxury exclusive trade and by various methods virtually eliminating those speculative businesses that offered the poorest garments with little to no intrinsic worth. The result would be a much greater streamlining of production, utilizing all that was successful in forms of factory and mass manufacture, in order to provide quality and fit-for-purpose garments at manageable prices for all.

# –3–

# Being Chic and Being British

This chapter takes the designs and silhouettes of the years immediately preceding the war as a starting point for a close, critical scrutiny of the practices and protocols that affected British women's fashion. The importance that attached to issues of dress and dress management are investigated as well as the developments in fashion silhouette and dress ranges during the last year of peace. These include the textiles and dress styles that reflected elements of a specifically British identity that would take on additional significance in the context of approaching hostilities.

In 1937, Alison Settle, fashion writer and editor of *Vogue* for eight years, published a book entitled *Clothes Line.*[1] In a series of short chapters, she covered a wide range of topics about fashion and style to provide women with an essential guide to the principles of successful clothes buying, keeping and wearing. While the book was clearly written with the more affluent woman in mind—a dress budget of one hundred pounds a year and how to manage it forms the substance of one chapter[2]—there is a tacit acknowledgement that these first principles behind quality in dress and dressing are simple rules that could be adopted by anyone given the chance. Even wealthier women could make style mistakes, particularly given the range of fashion choice now available, so while the book had a specific currency for the well-to-do, it also established ways of approaching dress and dressing equally relevant for those consuming fashion on more modest incomes. In fact, looking back on Settle's work from the vantage point of the war years, much of her advice seems to have a striking degree of prescience in advocating a set of less-is-more dress rules to create the careful and coordinated wardrobe indicative of true style.

In the introduction to the work, Settle establishes why, for her, fashion has a special significance. 'Fashion is the expression of the world we live in, a picture of what is going on inside our minds as well as outside in historic fact.' Fashion is both a personal and an historic narrative that contributes its particular discourse to the broader knowledge of period. As the hidden poverty of the long-term unemployed would be made visible through *lack* of basic clothing, warmth and hygiene, so the gradual assimilation of more stable incomes for the working and middle classes had revealed itself in the *desire* for fashion clothing as supplied by the burgeoning British high street. By 1937, the marketability of cheaper fashion selling across a broader range of price points highlighted this desire to own fashion goods, particularly amongst those on limited incomes.

The 'suburban shopping streets' had become 'a pleasure to look at',[3] but this had resulted in a glut of fashion possibilities in both good and questionable taste that made selectivity hard. A continuous theme throughout Settle's book is the problem that choice posed in terms of assembling outfits that were appropriate and well-groomed. The rich woman made 'more mistakes in her dressing than the poor because she sees more temptation to vulgarity and fussiness around her'.[4] When Settle speaks of the poor here, she is not consciously invoking the really poor but rather the less affluent components of the middle-class fashion-buying population, later referred to loosely as the 'budget women'. While the rich woman's mistakes don't really matter 'if she is lucky enough to discover that she has made them',[5] the same was not true for the woman of more slender means who had to live with her errors. Settle reiterates this idea in reflecting that 'the woman to envy in her dressing is not the woman with the excellent and complete wardrobe of clothes but the woman who, with a handkerchief from the handkerchief drawer twisted and tied with *chic* round the neck of a dull dress, causes you to forget the dress and only admire her *chic*'.[6] The essence of style lay in the intelligent use of what you had. Money was not an asset and offered the rich 'such awful temptations about buying just anything they fancy'.[7] A character in the chapter entitled 'Budget Conscious: A Dialogue' goes so far as to say: 'I believe that the best-dressed women are the women of moderate or limited income who think about their problems.'[8]

The biggest help here was the little black dress that 'no woman can afford to underestimate'.[9] The various ways in which this one dress could be reworked with thoughtful accessories—a scarf, a belt, flowers—spoke for economy rather than ostentation and confirmed style as residing in the paired back and clean lined. It is pertinent that this image of good taste emerges so clearly at this time. The idea of keeping clothing simple and worn with the addition of distinctive but appropriate accessories reflected something of a reaction to the consumer opportunities available.

Settle also urged women to be far more alert to the way all items of apparel were stored and maintained. Simply owning the pieces was not enough. The truly stylish woman managed her wardrobe with great rigour, washing and airing clothes sufficiently, keeping them in good shape by correct hanging or folding and, where necessary, mending, repairing or strengthening them for prolonged use. Settle suggested that an hour each day be devoted to perfecting the existing wardrobe, whether this be undertaken by the owner, if she had the skills, or someone hired to do the jobs required. It was an ongoing task to 'put on fresh collars and hooks and buttons, take stockings to the menders, cobweb darn the holes'.[10] She revealed the wealth of jobs that needed to be done and the skills that might have to be brought in to do them. While most middle-class women had some ability in basic sewing, home-crafting skills had diminished given the greater availability of ready-to-wear clothing. Settle now encouraged all classes of women to be adept at reviewing and repairing the deficiencies in their wardrobes in order to meet their first priority, which was to 'look well groomed, well-turned-out, as good-looking and as fresh-looking as possible'.[11]

Settle's preoccupation with clarity of line and unostentatious dressing would soon be reiterated in the spare and classic contours of wartime Utility wear. Superfluities of style would be shed in favour of a groomed simplicity. Her concern over domestic budgeting and appropriate planning and organization of clothing and accessories certainly prefigured the guidance issued during the inauguration of rationing in June 1941, after which the public were regularly exhorted to control and plan for their longer-term clothing requirements and develop a clearer picture of what their real needs might be. Similarly, *Clothes Line*'s advice on keeping up appearances through a strictly managed clothing care regime looked forward to the rhetoric of the 'Make-Do and Mend' and 'Mrs. Sew-and-Sew' campaigns that became an intrinsic part of wartime fashion and dress practice. Thus there is clear continuity here between elements of pre-war fashion thinking from someone whose opinion and expertise might be considered to count and the fashion philosophy that underlay the wartime wardrobe.

The main style stories of 1938, inspired by the couture houses and interpreted by the ready-to-wear manufacturers, had offered both classic and romantic dressing. The London collections for spring and summer 1938 had highlighted the tailored suit for the day, and this 'continued to be the mainstay of the classic English wardrobe'.[12] By autumn, the choice of fashion on offer 'had become a confused mix of period styles—Renaissance, French Revolution and Edwardian—', and 'Paris dragged up all the come-hither details of the early twentieth century: jewelled side combs, leg o'mutton sleeves, tiny hats, veils, muffs, hoods and other "heart-breaker" accessories.'[13] There seemed to be an outpouring of romanticism for the evening that allowed for a particular brand of femininity to be on show. Redolent of the times from which the fashions derived, evening wear was often narrow waisted, boned and corseted and carried connotations of wealth and leisure as much as history. The styles of late 1938, particularly those for the evening, saw women as 'mysterious, alluring, witty, veiled, gloved, corseted and even button-booted as any romantic, fairytale queen',[14] and it was this image of traditional womanhood that was carried through into 1939. While the more business-like and efficient suited look was clearly fashionable for the day, no matter what kind of feminine accoutrements might accessorize it, romance flourished thereafter. Tailoring gave way to more sexually pronounced curves through body shaping and décolletage, and clothes became reminders of the more traditional relationships between the sexes that had characterized the Edwardian era and arguably still retained much the same significance now.

Fashions for 1939 featured both the waisted suit, with accentuated peplum and flared skirt, and the boxier, rectangular look. On the high street, outlets like Jaeger were providing pleated skirts and longer-line jackets. There was a tendency towards the squared rather than sloping shoulder, moving nearer to the military rather than the feminine line. Immediately before the war, the two styles that would battle for prominence in the first months of conflict were already in existence: the British tailored suit, relatively conservative and angular, and the smoother-lined, sculpted, curvaceous Parisian suit that would eventually evolve into the New Look after the war. The overt flamboyance of the latter—with stiffened peplum, ascending shoulder and rounded hip line—celebrated a pre-war desire for historicism and Edwardiana which at the same time seemed to endorse, however consciously, all the connotations of traditional femininity.

How would these fashions be affected by the advent of war? Generous quantities of fabric would run counter to the need for fair shares for all, and the time, effort and craftsmanship that turned dresses into works of art would no longer be sustainable to the same degree or appropriate in the face of war restraint and service. In practical as much as ideological terms the exuberance of evening dress would soon be démodé[15] and retrenchments in clothing manufacture would inevitably dismantle some of those obvious class differences and divisions achieved through occasion dressing as these types of clothing became more limited. Metaphorically, the demise of more opulent styles would also reflect the changing roles of the women who had worn them, who were required now to rethink their identity and purpose as they took on war-related duties or joined one of the armed forces. For many women, their place within a social hierarchy would become visually less well defined as they began to wear overalls, boiler suits or service uniforms. A new and relatively unique sense of shared experience emerging with war promoted other social perspectives. People were not of the same class or background, but they might *look* and possibly feel the same under these changed conditions of living. Alternative dress protocols would help define and reflect these shared hardships of war.

Amidst the more conventional choices in clothing on the high street, *Vogue* raised the issue of the suitability and appropriateness of wearing trousers as fashionable dress in an article in May 1939.[16] Seen at this time as a constituent component of semi-tailored sportswear, slacks were also taking on the mantle of uncomplicated lounge clothing that moved the Riviera look of the late 1920s into a more modern and practical frame. Not seen as especially feminine—'from the swirl and rustle of femininity which characterises this season's clothes, we turn with relief to slacks for all our casual, informal living'—nor likely to be welcomed at ultraconservative locations—'wear them for yachting, too, if you keep away from the Royal Yacht Squadron lawns'—slacks nevertheless had their role. *Vogue* also suggested that unless your hostess was 'an Edwardian relic with reactionary views, take slacks away for all your weekends. . . . And live in slacks in your own country home; prune, potter and lounge in them.'[17] Slacks offered a more practical, easy style of dress particularly suited to physical activity, and De Courcy believed that by 1939 trousers in general for women 'were making headway, though still considered rather dashing. To be forbidden to wear them (as Newnham undergraduates were at their end of term examination) was newsworthy; to wear them would make even more news.'[18] It was a small blur between the sexes that war was to enhance to a much greater degree. *Vogue* advised women to own several pairs for the country wardrobe as well as a heavy silk or velvet suit for evening wear. The primary rules regarding trousers were that wearers were to be under fifty, weigh less than ten stone and never wear them on a grouse moor, which would be, for unexplained reasons, embarrassing.[19] Preempting the trouser that would become de rigueur wartime apparel, from siren suit through to Auxiliary Territorial Service (ATS) battledress, fashion slacks and trousers were important forerunners of the acceptance of a quintessentially male garment for female use. The hidden agenda of the female abrogating the role and authority of the male through use of the trouser was as yet muted and indistinct. While popular and habitual wartime wear would bring these ideas into focus, the practicality of the trouser was irrefutable.

Having established some paradigms for taste and style at this time and conducted a brief review of the kinds of clothes on offer, it is now useful to see how certain style genres that gained chic and cachet could be seen to be especially British and the way in which the more affluent wardrobe continued to reflect a variety of occasion-based clothing. In an article in *Vogue*'s June–July 1939 *Pattern Book*, a plan for 'five complete ensembles'[20] was suggested for the coming summer. These were to cover the following categories: 'For Town, Active Sports, For Afternoon, For Evening, Spectator Sports'. Settle believed that modern times called for far fewer changes of clothing than the past, with its constant preoccupation with the minutiae of 'appropriateness'.[21] Although the day was still divided into three periods, from the early 1930s there had been a move to create clothes with greater flexibility that would take the wearer through the day and from town to country and back without the need to change. These became known as spectator-sports clothes and were considered to be essentially British-inspired fashions, revealing a national flair for active and unfussy clothes which were 'right once and for all'.[22] This range was 'born in imitation of British country-cum-town life, wholly influenced by British type trade'[23] and provided informal, easy living, country-style ensembles that travelled well and might do service for a multiplicity of events. Yet within this modern approach still resided a classic tailored style. A signature British wool suit provided the starting point for this new brand of contemporary dressing, which was accessorized with knitted woollen blouses or jumpers and low-heeled shoes.[24] Such clothes emphasized the distinguishing characteristics of British textiles and design that would, in due course, contribute significantly to the wartime aesthetic.

This sense of history and tradition and the permanence they suggested were clearly important design elements of British dress, if generally more visible in its upper tiers. These clothes held their place and developed cachet within the fashion world as the 1930s progressed. In a chapter entitled ‘English Dress’,[25] Settle remarked on the greater chic now possessed by the Englishwoman that had emerged since the early 1930s. She believed that, rather than the Englishwoman herself changing, the world had changed in more greatly appreciating ‘the Englishwoman’s way of dressing, in other words of her attitude to life. For that is what we mean when we talk of fashions and ways of dressing’.[26] She went on to elaborate on this sense of stability in style that provided something firm and anchored amidst the vagaries of high fashion and seasonal variation. English women had always dressed ‘as if time were endless’[27] and would not be dictated to by the whims of fashion. Unlike the American woman who pursued change, the Englishwoman maintained her wardrobe of classic quality clothes throughout the years. Settle drew an interesting contrast here between British tweeds ‘built for wear’ and a ‘French wool intended for high fashion’. The latter, she contended, would not be ‘for continued service’ and would soon be rejected in favour of another.[28] A further nuance was added to an understanding of the difference between high Parisian fashion and British fashion in terms of durability. Its capacity to withstand time was seen as providing added value, while higher fashion was intrinsically ephemeral—beautiful, but transitory. The longevity of the British classic, with its heritage of bespoke tailoring combined with signature fabrics of the highest quality, had a particular relevance in the face of impending war. Settle remarked that ‘in a world where things seem to dissolve under our very eyes, the calm pursuance of the same path, a devoted attention to detail, an absence of fuss or flurry attracts . . . admiration’.[29] Foreign buyers were now distinctly aware of the British range of tailored separates, coats and accessories. All carried associations of established patterns of town and country life and of the leisure pursuits that defined the British character and way of life.

It has been useful to concentrate on *Clothes Line* as a way of opening up discussion on the taste and style of British fashion current at the time and appropriate to the broad range of the more affluent sectors of society comprising the middle, upper middle and upper classes. With emphasis on a less-is-more chic underpinned by scrupulous wardrobe management, Settle clearly wanted to establish a way of shopping for and wearing clothes that would avoid the pitfalls presented by commercial plenty on the high street. She also unwittingly voiced a fashion philosophy that would have increasing currency for the war years. Advice to spend carefully and select clothes of classic simplicity resonated with wartime calls for fashion economy and constraint, while praise for thrifty practice as a cornerstone of the well-turned-out woman would become central to later campaigns to care for the hard-to-replace contents of the home front wardrobe. Britain moved towards war, therefore, with an established reputation for more timeless, classic clothes less affected by the flux of fashion and continued to endorse a distinctively British design signature that would be so much associated with the future fashions of war.

# –4–

# The Healthy Body and the Politics of Fitness

This chapter explores the importance of a developing interest in health, fitness and personal well-being in the context of pre-war paradigms for health and beauty and the relevance of these emerging concerns for a future state of war requiring stamina and strength, both physical and mental. Evolving approaches to beauty, health and fitness and a new body consciousness had been in evidence since the years after the First World War, and fitness and strength began to be promoted as attractive for men *and* women. The appearance of frailty and vulnerability so long considered a natural component of femininity and often enhanced, if not caused, by restrictive clothing and dress practice was increasingly challenged as women continued to enter the more active spheres of work and sport. This developing philosophy of personal appearance that created a new focus for the body itself, as opposed to how it was adorned and dressed, grew out of a greater understanding of, and concern for, health and physical fitness and the disease and illness that mitigated against social improvement. New paradigms for health culture would prove of particular significance to the war effort for two reasons: there would be greater recognition of the importance of optimum *physical health*, essential for all the additional exertion of war life, and greater physical stamina would help engender more secure *mental health* on the basis of body and mind working together. This would produce a more psychologically balanced and energetic individual whose good health would contribute to the overall health and resilience of the nation.

The *Vogue Beauty Book* that went on sale on 23 August 1939 carried two articles on aspects of the ideal body. The first advocated sport as the best way to improve shape, acknowledging that modern living was 'death to the figure'. The article went on to suggest that 'we sit about too much, we drive in cars too much, we walk and run too little'.[1] This advice was clearly aimed at a more leisured sector of the population, and various types of exercise were recommended. Riding was considered good for 'posture and poise' and 'fine, too, for your general health, because it shakes up the liver and internal organs'. Exactly how this was supposed to be beneficial is not described. The sports suggested were indicative of a certain lifestyle: golf, bike riding, fencing—which promoted slim hips—swimming, riding and skating. All of these, bar swimming, required some level of expense and appropriate dress in order to participate, with golf and fencing also assuming some kind of club membership. It was easier to lead an active, more energetic life if you had money and time.

The second article considered body proportion and printed a chart showing 'the proportions of the ideal figure . . . these weights and measurements are ideal for women 20–35 . . . if you are over 35 you may weigh considerably more than the amount given for your height—and still be well proportioned and well-made'[2]—presumably age no longer required the same ingénue silhouette. The chart that followed revealed key proportions for the ideal height-to-weight ratio, with all the various measurements across the body taken into consideration, including ankle, calf and thigh sizings. The chart revealed the willowy figure, which had characterized much of the styling of the 1930s line, still very much to the fore. To take one set of figures as an example, the height of five feet three inches carried an ideal weight of just seven stone and nine pounds—the light side of this weight-to-height ratio, and the ideal body proportions anticipated were a thirty-two-inch bust, twenty-four-inch waist (twenty-three and three-quarters, to be precise) and thirty-three-and-a-half-inch hips. This would have produced for any plus-twenty-year-old a girlish rather than womanly figure, and the same shape was followed through in proportion for each height band. Glamour and sophistication for the younger woman began with a slim physique, although the fuller figure was clearly acceptable for a more mature woman.

The maintenance of this ideal could, as *Vogue* suggested, be achieved through various pursuits. These included a developing fashion for new communal exercise classes, dance, racquet sports and a wide range of active pursuits consonant with a more outdoor lifestyle. Holidays taken camping or hiking, for example, had for some years now allowed even those on modest incomes to spend limited free time in a healthier and more adventurous way, and this growing popularity had been reflected in the establishment of the British Youth Hostels Association in 1930.

The history of health and fitness during the 1930s reflects greater involvement by both men and women in sport, and female athletic activity was undertaken with greater freedom and more appropriate dress than ever before. In 1929, the National Playing Field Association had been formed under the aegis of the Prince of Wales to encourage participation in 'healthy athleticism',[3] and golf, still largely a male sport, became more available to the middle classes as 'new courses opened up on the fringes of the suburbs'.[4] George Topping remembered 'miner's bowling greens and tennis courts' being opened 'at a small cost',[5] and Stevenson describes the popularity of cycling between the wars, when 'more than 28,000 cyclists joined the CTC (Cyclist's Touring Club) . . . sharing in a general move towards the pleasures and enjoyments of the countryside. Hiking and rambling boomed.'[6] A cheap train or tram ticket could bring people to the countryside for a day out while outdoor enthusiasts of all classes, but particularly those with limited incomes, could now stay overnight in a youth hostel. These were 'strictly reserved for those who arrived on foot or bicycle . . . provid[ing] very cheap overnight accommodation, with the choice of a cooked breakfast and evening meal, or facilities for cooking. . . . It opened up a whole new way of life for many youngsters, who could not afford hotels, and were to be seen trudging the countryside with their rucksacks on their backs or packed on the back of bicycles. Some also took their own tents and sleeping-bags.'[7] The extended leisure time available through the shorter working week of the 1930s, with a half day on Saturday,[8] and a desire to 'escape from the grimmer aspects of the industrial scene . . . to unspoilt countryside', helps account for this new interest.[9] Stevenson quotes an unemployed man exploring Loch Lomond and the Campsie hills in 1930 who felt that 'during the slump there were many of the despairing and disillusioned who found a new meaning to life in the countryside'.[10]

Alongside of this positive approach to fitness and fresh air ran a more challenging reconsideration of the state of the nation's general health. The extent to which good health and physical fitness were reliant on specific social factors, such as good diet, a clean and manageable living environment and a viable weekly wage now began to emerge with greater clarity, particularly by 1939, and in the context of the need to be war ready. Poor housing with inadequate sanitation, living space or laundering facilities would predictably take its toll on community health. Concern for social hygiene and issues of public health played a significant role in modernist debate over the need for cleaner, brighter and more functional homes. In Europe, particularly Holland, Germany and Czechoslovakia, the social housing schemes of the 1920s had developed to help raise the standards of living of the poorer sectors of the community. Some flats included a fitted kitchen and bathroom, and apartment blocks could offer various communal features such as child care, medical treatment and sports facilities. Such new thinking on housing policy had endeavoured to create a better world and highlighted issues regarding 'the conditions in which working class people lived, and the problems of health and hygiene arising from them (alcoholism, crime, disease, poor housing) and their treatments'.[11]

Coming to terms with issues of national health in this way revealed some commonality with the pseudoscience of eugenics that aimed at improving and conserving the health of the nation. Given its long history of debate and conjecture reaching back into the nineteenth century, Wilk declares that it was 'indisputably true that eugenics underpinned or provided a framework for much contemporary debate on a variety of health-related subjects, especially among medical practitioners and policy makers, politicians and social activists'.[12] As part of a mass demonstration of health exercises in Hyde Park in 1935, the fitness and dance organization, known as the Women's

League of Health and Beauty, carried banners stating their aim as 'racial health', a seemingly innocuous and worthy belief in the possibility of health and fitness for all through improving physique. But as Wilson and Taylor point out, 'the whole obsession with the body beautiful was . . . profoundly ambiguous'.[13] The healthy body as an ethos increasingly found divergent meanings within the context of eugenics and in the hands of powerful propaganda mechanisms such as those operating, from 1933, within the Third Reich in Germany. Here the notion of health and fitness was taken to a new level as youth organizations were systematically trained in the arts of outdoor life, sport and games, often to the detriment of more academic programmes. Leni Riefenstall's famous Nazi peon *Triumph of the Will*, which records the sixth Nazi Party Congress held at Nuremberg in 1934, reflected on this desire for a new racial energy and zest at the service of the führer and the Fatherland. With scenes capturing the mass rallies of the Hitler Youth organizations and young people in their thousands camping and taking part in parades and displays, the myth of the clean and healthy-living new German *volk* was underway. Fitness for family life underpinned much of this training and reflected a new emphasis on the importance of personal fitness for parenthood and the capacity to contribute appropriately to the *Volksgemeinschaft*, or national community, of the Third Reich.[14]

Interest in healthy pursuits was not politicized in Britain as in Nazi Germany, and it was never made part of a national programme of compulsory training. Three distinct approaches to the idea of health and well-being, however, do emerge in Britain during the 1930s. The first was enthusiastic participation in active hobbies and leisure pursuits. These could be undertaken by all those with enough time and money—even if both were relatively limited. The second constituted a slow and somewhat grudging recognition on behalf of government that there were elements of the community whose particular social and economic culture was inimical to good health. These people, without either time or money, were discovered to be suffering from poor or even chronic ill health that only some level of national welfare could assuage. The third concerned itself exclusively with the mental well-being of the nation, the relationship between mind and body and how a particular type of warfare that was increasingly on the government's mind might require new mental health initiatives for the good of the nation. It is to these three elements of health culture that we now turn for a closer investigation.

The promotion of physical activity and the concept of the body beautiful had begun in the years immediately after the First World War. Prunella Bagot Stack, daughter of the founder of the Women's League of Health and Beauty, writing her mother Mollie's biography, believed that at this time, 'a different physical ideal was emerging'[15] and that this had become noticeable through dance: 'Isadora Duncan . . . had freed dance from the limitations of classical ballet and advocated natural movement in bare feet, free from constrictive clothing. She was followed by other innovators like Ruby Ginner and Margaret Morris, who were inspired by the art and ideals of ancient Greece. Mollie was working along the same lines.'[16] With freedom of movement and natural rhythm as key elements, Bagot Stack pursued her belief in the benefits of body training, initially through her 'health' school started in 1925.[17] Here participants were invited to 'Build the Body Beautiful'[18] and achieve a professional qualification in movement and dance. But training professional teachers was not Stack's only interest. She also became 'much concerned with the needs of working girls and women, the sort of people who could not afford an expensive course and had not the talent to become professional dancers but who nevertheless wanted to train their bodies and enjoy movement'.[19] This part of her work led her to found the Women's League of Health and Beauty in March of 1930 and write a book outlining exercises for all, entitled *Building the Body Beautiful*, published in 1931. She initially ran classes for women in the offices or shops where they worked and then began public classes for anyone able to attend. Her objective was to help women whose long hours of work and low pay left them little time or opportunity to take on leisure activities. The League classes were an immediate success. Her daughter Prunella suggested that 'people were enthusiastic about joining associations at that time, and the word League was in vogue. There was the League of Nations, an Overseas League, and the League of Health and Strength (for men).'[20] Fitness became fashionable, and the movement went from strength to strength. Stack wrote that 'everyone was on first name terms and everyone wore the same exercise kit, so that differences of class or background disappeared'.[21] By 1934, membership had risen to sixty thousand. The Stacks began putting on larger public displays in arenas such as Hyde Park and the Royal Albert Hall, where dance and fitness routines could be brought to a wider cross-section of the public. In her book, Mollie Bagot Stack had written about the very clear 'vision' that she had for a world where 'the women are so beautiful that they are an inspiration, not a temptation, for thus the happy future of the whole human race will be assured'.[22] Health was a pathway to beauty and happiness, a joyous participation in a free and fit body. In a speech from the platform of the Royal Albert Hall during a display in 1934, Mollie Bagot Stack described 'a goal further ahead than Health and Beauty, in the ordinary sense, and that is Peace, and further on stands Love—Universal Love and Service. Human health and Beauty are but the stepping stones to that ideal. . . . Health represents peace and harmonious balance in the innermost tissues of mind and body. Beauty seems to me to represent this idea carried out by every individual, by a humanity universally. . . . Peace must finally come to the world by our own determination to make it come. Each individual counts.'[23]

Stack's work and the League she founded were based on a deep-seated belief that health and well-being together provided a wellspring of something much more profound. All, irrespective of class or culture, were invited to share in this goal of social harmony and peace brought about by happy, energetic people aware of life's rich potential.

The League continued to grow in popularity and by 1936 had a membership of 'close to 100,000'.[24] After her mother's death in 1935, Prunella Stack was approached, on behalf of the League, to join a new national sports venture called the Central Council of Recreative Physical Training. This organization had as its remit the bringing together of all aspects of physical training across the country and was intended to direct government attention to the fact that 'Britain was physically far from being an A1 nation'.[25] This in turn produced a new Fitness Council in 1937, whose aim was to improve the nation's general health. The council undertook to promote a national fitness campaign with rallies and speaking events publicizing the cause of fitness, and while Stack spoke of the council as 'smothered by the bureaucracy of the Civil Service',[26] it was, by 1938, supporting groups like the League with grant aid.

But as war became imminent, it was clear that there remained a significant element of the population untouched by any of the new health and fitness initiatives. Social enquiries from both before and during the war revealed levels of poverty here that, in association with the strain and pressure exerted by sustaining family life on a very low income, were having a deeply detrimental effect on physical strength and mental health. Margery Spring Rice's important research entitled *Working Class Wives*, published in 1939,[27] emphasized the serious health issues, both physical and psychological, that had poverty as their root cause, often exacerbated by unemployment, whether long- or short-term. The living conditions she witnessed were, in the main, unwholesome, and diet was poor. Taken in conjunction with large and usually uncontrolled or unplanned families, the unremitting grind and drudgery of many women's lives were now revealed as part of a seemingly inevitable and inescapable downward spiral of deprivation and need. The world of health, beauty and happy recreation was simply not achievable here.

Spring Rice's study involved interviewing 1,250 working-class women across the country with incomes ranging from an extremely meagre four shillings or under per head per week, to those with ten shillings or over per head per week.[28] She revealed the numbing and monotonous workload experienced by many women struggling to make ends meet each day on too little money. The pressures of family life played out under such adverse conditions had inevitably led to a worsening of general health, further undermined by the physical duress of regular pregnancies. Many women were reluctant to seek medical help, and most were not covered by any health insurance so only received health care for free when pregnant or nursing an infant. Chronic ill health for many was a direct result. Husbands—if working—might be covered by National Insurance in the event of sickness or unemployment, which entitled them to see a panel doctor and receive free medicine.[29] All other medical care for a family had to be paid for. The level of welfare was clearly inadequate, appeared incapable of regenerating health and well-being and provided little in the way of preventative care.

Over the course of Rice's study, it had become apparent that those on the lowest incomes found little or no time for any type of leisure activity. Sitting down for an hour or so mending or making clothing was the nearest many got to any form of relaxation. Rice believed that without a measure of release from the physical and mental grind of daily life, it was predictable that health and outlook would suffer. Early on in her study, Rice commented on how 'heartbreaking' it was 'to see how rapidly a pretty attractive girl grows old and drab after a few years of marriage. She loses her looks and ceases to take a pride in her appearance; minor ailments are neglected, her temper is frayed and household worries weigh unnecessarily heavy.'[30] Barbara Cartland, writing of her initiative to provide white wedding dresses for wartime service brides, speaks of a similar experience. Having advertised for dresses, she travelled to inspect them 'in all sorts of places. . . . In mean streets, poverty stricken houses, a tired, down-at-heel woman would show me a lovely dress which must have cost her at least £15.00 or more. Sometimes when they showed me a photograph of their wedding it was hard to recognise the radiant girl in white as the same woman that stood beside me. How many dreams had been unrealised, how many hopes dashed, how many tears shed since the day that photograph was taken.'[31] Many women had few opportunities to escape from what Rice described as the 'wear and tear of family life',[32] and the need for leisure, some form of release from perceived duty, as well as access to health care, seemed essential. It is important to mention that Rice saw 'all aspects of a woman's physical and psychological life' as treatable under the auspices of new 'gynaecological clinics',[33] clearly suggesting that a significant number of both physical and mental health problems were allied to childbearing and child rearing under very straightened circumstances.

The Stacks had believed that mind and body needed to work in harmony for inner peace and outer strength, and psychological well-being was clearly to be linked with general health. One of Rice's interviewees both reflects this belief and introduces a common portmanteau term used throughout the war for a variety of vague ailments and referred to as *nerves*. Her battle against poverty had resulted in her feeling 'nervy and irritable', while worry had often induced a physical lethargy that she found hard to explain.[34] Beddoe suggests that during the 1930s, the condition of nerves became increasingly common 'if the amount of column inches devoted to the topic is any indication'.[35] She saw this problem as 'clearly related not merely to the house-bound condition of many young wives, but to being house-bound with young children'.[36] The popularity of editorials on family life, child care and child health may well have subliminally endorsed women's perceptions of their role as wives and mothers,[37] tethering them further to this exhausting and often debilitating way of life.

Beddoe goes on to state that it was not only the poor and harassed who suffered from nerves, but also some better-off women. She mentions the phenomenon of 'suburban neurosis' connected with cases of depression experienced by the lower-middle-class residents of the new housing estates.[38] In these new locations, and without the company and guidance of family relatives, a marooned wife might find child rearing on a relatively low income increasingly stressful.[39] Taken in conjunction with the sheer amount of advice given to women in the popular press about keeping nerves in check and maintaining a healthy and balanced life, there is a case for suggesting that mental health issues were both recognized and caused some concern. These problems, however, were seen very much in the domain of personal self-management. Women and occasionally men, too, were exhorted to keep going for a more important cause, whether family support or, in due course, war work. The psychological or psychiatric aspects of health appeared to have low political visibility and were to be managed at the level of popular journalism.

While research by Rice could clearly account for aspects of worry, low self-esteem and other stress-related symptoms as *already in existence* and related directly to the relentless pressures of domestic lifestyle, Titmus reveals an alternative source of concern regarding mental health issues in his official war history on social policy. As war approached, the fear associated with air raids and the growing strength of the German air force had begun to lead to what Churchill called an 'obsessive' preoccupation with air strike and bombing.[40] Titmus does not mince his words: 'It is uncomfortably easy for the historian to look back on this period and to imply criticism of the temper and mood which Ministers and officials brought to their task of planning the war-time social services. For this mood, this fear of a war which might end civilisation, was something which infected both Government and people.'[41] The fear of the slaughter and mass disorder that could erupt during air attack had haunted official thinking since as early as the 1920s. A first meeting of the air-raid precaution committee of the Committee of Imperial Defence in 1924 believed that 'the moral effect of air attack in a future war would be "out of all proportion greater" than the physical consequences'.[42] Over the years that followed, there remained an 'underlying anxiety about human behaviour'[43] that would have to be addressed, as far as it could be, through civil defence measures and social service provision. Titmus records that 'it seemed sometimes to have been accepted almost as a matter of course that widespread neurosis and panic would ensue'.[44] He makes the following key statement: 'In planning the emergency social services the Government thought it necessary to bear constantly in mind the possibility that civilian steadfastness might fail. For the war that threatened was seen to be something new. That this was recognised, and recognised many years before it came, was unprecedented. Never before, in the history of warfare, had there been so much study and so many plans which were concerned with the protection and welfare of the women and children of the nation.'[45] While women and the young were clearly seen as especially vulnerable, plans were hatched for the mass evacuation of large elements of the community away from danger zones, and civil defence units and air raid precaution teams were prepared to mitigate public distress and invoke order and control.[46]

There was a consistent and genuine concern expressed over how people would behave at a time of possibly unprecedented disaster. While the rank-and-file organization of the military, uniformed and disciplined, might be relied upon to some degree, the reaction of the individual was unknown territory.[47] In 1938, a group of eminent psychiatrists met to discuss their view of the way the civilian might act under such duress. Their conclusions are worth recording in full as they provide a very clear picture of the assumed danger facing the nation and the radical new thinking that now underpinned war planning. They 'envisaged a large and elaborate organisation providing immediate treatment centres in the bombed areas, out-patient clinics running a twenty-four hour service on the outskirts of cities, special hospitals, camps and work settlements in safe areas, and mobile teams of psychiatrists and mobile child guidance clinics. It was suggested that psychiatric casualties might exceed physical casualties by three to one. This would have meant, on the basis of the Government's estimates of killed and wounded, some 3–4 million cases of acute panic, hysteria and other neurotic conditions during the first six months of air attack.'[48]

It was believed by the Mental Health Emergency Committee that the number of people suffering from nervous disorders would 'increase to an extent never before experienced'.[49] In the light of this type of information, it is possible to see the significance of so many of the subsequent actions of government and local authorities, support services and media. On all different levels, from the strategic planning of civil defence, hospital reorganization and evacuation, through to public information broadcasts, public safety films and home front media campaigns, the need to maintain public morale and sustain community spirit was paramount.

Advice on diet, exercise, relaxation and a whole host of self-help remedies for the many and various symptoms of war strain would now come to the fore in new government and advertising campaigns designed to promote the physical stamina and psychological fortitude of the whole nation. Improving levels of fitness and well-being became key elements of sustaining morale on the home front, accompanied by a new, more active visual aesthetic promoting the healthy, energetic and resilient individual. To stay well both physically and mentally was increasingly seen as the personal responsibility of every individual and would be at the heart of famous war slogans such as 'smiling through', 'keep calm and carry on', and 'going to it'.

–5–

# Evacuation

While information and education on health and fitness increasingly reached out to a wider audience, there remained an element of the population for whom such initiatives were of little or no consequence. The poorest families in Britain experienced an endless struggle to feed and clothe their families adequately, and the living conditions of many in this social class mitigated against higher standards of cleanliness, hygiene or diet. When the programme of assisted evacuation began, the appalling truth about the poverty some parts of the community endured began to emerge. The poor clothing and unprepossessing personal appearance of those evacuated from near-destitute families became metaphors for the unresolved want and neediness that had been obscured by more secure economic and commercial growth elsewhere. As children and families of different classes were constrained to live together, the gulf that existed between their lifestyles and outlook now became evident and conflict arose. Standards of dress and hygiene were immediate indicators of difference and where these were perceived as threatening the health and well-being of reception families, there was fear and anxiety. The government now had to confront the deprivation of the poorest evacuated classes and look to create economic adjustments that would offset necessity and bring greater social security for all in the face of impending war.

The population at large would not have been uninformed about poverty. Its connection to unemployment had been well publicized throughout the decade. The National Unemployed Workers' Movement (NUWM) had organized hunger marches in 1930, 1932 and 1934.[1] In October 1936, Ellen Wilkinson, Labour MP for Jarrow, and the Jarrow Town Council organized the Jarrow Protest March of two hundred unemployed men who carried a petition to London with 11,572 signatures asking for work.[2] The march 'co-operated with the authorities [which] earned it more sympathy and publicity than any other' and it became 'the symbol of mass unemployment'.[3] Rose describes a number of other passive protests by the NUWM during Christmas 1938, including one hundred men 'entering the Grill Room at the Ritz to ask for tea, petitioning the king and picketing of the main railway stations on Christmas Eve'[4] and while this 'yielded no change in Government policy [it] . . . did attract widespread press coverage and public attention'.[5]

With regard to the number of people who were unemployed before the war, Titmus reported in 1950 that during 1939, the 'average number of insured persons unemployed in the United Kingdom was 1,480,324, and there were 1,049,718 persons in receipt of poor law relief in England and Wales'.[6] While these figures did not represent 'a standing army of permanently poor, long-unemployed persons', they did give an indication of a basic number that was, in all likelihood, much higher. Titmus suggested that by multiplying the unemployed figure 'several times' and factoring in the families that shared in this hardship, a much-higher experience of unemployment would arise. This would later help account for the large numbers of extremely poor evacuee children emerging from the urban industrial areas where opportunities for work had fallen.[7] Unemployment was much higher in urban areas than rural, and Liverpool was cited as spending over five million pounds on public assistance between 1936 and 1939.[8] The very poorest could obtain only the most limited financial help from the means-tested Poor Law, administrated by the Assistance Boards, and unemployment insurance, which, like poor relief, was also of limited duration and intended to stave off destitution until further work could be found.

One way of tracking the effect of low income on children was to undertake periodic medical checks through school that also registered how pupils were dressed. The statistics on clothing kept by the school Medical Officers of local authorities were found, in retrospect, to have considerably underplayed the reality. In *Our Towns*,[9] Dora Ibberson cited the Chief Medical Officer in 1935 suggesting that standards of clothing and footwear were 'very satisfactory', when in fact figures showed 'nearly half the children, even on . . . pre-announced occasions, as less than satisfactorily dressed'.[10] Ibberson pointed out that the data collected was turned into an average figure that included the best schools so that the reality of the poorer schools being well below this average was not visible. The situation was not satisfactory at all. A similarly unclear picture had arisen from routine school medical inspections undertaken by London County Council nurses during 1938. Ibberson suggested that children probably wore their best clothes on these days and had underwear 'bought for the occasion', which skewered the results.[11] Real deficiency was therefore obscured in the interests of what Titmus called the 'worship of the statistical average'.[12] As the time for evacuation drew nearer, the Ministry of Health clearly grew more concerned about the financial capacity of those living on public assistance or unemployment insurance to provide the clothing and footwear children would need. While Titmus cited no specific reason for this, the answer seemed to lie in the disparity between official reports on clothing, which implied a sufficiency commensurate with health, and a reality that saw local authorities supplementing obvious clothing need. Titmus observed the Glasgow Public Health department doing just this despite reports largely defending the state

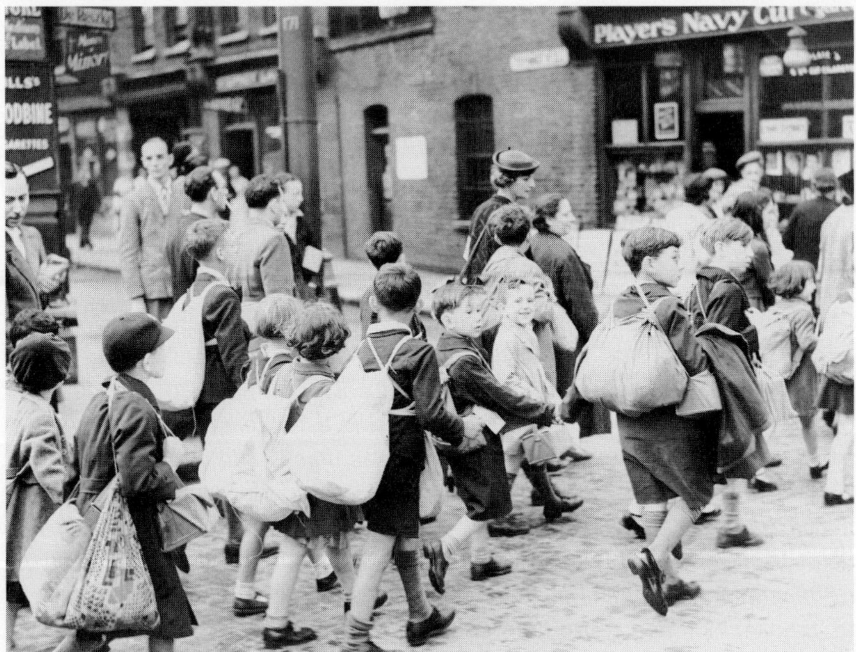


**Figure 2** Evacuation, undated. Children leave London's East End for homes in safer areas. Ministry of Information Second World War Press Agency Print Collection. © Imperial War Museum (HU36238).

of children's clothing.[13] The Treasury finally released money for local authorities to spend on child evacuees, providing one pound 'for every 200 children, on the understanding that no publicity was given to such assistance'.[14]

The scale at which they envisaged need was nothing like the reality. But this would not be known until evacuation had begun and reports began to surface about the quality and type of clothing worn. London received the order for evacuation to commence at County Hall at 11:07 a.m. on 31 August 1939. The exodus of six hundred thousand school-age children and mothers with children under five began the next day. Also included were three hundred special parties of handicapped and nursery children, nearly four thousand pregnant women within one month of confinement, and just over two thousand blind adults. This was only about half of the people originally catered for, and the whole operation was concluded in three days—one day less than expected.[15] The same categories of people also began their move from evacuation zones across England and Scotland, including the teachers and helpers who superintended unaccompanied children in school parties. Titmus recorded that the total number of 'official evacuees' in England came to 89,355, and in Scotland, 13,645. This made a total of

1,473,391. These figures did not include the two million private evacuees who had made their own arrangements, but added to this figure gave the total number of the population that had chosen to evacuate as 'between 3,500,000 and 3,750,000'.[16] Between the commencement of evacuation and 1944, there would be several more waves of evacuation from London and the rest of the country in response to the changing conditions of war,[17] but none would be quite as dramatic in their impact as the first, revealing as it did such large disparities between different sectors of the population in terms of living standards and expectations.

Mass Observation (MO)[18] recorded school parties leaving from Victoria station in London. The atmosphere was positive and the children well organized and mostly smiling. Buckingham Gate School marched in under their own banner, with the girls and boys carrying a range of personal possessions, from shoe bags and haversacks to gas masks and paper parcels. The children wore London County Council red-and-white arm bands to distinguish their point of origin, a device used as an early element of service and civil defence uniform, and teachers also adopted coloured arm bands.[19] In quasi-military manner, the children marched towards their platforms with no attempt to 'break ranks' and get to their watching parents.[20] The *Times* official advice had stressed children were to take with them no more than they could carry,[21] and MO noted that each child had 'bundles of one sort or another hung round it in all directions'.[22] The *Times* had advised parents to provide their children with 'a change of underclothing, night clothes, house shoes or plimsolls, spare stockings or socks, a toothbrush, a comb, towel, soap and face-cloth, handkerchiefs, and, if possible, a warm winter coat or mackintosh,[23] and each parent had been given a list of required articles by the school. MO recorded the comments of a school teacher involved with preparation for evacuation on what mothers did to make sure their children had the right clothing with them: 'The school where I was working was in one of the poor districts, and I was surprised at the thoroughness most of the mothers had displayed in equipping their children. In a batch of twenty . . . only one family of four had not all the listed articles. . . . About half of the twenty had brand-new pyjamas, new soap, new toothbrushes, new plimsolls, new shirts for the boys and new knickers for the girls. . . . A teacher told me that one of the mothers would be paying for her children's new clothes till Christmas.'[24] The fact that she could finish paying for them at all reflected that she was not of the very poorest, but the general care witnessed here was not unusual. Many poor families had clearly made an enormous effort to get everything required, even though this had entailed hardship at home. MO quoted the findings of a report carried out by Dr Gertrud Wagner in Liverpool shortly after evacuation had begun and based on 356 interviews with mothers of evacuees.[25] She found that over half of them, whose children had not returned home, remained in 'serious financial difficulty' and that 'Mothers who might have let their children go on wearing their old things if they had been at home, felt bound to raise the standard when they were staying in other people's homes'.[26] Another mother, described as 'shabby, thin and very anxious', had packed extra toiletries, towels and new clothing so that her children would not be 'any bother to the people they're going to'.[27] It appeared parents wished their children to have the right things, and where this was possible, even if it caused hardship, many worked to achieve a good send-off. This puts into some perspective the torrent of stories that began to emerge about inadequate and squalid clothing. As Titmus remarked, 'It is highly probable that most of the children were sent away in the best that their parents could provide. Apart from the question of pride—and the clothing of children still plays an important role today in matters of social status—it is unlikely that the children were sent to safety while their best clothes were kept at home.'[28]

Getting to the reception areas was not always easy. Some journeys were long and tiring, and trains without food or toilets caused additional discomfort. On arrival, as Calder suggests, 'normally clean children were at their worst, and the condition of the really scruffy ones was unspeakable'.[29] For some, the start was not good. On arrival, children were met by Women's Voluntary Service (WVS) members or similar and taken to halls or village greens to be allocated their new homes. A number of MO respondents described the subsequent ordeal of billeting children, and later mothers and their younger children, as 'akin to a cattle- or slave-market'. The children from Buckingham Gate School were taken to a village green where prospective foster mothers, 'who should not have been allowed on the field at all, just invaded us and walked about the field picking out what they considered to be the most presentable specimens'.[30] For those children from really poor families whose standards of dress and personal appearance were distinctly unprepossessing, the experience was appalling. Harrison provides an indicative and revealing account of some evacuees from a slum-clearance scheme in Edinburgh arriving late at night in their reception area 'in a shocking condition of neglect . . . lousy, afflicted with impetigo and ringworm etc . . . [which] led to a great deal of dissatisfaction on the part of the hosts, where these hosts were well-to-do. Working class hosts either got down to it and cleaned their guests up, or being of the same temper, felt quite at home with them.'[31] While 'social mismatching'[32] had much to do with the outcry over disparate standards, the Women's Group for Public Welfare (WGPW) endorsed that children were arriving in dirty and inadequate clothing and without spare clothing to change into. Ibberson cited children evacuated from the slums of Grimsby, Hull and Manchester as not only very badly equipped and without additional clothing but also in possession of garments that 'often had to be burnt as they were verminous. In other cases the householders had to keep the children in bed

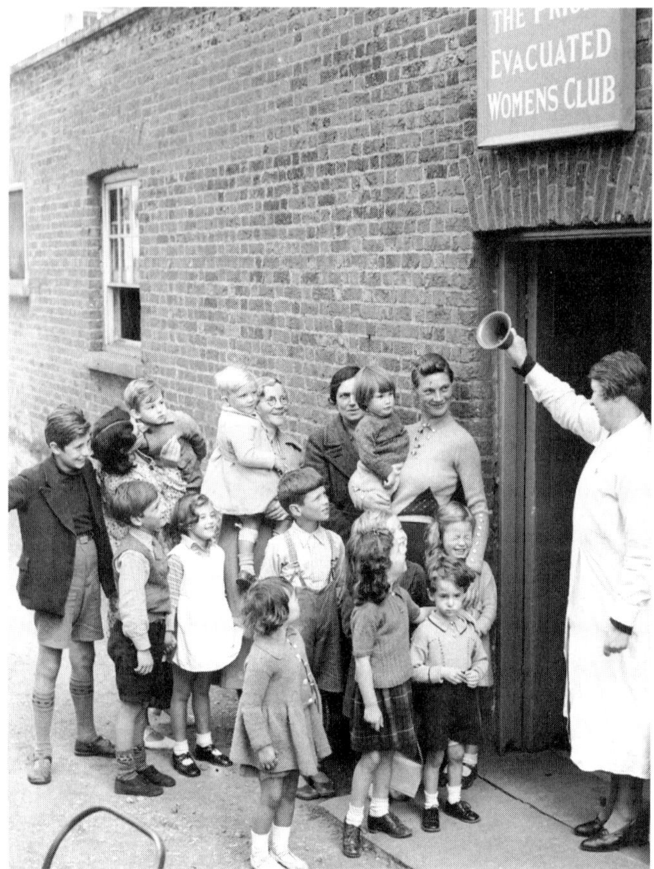


**Figure 3** Evacuees Club, 28 September 1939. 'A member of the Women's Institute rings the lunch bell at The Priory Evacuated Women's Club in Hitchin, Hertfordshire, where evacuated mothers and children meet over a cheap meal'. George W. Hales/Fox Photos/Getty Images. Getty Images (3317827).

while they washed their clothes. Some children arrived sewn into a piece of calico with a coat on top and no other clothes at all.'[33]

Complaints surrounded three areas: the quality and type of clothing, its state in terms of cleanliness and the level of personal hygiene practiced by the evacuee. The latter also included the various illnesses and conditions a child arrived with, including skin diseases and head lice. The poorest children, with little or no appropriate clothing, were also, predictably, the dirtiest and least healthy in general. Clothing here was either ragged and incapable of mending, very dirty or both. Where clothing had been purchased from second-hand stalls, the risk of infection was rife and was a threat to the health and well-being of the host family. Ibberson had identified second-hand clothing as being one of several ways of buying new-to-the-family clothes as outright purchases, as opposed to undertaking some kind of weekly payment scheme. But she associated this practice with women who were 'less good managers' because although the goods bought were cheap, the purchaser ran the risk of receiving 'infective' clothing or clothing that might 'contain the live eggs of lice'.[34] This type of infestation was not just unpleasant, it was potentially dangerous. In an information leaflet entitled 'War on Disease',[35] published by the Central Council for Health Education (CCHE), the concern about lice was made clear. Typhus fever could be spread by infected lice, and although the disease was 'almost unknown in this country . . . it might easily break out if a large number of people became infected with lice. The eggs of the head louse stick to the roots of the hair and are called "nits". The body louse lays its eggs chiefly in the seams of underclothing. . . . The best protection against lice is cleanliness—clean bodies, clean clothing, clean bedding.'[36]

If the householder was anxious, the best recourse might be to delouse, information about which could be found in a follow-up leaflet from the CCHE called 'Unwanted Guests'. Information was also made available on troublesome skin diseases that were contact contagious, such as scabies, ringworm and impetigo, as a number of evacuees had been found suffering from these conditions which could be caught either by direct contact with an infected person or 'from infected towels and bedding etc.' Cleanliness was the best safeguard, and householders could apply to the local authorities for assistance in having 'clothes and bedding disinfected'. To stay healthy, people were advised to 'wash the hands after going to the W.C. . . . Change underclothes regularly. . . . Bath at least once a week.'[37]

It was a relatively easy, if unpleasant, matter to wash dirty and soiled clothing, but less easy to find the clean garment almost unwearable through age and raggedness. An associated problem was training children with little or no understanding of the common practices of hygiene into new routines of toilet use and bathing. Oliver Lyttelton, later President of the Board of Trade, was shocked when he found his evacuees 'completely ignorant of the simplest rules of hygiene' and using 'the floors and carpets as suitable places upon which to relieve themselves'.[38]

Even modest homes found themselves in the position of needing to replace evacuee clothing at their own expense because the poorest children 'do not know what it is to have a spare set of underclothing; they have no nightclothes, but sleep in their day underwear; warmth is provided by accumulation of cheap garments worn one above the other and excluding air from the skin; overcoats and mackintoshes are never worn, and satisfactory footwear is rarely found. Some boys are brought up to wear no underclothing but a shirt, cotton or union, and the effects of this upon health should be urgently examined.'[39] That the dress practices of the poor were not only at variance with the classes above them but also often unsanitary and unhealthy was alarming. It highlighted the gulf that existed between the poorest and the rest and revealed alternative clothing protocols that were a reflection of the poverty of circumstances. The socialist Lord Provost of Glasgow, Lord Darling, defended the evacuees: 'These children . . . are more deserving of sympathy than censure. They come from houses which have been denied the amenities of modern civilisation, and are the victims of an environment that would have been impossible if in bygone years men had thought more of homes and families than of profits and dividends.'[40] The power of clothing to act as an indicator of pernicious social disadvantage and to represent a society at once divided and unfair had significantly increased in the context of the evacuation scheme. It revealed a culture of poverty that had learnt to function despite squalor and insolvency, self-contained within communities where self-help and shared neighbourhood ills had sustained an insecure and unstable way of life.

Two questions were raised. Where had the clothes come from that these children did own, and what could be done to ameliorate the needs they were now seen to have? The first question brought to greater consciousness the role of the clothing clubs and pawnbrokers of the preceding years, the second a requirement for government intervention and support for new social welfare initiatives. These needed to address not only the most pressing needs of the poor for decent clothing, boots and shoes, but also create a new infrastructure of support that could continue to uphold higher and healthier standards of dress.

Pawnbrokers lent money on clothes for redemption later. A survey conducted in 1935 and cited by the WGPW in their 1943 report showed that pawnbrokers and second-hand markets were the most used methods of obtaining clothing. The survey had been carried out in London and Birmingham, and the WGPW believed it still reflected 'a fair picture of the buying of the poorest class in the towns mentioned'.[41] With 27 per cent of the total, the pawnbrokers and second-hand merchants offered different types of service, but to similar ends. Pawnbroking was described in detail in Walter Greenwood's novel *Love on the Dole,* published in 1933.[42] Set in the industrial north of England in an area not too far from Salford, Greenwood depicts the lives of several families living at the borderlines of poverty. All worked, bar the married women, but jobs were either very poorly paid or seasonal, resulting in hand-to-mouth living. The women regularly visited the pawnbrokers on Monday morning to borrow money on clothing for the week ahead. When Friday—payday—came, the best Sunday suits of the men, for example, could be redeemed, if only temporarily, to be back at the pawnbrokers the following Monday. In this way, Greenwood depicted the pawnbroker as a money-lending service located largely around clothing: 'Next Friday or Saturday . . . they would hand over their wages . . . in return for whatever they pawned today. And next Monday they would pawn again whatever they pawned today, paying Mr Price interest on interest until they were so deep in the mire of debt that not only did Mr Price own their and their family's clothes, but also the family income as well. They could not have both at the same time. . . . The women were come to redeem the moneys with the family raiment so that they might pay off their tick account for food which stood against their names in the books of Mr Hulkington, the street corner provision merchant.'[43] Debt was relentless and food and clothing inextricably bound up with it. When families were no longer able to redeem clothing, it could be sold, and on this basis the pawnbrokers became another type of second-hand outlet, running the same risks as the second-hand shops. Greenwood depicted a temporary escape of a type from this cycle of deprivation in the earning capacity of the young sons and daughters living at home who, although they gave up much of what they earned for keep, nevertheless had a little for themselves. He described the mill girls as wearing 'cheap artificial silk stockings, cheap short-skirted frocks, cheap coats, cheap shoes, crimped hair, powder and rouge'. They would work five and a half days weekly 'until they married when picture theatres became luxuries and Saturday dances, Sunday parades and cheap finery ceased altogether'.[44] The family—and the larger family, in particular—was seen as intrinsic to the slide into poverty and need that had so characterized the poorest evacuees.

Pawnbroking allowed clothing to be used as a redeemable asset over hard times, while second-hand offered the chance of a cheap but outright purchase. After these options, the second most popular choice for clothing was the clothing club, or Tallyman method, referred to earlier.[45] This required buying on an instalment system of so much a week. The WGPW had found many of these clubs to be especially iniquitous in charging inflated prices for very shoddy goods. They went to some lengths to explain how this was done by the combined efforts of the club, the club salesman and the shops associated with the clubs. These all took their margin of profit, causing the price of goods to escalate.[46] Women were often constrained to exchange club checks at shops offering very poor quality so that inflated prices and debt went hand in hand with badly made clothing that did not last. The WGPW report quoted a caretaker from a large block of working-class flats explaining the club system as he understood it: 'To get people into debt and then keep them in it is the sole aim of firms that I shall discuss . . . they are not concerned whether a man's children have shoes or blankets on their beds, but they are concerned in selling "tripe" at exorbitant prices . . . by this I mean shoes with compressed cardboard soles, cotton blankets, kiddies blazers of very inferior flannel, in fact most "Tally" goods are very conspicuous by their poor quality.'[47] This type of buying formed the basis of many working-class wardrobes and goes some way towards explaining the small amount of inferior clothing possessed by the poorest evacuees.

The WGPW noted how few purchases were made for cash in the 1935 survey. On a more positive note, there was some security in buying from 'unpretentious and old-established shops . . . or clothing club run by a neighbour'. This smaller type of local club might not charge commercial premiums and so represented 'a genuine effort to meet the difficulties of people on low income'.[48] Apart from these possibilities and buying at sale time, the only other way clothing or footwear could be obtained was through charity. There seemed a variety of different charitable mechanisms ranging from school needlework and knitting classes in better-off schools that made gifts for the poor to church charities that distributed goods where need was perceived. Ivy Green remembered being 'made aware of "others less fortunate than ourselves"' and was 'encouraged to join the Working Party, making articles of clothing etc for the poorer children of Battersea. These items were put on display in the hall before being collected by the Mayor.'[49] Other forms of charity were associated with the welfare provided by the Assistance Board, organized at a local level, and beyond that the help and kindness of family and close neighbours. When much of the infrastructure of this level of support was removed by evacuation, particularly for mothers and young children, it was not surprising that inadequacy and need could no longer be staved off or hidden.

How were these needs to be met? Titmus recounted that in the first instance, 'charitable schemes' were organized quite widely to offer immediate aid in terms of money and gift clothing, and as early as 8 September, the Ministry of Health broadcast an appeal for second-hand clothing.[50] Other schemes followed, but charity was not the right way to deal with ongoing need of this kind. On 7 November 1939, the Ministry of Health informed local authorities that if help with essential clothing and footwear could not be had from unemployment benefit, the poor law or other charitable organizations, a fifteen-thousand-pound grant would now be available from which money could be drawn to help specific cases of need. Once again, this offer of financial aid was not to be made public by the Directors of Education in the evacuation areas who would now be responsible for disbursing the money. Cases of need were referred by the head teacher in the reception area. Thus a clothing scheme of sorts arose.

In the climate of social welfare prevalent at the time, two elements underpinned this first tier of the scheme: parental responsibility to provide for their children was still considered the first priority, so no money could be given out until the parents' ability to pay had been means tested, and no aid from taxpayers' money could be made available until such an investigation had occurred. Separate clauses outlined the special conditions pertaining to families already in receipt of other state benefits so that, taken all together, the scheme proved laborious and time consuming. Administrative procedure was put before child welfare, which in the meantime was sustained by the good offices of host families and voluntary handouts.[51] Clothes prices continued to spiral,[52] and the needs of a country winter were fast approaching. The *Daily Worker* reported on 4 November that the London County Council (LCC) had decided to provide clothing where necessary for parents receiving public assistance.[53] To what extent this might have influenced, or been influenced by, the work of the Ministry of Health is unclear. The *Daily Worker* also reported that a full list of the items children who were going out on the supplementary evacuation scheme would need had now been issued by the LCC. This list was later endorsed by the WGPW, who upheld it as something of a standard of adequacy where one had not previously existed.[54] The full list asked for the same toiletries and towel as before but made explicit the need for a second pair of boots for all and the type of daywear expected for both boys and girls commensurate with climate and environment.[55]

This system rumbled on for a year. Titmus believed that had bombs fallen earlier than they did, the scheme's inadequacies would have been revealed much sooner.[56] In the meantime, the Women's Voluntary Service (WVS), who had ample opportunity to assess the workings of the evacuation scheme as they organized the reception of, and some level of oversight for, evacuated children, put together some guidelines on clothing for 'those caring for unaccompanied children in the reception areas'. Their leaflet spelt out the rules and enabled some level of monitoring to take place.[57] Foster parents were reminded that while they had a responsibility to launder and care for clothing, they were not required to replace it, and that mending parties and voluntary laundries had started up—largely run by members of the WVS—to help them with the extra household chores occasioned by evacuation. The leaflet asked the teachers, welfare committees and billeting officers who had to contact parents if new clothing or footwear was becoming necessary to remind them of the need for more durable items for country living and not to send smart but rather 'sensible' goods. Another list was appended that underlined necessary items for children to have as opposed to those deemed desirable by hosts who enjoyed a higher standard of living. In March 1940, the LCC issued a further notice in readiness for the next wave of evacuation in June 1940, known as Plan IV, laying out clear guidelines for the continuing assessment of evacuee clothing and footwear by teachers as well as providing information on the health checks each child would have to comply with prior to leaving home.[58]

Small refinements were therefore made to shore up the first clothing scheme. The second and third waves of evacuation from London continued in June and July 1940 (LCC Plan IV and Plan V) in response to the blitzkrieg in Europe and the increasing threat to home security, but it was not until the heavy bombing of Britain had already begun that any real changes were made to the provision for necessitous children. Under these new conditions of war, women and children were now leaving industrial and city centres both because they wished to and because they had been made homeless. In this context, the requirement for shelter, food and clothing now took on a whole new dimension. By October 1940, 'it was no longer the recovery of costs from parents but the need to clothe the children that took first place'.[59] The original allowance of one pound a year per two hundred children was revised to one pound per thirty children, still without publicity, and local authorities could now choose how best to implement the provision of clothing and footwear to speed the process up. The WVS was brought in to help by running county clothing depots and clothing exchanges amongst the large number of other duties they also masterminded.

Titmus recorded that by 1942, there were 'some 1,500 W.V.S. issuing depots in the country helping to supply the needs of evacuees, refugees and homeless people. The value of clothing and footwear was then estimated at £5,000,000, much of it having originated by gift from the American and Canadian Red Cross Societies and other voluntary sources.'[60] As people moved around the country, clothing clubs and Tallymen could no longer operate, and, with the advent of better ways to procure necessary clothing and footwear, a greedy and profit-driven system was superseded. The London County Council Clothing Scheme was instituted in November 1940 under the WVS and provided reception area clothing depots with two kinds of material. The records of the LCC recalled that these were either 'official' or 'gift'. Gifted Goods

> were received in large quantities, particularly from the American Red Cross, [while] material supplied by the Ministry [of Health] was made up by the W.V.S. and purchases were made with official funds. Clothing was issued from the depots when parents did not meet their children's needs, and recovery was made from the parents according to means. Thus if the child's need was for clothing to the value of £3 and the parent could afford £1, official stock was issued to this value and gift stock to the value of £2.[61]

No child now left the LCC area without proper clothing, and there was a reserve depot for any additional needs.[62]

For parents who simply could not afford to provide clothing and footwear fit-for-purpose and in the right amount, a system was devised that, while it took advantage of charitable giving, also established new government welfare initiatives. These were an acknowledgement that the health and well-being of the poorest could be maintained in no other way. Endemic poverty could not heal itself. Only with the move towards full employment and better wages would the situation begin to mend gradually from within.[63] Smith suggests that evacuation became 'something of a minor social revolution . . . one of those unforeseen and unavoidable consequences bequeathed by the 1930s on 1940'.[64] Nowhere were the living conditions of the poor so clearly reflected than in their lack of basic clothing and personal dignity. Clothes became politically powerful tools that illustrated the divided social reality that existed in Britain. The inequality they reflected was both shocking and alarming. Dirty laundry had indeed become public, compromising not only the humanitarian objectives of the evacuation process itself but the national unity of purpose it sought to promote. Prior to rationing, therefore, the principle of fairer shares had already been acknowledged and acted on. The provision of essential and sufficient clothing now stood as a symbol of an increasing sense of local and national government responsibility to safeguard the well-being of the least advantaged of its citizens and laid a foundation for future advances in social welfare.

That social and state intervention, no matter how gradual or recalcitrant, took place to ameliorate the conditions of these people demonstrated both public and governmental conviction that all sectors of the community should be entitled to good health and hygiene. This belief had to underpin any new politics of fitness. Even if expediency had motivated governmental intervention, continuing improvements in welfare and the opportunity for full employment would bring about real and lasting benefits which would render such unmitigated poverty in Britain a thing of the past.

# –6–

# Fashions for a Phoney War

At 11.15 a.m. on Sunday, 3 September 1939, Neville Chamberlain confirmed that Britain was at war with Germany. For the eight months of 'peace-in-war'[1] that followed, Britain was to experience very little direct conflict on home soil, although there was much action overseas to engage attention through newspapers and cinema newsreels. During this time, however, there were significant shifts on the home front in terms of cost-of-living rises, changing employment opportunities and the effects on the public at large of the state of being at war. These factors combined to produce different perspectives on dress practice that would subsequently underpin more permanent shifts in fashion consciousness. During the early months of war, some changes were already noticeable on the streets. Amongst these was the wearing of uniform, 'one of the war's strongest images',[2] for both the armed services and various civilian occupations. The uniformed woman became a prime influence on both the developing war aesthetic and the expression of a new attitude towards the use and wear of clothing. Other indications of war ranged from the practical necessity of carrying gas masks to the military references adopted by some civilian styles.

Harris cites that ATS volunteers had been complaining that they had to wear uniform even when off duty.[3] This had clearly meant a much higher profile of uniform wearing in social and civilian environments and caused the owner of Mercia and Co., Mr H. Scott, a specialist retailer in debutante dresses and designer daywear, to express heated concern over the state of dressing since war had broken out. In conversation for Mass Observation in December 1939, he vented his anger and irritation over dress codes breaking down through the wearing of uniform, particularly during the evening. Civilian dress had responded by becoming less formal, and this had led to repercussions for trade in luxury wear. His cure for the situation was that 'every man and woman in H.M. Forces should be allowed to get into mufti on any leave, daily, weekend, any time they have any leave but wearing a miniature badge. Somebody should put it to Belisha.'[4] The service rules were changed by early 1940 when civilian clothing was allowed for home leave,[5] but the presence of uniform in everyday life would only increase as women volunteered for the services and took up uniformed civilian employment.

As the wealthier classes still tended to be made officers, particularly at the beginning of recruitment and the early stages of war,[6] they obtained their uniform more quickly through military tailors such as Savile Row's Huntsman and Gieves and the less exclusive Austen Reed, Hector Powe and Moss Bross, amongst others. Uniform—and good-quality uniform well cut and in excellent materials—therefore, became much more noticeable more quickly in just those social circles where it would have most impact on other forms of dress. The fight to retain evening attire was one of the most significant early responses to war by the fashion trade and will be returned to shortly.

At peak strength, the number of women serving in the Women's Auxiliary Forces would lie in the region of 463,000.[7] In civilian life much larger numbers of women would enter either full- or part-time work many of whom would wear some type of uniform. Braybon and Summerfield estimated that by 1943 '7,750,000 women were in paid work' and went on to summarize that 'if part-time and voluntary work were taken into account, fully 80 per cent of married women and 90 per cent of single women were by now contributing to the war effort'.[8]

One of the largest forces of women workers was that of the WVS, the Women's Voluntary Service. With over 250,000 members already in place immediately after the Munich crisis, membership rose to 370,000 in September 1939, of which 200,000 were involved exclusively with evacuation work. Over a million women served with the WVS during the war, and another 750,000 took part in the 'Housewives Service' from their homes.[9] Uniform pieces were paid for by the member herself, and coupons surrendered after June 1941 with the advent of clothes rationing. The WVS featured significantly in a wide range of social and welfare roles, and their dress code of grey-green tweed coat or suit, red blouse and grey-green summer dress, or more simply badge or arm band, would have been well known.[10]

Other occupations might feature specific arm bands or badges. For example, women in the Home Guard auxiliary had no uniform but could wear a plastic badge featuring the Home Guard initials surrounded by a wreath.[11] The whole range of civil defence services was rather haphazardly dressed as war began, but through a variety of overalls, battle dress, arm bands and helmets were able to differentiate themselves to reflect their authority and responsibilities. The many services that built up the home front, as featured in the Ministry of Information's *Home Front Handbook,*[12] first published on 15 September 1943, only revealed to what extent people would have been accustomed to seeing uniforms on the streets and in their homes as much as in service barracks and camps. Women's war work was celebrated in Arthur Wauters's *Eve in Overalls,*[13] published after September 1942, which reminded the public, if they needed it, of the enormous variety of roles women were now taking on, many of which had quite specific dress codes clearly differentiating their new working lives from those they had been leading in their homes.

Traditional patterns of life, roles and aspirations began to undergo enforced changes. For some this shift would be temporary and for the duration only, while for others it represented a more permanent break from pre-war life, resulting in different hopes and expectations for the future.[14] As women, both single and married, took on new roles, they often adopted appropriate forms of dress to accommodate their working lives, so reflecting a broader cultural shift into what might be seen as a predominantly male order. Uniform and workwear signified a break with traditional paradigms of femininity. The divisions between the sexes became less visually rigid. Clothing, in many ways unintentionally, became an arena for reviewing gender definitions and clarifying issues of status and identity. On one level, clothes moved simply and logically towards practicality and ease of wear. On another, they challenged what it was to be a woman and raised issues about the nature of equality and freedom of choice.

In an interview for Mass Observation in March 1940, the fashion historian James Laver had remarked, 'Women wear uniform when their function is more important than their sex. Men always wear uniform because their function is usually more important than women's. A man dresses not as a man but as a banker.'[15] This view clearly expressed the relative positions of men and women as they had been, but not as they might now be. Traditional adornment practices that had expressed femininity in predictable dress codes appeared to be happily accommodating a new functionalism that moved away from the safe, known territory of feminine attire. This in turn reflected women encountering new working horizons where they would experience the inevitable conflict between old and new ways of living and self-expression. How they navigated their way through the various dress options open to them and what this revealed about conceptions of femininity and identity can now be investigated.

Looking back from the vantage point of January 1940, the *Vogue Pattern Book* recorded that full evening dress had been fashion's first 'casualty of the war'. It went on to explain that 'in those early uncertain weeks it was obviously out of place'.[16] For the more affluent woman, the wearing of evening dress quickly became not merely out of place, but also against the protocols of dress in terms of not mixing with uniform. The new, more informal styles of dress that took over at nightclubs and restaurants not only meant less elaborate dress routines for the wearer but less profit for the dress trade. Businesses had been affected right from the outbreak of war as many houses were preparing, in the early days of September, to show their new seasonal offerings. As Jean Smith, secretary of the London Fashion Group,[17] explained to Priscilla Feare of Mass Observation, 'everything went haywire for the first three weeks. Most fashion houses simply closed down altogether. Everything was in a terrible mess. You see it came at a bad time, just when designers should have been bringing out their new collections, designs that had first been thought out before the war ever started.'[18] Mercia and Co.'s Mr Scott concurred. 'The most disastrous thing about the war is that all the model houses were going to show their evening collections when war broke out. It wasn't so much a question of a buyer coming in and buying a collection of evening frocks and then showing them straight away. In September they buy evening stuff to show at the end of September and beginning of October. All that trade was immediately annihilated. And everybody was already committed for peace goods . . . nobody bought any evening stuff at all. There was that awful atmosphere about, that it was bad form to wear evening clothes.'[19] Profits dropped at Mercia from between seven and nine thousand pounds at the same time the previous year to just ninety-nine pounds. Interestingly Scott does see this as the extreme end of a trend that had already been 'growing steadily for the past two years' and cited his own company's advertising campaigns in both *Vogue* and *Tatler* condemning 'dress laziness'[20]. He blamed men's increasingly less formal dress styles for this. Now, and on top of this movement towards informality, short frocks were being worn by women in place of full evening dress to accompany men who were no longer wearing dinner jackets in deference to those required to wear uniform.

While war clearly affected one particular aspect of the fashion market, the public were asked to curb their spending on clothing in general by the Chancellor of the Exchequer, Sir John Simon. In a speech in the last week of November, reported as headline news in the *Drapers' Record* for 2 December, Simon's request to the public to buy nothing unless it was absolutely necessary was taken severely to task by trade interests. The report cited the National Savings Committee's statement, which twice asked people to 'refrain from buying new clothes'. *Drapers*' commented that 'thousands have already done so, hence the existing unemployment in the dress industry . . . Surely the most sensible way to help raise the vast sum needed by the Treasury is for spending to continue steadily, as far as possible on home produced goods, thereby maintaining employment, the number of wage earners and tax payers.'[21] It was certainly true that civilian spending had already fallen off noticeably without prompting from government. The *Tailor and Cutter* had reported as early as 15 September that 'civilians have almost stopped buying clothes', although they predicted a change coming. They suggested that the morale of the home front would soon be affected by such a 'sackcloth and ashes' approach to clothes rather than 'dressing well' and reminded readers that a 'spick and span nation remains cheerful and buoyant'.[22] But trends did not reverse significantly enough for the clothing and dress trade. There were lay-offs and redundancies to the extent that Simon soon revoked his previous appeals for thrift. The *Drapers' Record* reported on 16 December that Sir John was now saying 'go on spending if by so doing you keep other people at work'.[23]

Jean Smith suggested the downturn in spending, particularly for those buying clothes for social entertainments, was almost inevitable in the early weeks of war as 'the Government closed everything—cinemas, amusements, theatres, evacuating everyone'.[24] *Vogue*'s advice on the outbreak of war had been to encourage women to go ahead and shop for their autumn wardrobes, telling their moneyed readers that 'every time you hold back from buying, you throw the national economy a fraction off its balance. Multiply that by millions, and it becomes a considerable punch on the very chin which the dress trade is trying to keep up.'[25] But prices were rising, and there was confusion from shoppers as to whether to buy or not. Harrison and Madge recorded this dilemma in their Mass Observation survey of changing social attitudes, *War Begins at Home*. On the cautionary side, one saver raised the issue of the wastefulness of spending more on poorer quality, while another thought that, with supplies becoming scarce and prices therefore high, having a little money in hand was no bad thing.[26] Other respondents who had been practicing careful buying to supplement what they already had believed goods could be of more value than money or wanted to maintain supplies while they could still afford to. Sir John's own vacillations had not helped, and it was left up to the trade to engineer new approaches to encourage spending. Creating new war lines and diversifying around emerging trends were ways to do this, both to satisfy public demand and combat distress in the industry.

New perspectives on evening wear now connected to broader considerations about what was appropriate apparel for daytime. By December, the daywear section of the clothing industry had clearly moved towards less formality, with work clothing such as 'slacks, boiler suits and uniforms' all now 'popular for normal daily wear'.[27] Elements of the luxe dress trade fought a rearguard action to retain evening elegance, ostensibly for reasons of morale, by trying to shame women into dressing more glamorously. The *Drapers' Record* reported that 'some fashion producers are acting individually in an effort to revive interest in evening wear. They are sending women relatives or mannequins to attend restaurants and night clubs attired in elaborate evening creations.'[28] Mary Joyce, editor of *Woman's Wear News*, was not in favour of this type of action: 'I don't think it's any good sending beautifully dressed mannequins into restaurants, as some fashion specialists have suggested. It wouldn't make women ashamed. It would be more likely to have the opposite effect. If I went into a restaurant in a décolleté evening gown and sat next to a woman in Service uniform, I should feel most embarrassed.'[29] Her view was that to try and keep reinteresting people in this form of dress was a mistake and that more emphasis should now be placed on the types of short daywear dresses that were doing double duty for a range of social events throughout the day. A fashion gala was, nevertheless, arranged for 12 December at Grosvenor House with the object of helping Christmas sales of more glamorous day and evening wear. Proceedings were opened on the offensive. Lady Hart-Dyke, presiding, asked women, 'Do the men like to see you dressed badly? . . . Of course not!'[30] The idea that practical dressing was either slack, lazy or just bad was easy to raise not only in the relatively safe environs of the Grosvenor amongst women with similar interests and spending power, but also in the context of a phoney war that had not, as yet, made some of these less formal approaches to clothing essential. But appealing to women's vanity was not necessarily a successful tactic beyond Mayfair. There had been, as Mary Joyce surmised, a definite shift in the way women were approaching clothes, and recognizing and adapting to these changes would now be the way ahead for the fashion industry at large.

The sort of clothing Joyce suggested were daytime-length outfits, kept quite simple in design, dressed up with 'lots of chunky gold jewellery at the neck and that sort of thing'. For evening she suggested the 'evening jumper—again with gold trimmings and braid, and worn with a dark skirt. Styles like these are the things to push, because they are so practical, and if you have what the Americans call a background dress, you can vary it with all sorts of different accessories.' Her advice for fashion was to move away from peacetime practice 'because conditions are different now, and we need new styles to meet the new conditions. . . . I wouldn't feel like going out in the evening in a backless chiffon dress when you might have to rush to an air-raid shelter any time, would you?'[31] The status of being at war, it seemed, was too strong not to have an effect on fashion. It began to change people's everyday lives and maintained an imaginative hold over them in terms of what war might bring at any time.

The November issue of *Vogue* had endeavoured to sum up exactly where fashion was after two months of war preparations. In an article entitled 'Fashion Meets the Challenge of War', it confirmed that 'a picture gown looks as démodé as a picture hat'. Fashion had turned an 'acrobatic somersault' away from the 'wasp-waists and fragility' that Paris had launched back in August towards a new 'robustness and shrewd common-sense' for day clothes. With practicality as the new key note, *Vogue* reflected on the serviceability of town clothes that had to be less rigidly urban in colour, cut and silhouette. Sharper lines were displaced by clothes with an 'imperturbable ease', made in tweed fabrics by choice and with coats cut generously to 'swallow up suits without trace'. Larger pockets now became more popular on swing-style coats and would gain even greater currency as practical accessory features for blitz conditions. Shoes were 'built for business . . . solid-soled [and] square-heeled', and sensible was now fashionable. Hats too had to fit properly as a 'flighty hat, tugged by the wind, is as incongruous in town, with gas mask satchel and flat shoes, as it ever was in the country'. *Vogue* somewhat diplomatically did not outlaw all long lines of evening dress at this stage, although November's *Vogue* would have been put together at least a month earlier, but rather recognized a significant shift in the way remaining long lines could be worn. They promoted slim-lined 'restrained evening elegance' and dressing down in quiet jersey silk or wool dresses that fitted warmly around neck, wrist and ankles. The less formal cut of clothing became, therefore, one of the first elements of the changing war aesthetic. While a smart fitted look remained important, clothes in general had to be easier to wear, move in, put on, take off and keep looking good. With less time for, or interest in, the more studied and elegant

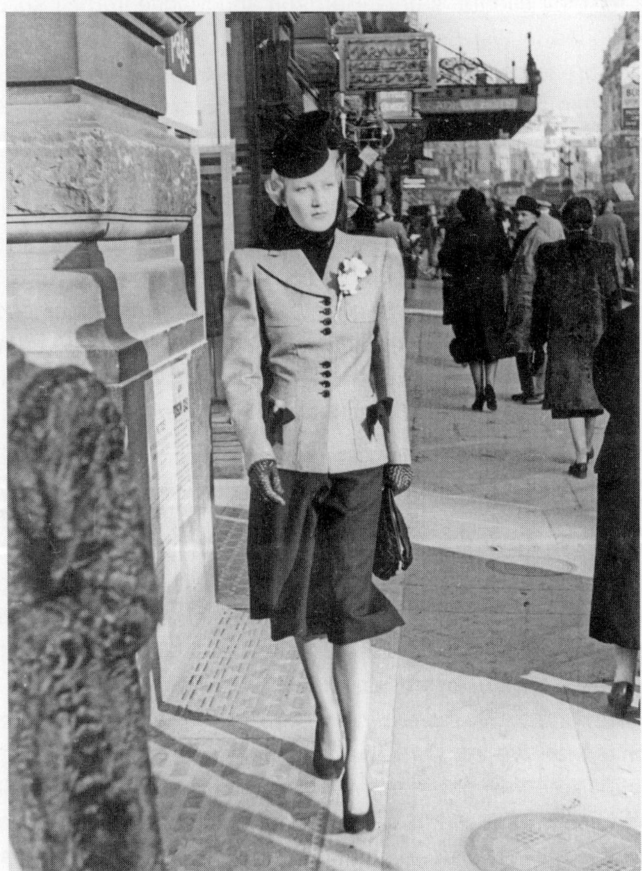

**Figure 4** 'A Pretty Girl Goes for a Walk', 1 January 1940. This *Picture Post* image featured a tailored square shouldered suit with jacket buttons and trim matching the pleated skirt. Zoltan Glass/Getty Images (2696645).

refinements of dress, simpler styles in more relaxed fabrics created softer silhouettes. These, as far as *Vogue* was concerned, still exhibited 'immense charm'.[32] Popular colours to offset both khaki and the blackout included the darker shades of pink—*Vogue* suggested raspberry and prune—and cocoa brown, with a range of white fabrics and accessories.

In terms of fashion trends for the early months of the war there were some that looked likely to prove influential yet failed to sustain public interest and others that were criticized and pilloried yet survived to become important stories for war fashion. One such unsuccessful trend was for blackout clothing and accessories. As war began it appeared that the extremely dark conditions that prevailed for a few weeks would influence colours for garments and accessories and various retailers were quick to produce fashionable coordinating pieces for their clients' safety. Harrison and Madge in their survey on the blackout included in *War Begins at Home* reported that 'the whole structure of British leisure is being changed by the black-out'.[33] Women were more affected by it than men, with women tending to be more intimidated by the lack of lighting in public spaces, while men found it boring rather than frightening.[34] Lights had been doused to hinder the accuracy of aerial bombing, and the restrictions it caused made any form of travel after dark hazardous. Traffic accidents and road deaths went up,[35] and while entertainment establishments had reopened by December,[36] the difficulties of travel to and from these venues operated against frequent trips out. Petrol rationing for domestic cars complicated travel plans and cars that were in use had to be suitably blacked out.[37]

The problems attendant on blacked-out journeys had repercussions. Of more lasting significance, entertainment hours and locations altered, particularly for those used to partying well into the night. *Vogue* reported that 'playtime hours' had changed. Evenings were now beginning at five o'clock, instead of eight, and ending at the much earlier hour of eleven compared to two the following morning. The Berkeley Hotel had instituted tea dances to accommodate these earlier starts.[38] As the blackout made travelling more precarious, dress not only had to be practical to facilitate more walking, and on cold nights, but also to provide the wearer with elements that could be seen after dark. Jean Guest reminded retailers in the *Drapers' Record* that 'white accessories are sought eagerly by many shoppers; what can you supply for "safety wear" during black-out time?' The accompanying illustration showed a young women with 'gas-mask case, hand-bag and broad belt in white'.[39] *Vogue*, too, advertised an ensemble from Fortnum and Mason comprising a 'shining white silk waterproof' at five and a half guineas with a matching white waterproof hat at two guineas. Both were practical and bright for 'November's bleak black-out days' and were accessorized with a white umbrella. Lilywhites offered a white curly wool coat with hood in white with a red lining.[40] Items across the price band became available and in the first flurry of the blackout appeared desirable as well as sensible. Yet it is hard to gauge just how popular wearing some form of white garment or accessory was at this period given that the skies remained quiet and blackout restrictions were soon relaxed. This allowed a subdued level of street and shop lighting to be reintroduced, which continued until restrictions were reimposed during the blitz.[41] In November 1939, *Vogue* featured a white armband on a dark-brown suit[42] that anticipated an official campaign run the following year during the winter of 1940–1941 to promote wearing something white during the blitz. A Mass Observation report that monitored the success of 'For safety's sake wear something white' came to the unexpected conclusion that almost no one was taking the wearing of white seriously despite the now hazardous night-time conditions. Notwithstanding intensive publicity in the press and through posters, 'an average of only one person in a thousand was wearing a white arm-band after dark in London'. The highest figure for members of the public in London wearing some form of white at night during February and March 1941 was only 9 per cent.[43] It is difficult to imagine why people chose not to take these precautions, but in the absence of evidence to the contrary, the dangers on the ground, if not from above, must have been considered overrated.

Another trend that did not sustain initial enthusiasm was for carrying fashionably customized gas mask containers. The trade's attempt to create a quasifashion statement out of the necessity to carry a gas mask soon lost public interest despite the risk still connected with gas attack. The public had been asked to obtain masks in September 1938, and thirty-eight million were given out. They were carried in small square cardboard boxes on a long piece of string, and there were Mickey Mouse masks for very young children and glass cylinder masks, where air was pumped in, for babies. Calder suggests that at this stage, 'fitting on these grotesque combinations of pig snout and death's head, sniffing the gas-like odour of rubber and disinfectant inside them, millions imagined the dangers ahead more clearly'.[44] When no gas attacks happened at the outset of war, people were still prepared to carry them around just in case. Retailers were beginning to recognize marketing opportunities in offering replacement carriers for the rather inadequate official cardboard and the *Drapers' Record* suggested, in early September 1939, that there could be 'a big potential market here (among women at least) for coloured straps to tone with their clothes and counteract the grimness of the situation. Also why not sell waterproof covers . . . in gay colours.'[45] Gas mask handbags appeared and Harrison and Madge spoke of the competition between women to obtain 'coloured or unusual containers'. According to their Mass Observation reporters, women 'favoured cylindrical (not tin), conical, purse and bag carriers which were practically never carried by men . . . [whilst]

very few women, [and] many men carried their masks in knapsacks or tin containers'.[46] In November, *Vogue* was advertising a 'gas mask container and bag combined', made by Tallulah's, in black, brown or navy calf leather costing twenty-one shillings.[47] Jan Struther, writing as Mrs. Miniver in early October 1939, described the practice of gas mask carrying: 'Of course, the people who are natural born dowds still manage to make their gas masks look dowdy, but those who are normally well-turned-out somehow contrive to make them into a positive decoration. It isn't only a question of having one of the many expensive and pansified cases which are on the market. Though I admit they help; it's more that most people have now learned to carry the thing with an air—with panache. You might think, walking about London, that everybody was going off to a picnic with a box of special food.' The humour endeavoured to

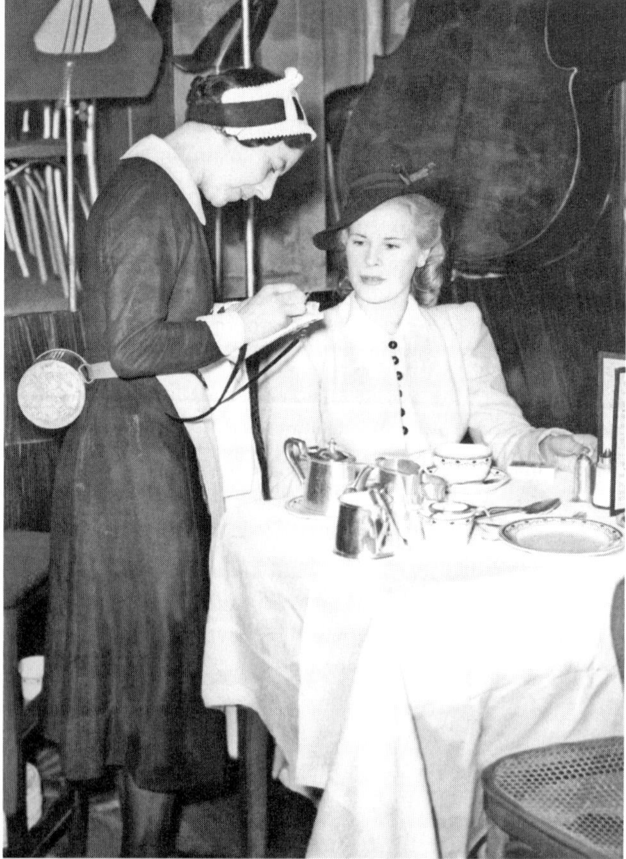

**Figure 5** 'Waitresses Carry Gas Masks on Duty', 6 September 1939. Keystone-France/Gamma-Keystone via Getty Images (107414603). © 1939 Keystone-France.

neutralize anxiety by turning an object of distaste and fear into a fashion accessory. Also, in this vein, Mrs. Miniver expressed her view that 'Hitler, poor misguided man, has made the biggest mistake of his life in giving us a month of this kind of peace-in-war in which to become calm, collected and what is more, chic'.[48] By December 1939, however, Harrison and Madge were reporting that very few people now carried gas masks. For them, 'one important outward symbol of "unity" has gone by the board'.[49]

Other elements of a developing war aesthetic proved far more durable, however, reflecting a willing adaptation to changes in the home front environment. In this category came the much larger and sustained trade in overalls for women, and their derivatives, known as siren suits. These garments signified an acceptance of new working paradigms through the overturning of more traditional dress codes. Overalls were already part of the hard-working and durable battery of service clothing and had long been a staple component of heavy civilian workwear for men. Often made in denim or other close-weave cotton fabric, overalls were an all-in-one garment with button or zip closure that went,

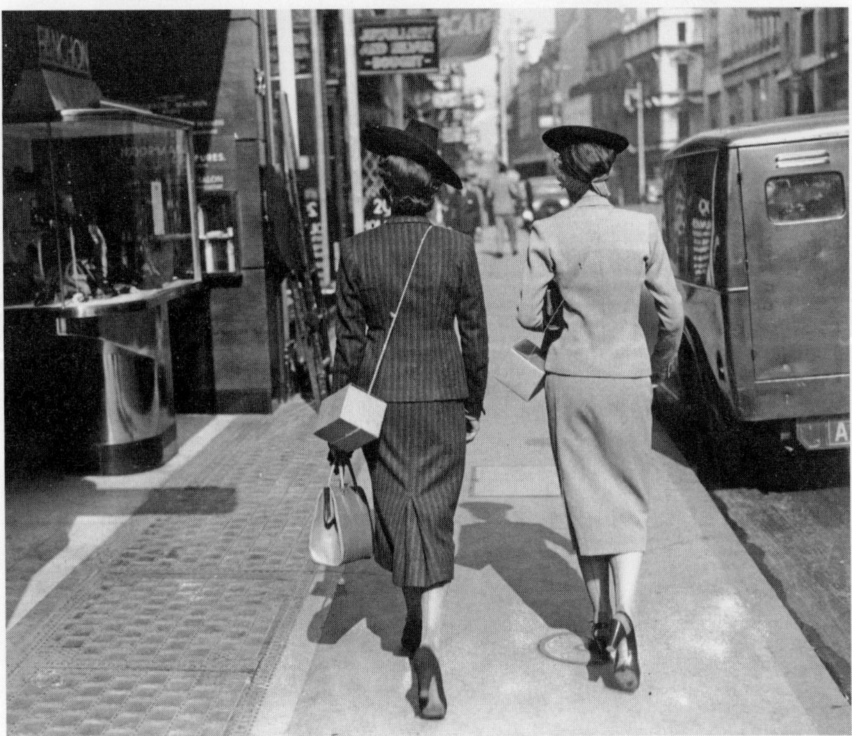

**Figure 6** Women shoppers in Bond Street with their gas masks in cardboard boxes, 1 September 1939. Davis/Getty Images (2664778).

as the name suggests, on top of other, smarter, clothing. In September, the *Drapers' Record* were talking about overalls and Air Raid Precaution (ARP) departments in stores and suggesting retail activity diversify to meet new demand. Overall retailers were advised to sell dungarees as well as overalls as both were popular for all types of 'fatigue' work.[50] As war service began to absorb both men and women previously in domestic service, new routines developed at home for many women now doing their own housework, gardening, cooking and general maintenance. Overalls and dungarees proved of good service here, along with decorative aprons. The *Drapers' Record* carried an advertisement in December for some rather glamorous Christmas aprons available in art silk (rayon) and silk slub pinarette in pinafore and Dutch pinafore styles. They also offered a special assortment of taffeta aprons. It is

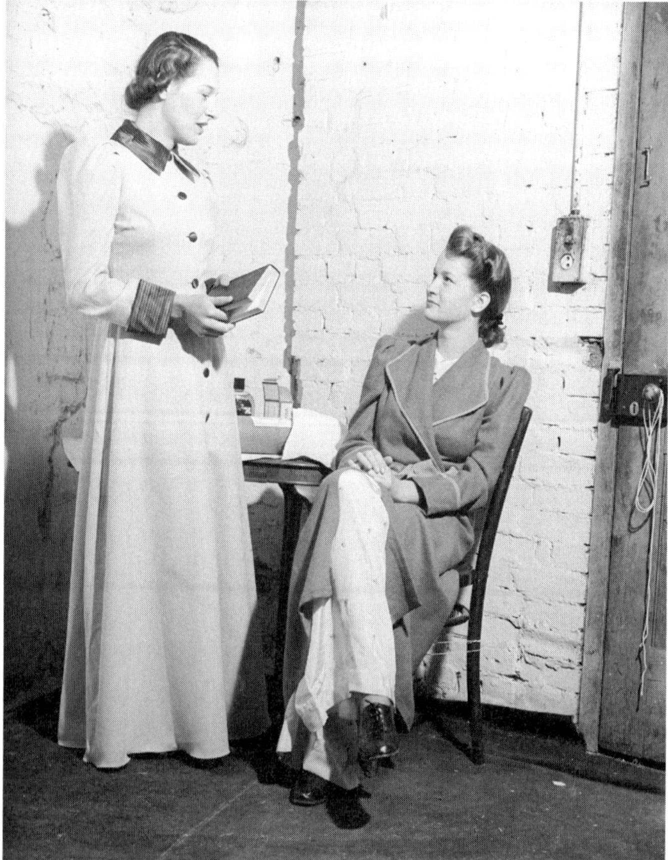

**Figure 7** Dressing Gowns, 21 September 1939. Warm woollen dressing gowns for night air raids (p. 18). M. McNeill/Stringer. Getty Images (2667641).

questionable how practical these would have been, but these fabrics, replacing standard cotton, no doubt added elegance to domestic routine.[51]

Perhaps the best-known garment that appeared at the onset of war was the siren suit. This all-in-one boiler suit-style garment had originated from garments worn by First World War munitions workers. They were hooded and constructed with many and capacious pockets. The need for practical clothing, easy and quick to put on in the event of an air-raid warning, had arguably produced the first fashion of war. The siren suit initially came to prominence as a protective item of clothing that would provide warmth in the often inhospitable environs of the air-raid shelter. Homes in the twenty-eight metropolitan districts of London and other provincial regions felt to be vulnerable to air attack had received steel-built shelters after a decision to protect householders back in February 1939. Measuring 6'6" x 4'6" (although larger families could

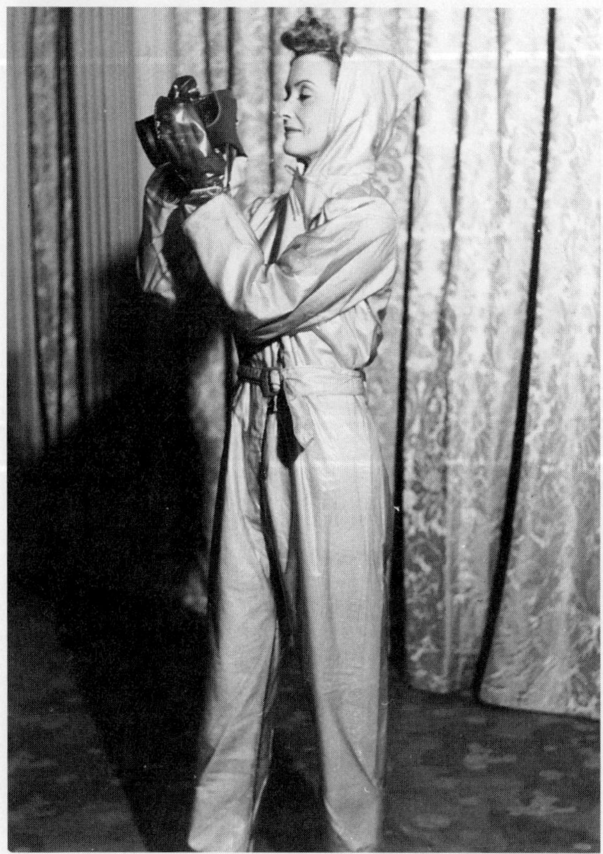

**Figure 9** Siren Suit, 1 January 1940. Popperfoto/Getty Images (79621828).

get bigger), the tunnel-shaped shelter had to be partly buried in the garden for greater strength. This often resulted in water seepage and robust clothing was therefore needed to keep out the cold and damp. Use of designated communal shelters at night also required easy-to-slip-on garments that were modest in coverage as well as warm and practical. Variants of the siren suit for nocturnal raids included the hooded and belted dressing gown, as featured in September by the *Draper's Record*, which could be left open at the bottom or zippered up the legs to create 'pantaloons'.[52]

When no air raids took place, the siren suit had to be marketed another way. Shops like D. H. Evans were promoting their practicality and good sense

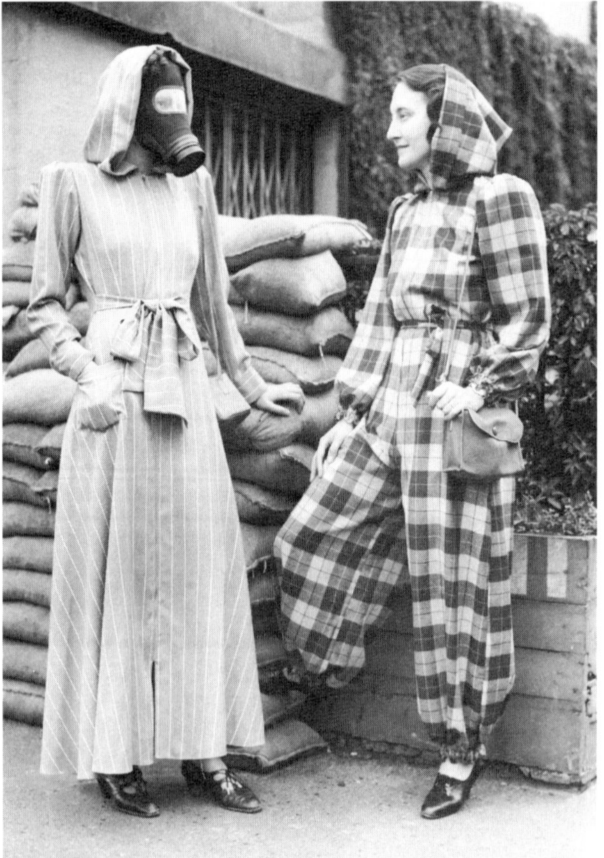

**Figure 8** Air Raid Shelter Fashion, 1 September 1939. *Drapers' Record* featured this photograph on 23 September 1939, illustrating the 'slip on hooded dressing gowns, slider fastened [which] can be left open at bottom or fastened to form pantaloons' Keystone-France/Gamma-Keystone via Getty Images (107414253).

for the chilly evenings of October[53] and by November were mounting window displays of slacks, jumpers and siren suits with the caption 'Keep cheerful in slacks'. On offer inside was, for example, a fashionable wool, zip-fronted siren suit in cyclamen, with the belt, cuffs, edge to hood and pocket flap all in cobalt blue, for 45s 9d.[54] An interview with a buyer from D. H. Evans, Oxford Street, London, confirmed that there had been a steady sale of siren suits since the war began: 'People buy them for sitting about at home in and ARP. They are comfortable . . . People are buying warm and practical clothes now'. The store was selling them for a reasonable cost because 'people have to buy them themselves and when you're doing voluntary work you aren't going to pay four or five guineas for one.'[55] Fortnum and Mason, however, were offering dungarees and boiler suits for three and a half guineas in the 'on duty' section of their new Service Equipment Department and ARP suits for six and a half guineas in the also new Shelter Equipment Department.[56] Prices reflected fashionable uptake of basic workwear, now also in quality tweed and wool mixes, and Viyella commissioned Digby Morton to design a couture version of the siren suit in their cotton and wool mix fabric.[57] This appeared to give the new trousered image the seal of approval.

Siren suits and boiler suits were the hardest working face of a close relative, the pair of slacks. These began to be worn with increasing frequency for practical work but also as informal daywear for both domestic duties and relaxed social events. This much-maligned garment came in for vicious criticism from designers and fashion gurus alike as slacks appeared to undermine traditional aspects of femininity and reflect changing perceptions about the nature and use of fashion. Such ideas were viewed as clearly at odds with the industry's own thoughts and a threat to the type of fashion they were selling. Vested interests now played against a developing war aesthetic of practical modernization, with revealing consequences. During the early months of the war and into the winter, trousers weathered protest and condemnation. Yet public demand proved too strong for trade interests to ignore, and by spring 1940, the battle for the trouser had been all but won. This process is interesting to investigate.

As we have already seen, the fashion for slacks had been acceptable before the war while it played its part alongside other forms of daywear, notably dresses. *Vogue*'s condemnation of 'slackers in slacks' during November[58] aired the view that while service personnel could wear uniform with some level of impunity, it was not yet acceptable or even necessary for women to abandon the usual fashion protocols and adopt what they—representing the fashion cognoscenti—saw as slovenly and outlandish. Designer Victor Stiebel vented his wrath in an interview with Mass Observation on 1 December 1939. After recognizing an initial enthusiasm for buying practical and essential clothing, he denounced women who 'seemed to feel that now at last they could forget all about fashion and do just as they liked. The way they walked about Bond Street and Piccadilly with no hats and those disgusting slacks! Horrible! Of course, lots of them still do, but it's getting better.'[59] Fashion Group's Jean Smith declared, 'It was too awful. Women dashed into slacks and things immediately.' She put this down to a psychological reaction: 'Men were being called up, and women were taking on men's jobs, driving ambulances and changing wheels, doing housework and all sorts of things they'd never done before, and that's why they gave up feminine clothes.' Clearly referring to a particular social class of woman, she also believed, like Stiebel, that there had been something of a turn round: 'It's not like that now.'[60] Yet trade figures did not bear out that sales in this type of practical wear had slowed down. Taking all forms of trouser into account, demand continued throughout the autumn, with designers, including Stiebel, reporting that trousers were selling well.[61] Fortnum's were selling split cycling skirts, dungarees and slacks in late autumn, and by the beginning of the following year, the *Vogue Pattern Book* was agreeing that 'women must work—and when it's a tough job, most women tackle it in slacks. . . . Add a tuck-in shirt, a many pocketed jacket, and you're ready for anything.'[62] Anne Seymour, editor of *Women and Beauty*, had believed trousers would not prosper for the simple reason that men did not like them,[63] and Madge Garland from *Vogue,* who did not refer to slacks directly, deplored the general change in feminine style, presumably as adopted by the social class she catered for in *Vogue.* The extreme 'carelessness' and 'slackness' she saw left her inarticulate: 'I can't say strongly enough what I think. I can only call it dastardly behaviour on the part of British women since war broke out. Once you start letting yourself go, nothing's going to matter.'[64] Referring to the lack of desire to dress up and a new focus on comfort clothing, particularly going without a hat, Garland was representing, if in an extreme way, the response of the traditional fashion world to difference and progress. New practices might be met with hostility and derision but would not now be overturned.

The battle that was being fought in the first few months of war was between two sets of values. The more traditional of the two wanted to maintain the existing dress framework for what it said about being a woman and what it meant to dress properly—that is, according to established sartorial rules originating from privilege but affecting all classes. The new war aesthetic, in adopting dress practices outside of this strict framework, threatened recognized ideas about femininity and, as it offered alternative dress codes, began to deconstruct clothing as an indicator of class. After a knee-jerk reaction of distaste from the fashion hierarchy, the only way forward would be some kind of compromise that put this hierarchy back in control. By January 1940, *Vogue* was explaining the right way to wear practical clothing including slacks. It was even providing several slacks patterns while firmly corralling them within a varied wardrobe full of *other things*. In particular, they promoted the divided skirt. 'More versatile than slacks' (but of course), 'it slips by as an ordinary skirt when occasion demands. And it is kind to the figure on whom slacks are unwise.'[65] Much of the fuss about careless or sloppy approaches to dress actually came to nothing. Women did not throw away skirts and dresses, and female fashion found its own natural balance between old and new styles without interference from the older guard of the fashion elite. By March 1940, the *Drapers' Record* was reporting on how the '1940 Open Air Girl will dress', highlighting a modern spirit of freedom and movement in clothing that had arguably emerged victorious out of the conflict with older styles and philosophies. The article looked forward to spring fashions with slacks continuing to be popular. Styles were staying much the same as the previous year, with turn-ups remaining and 'sleek hip fitting . . . essential'. There was a demand for both the jacket and slacks suit and a three-piece suit with skirt. It was reported that 'the heavy sales of slacks last autumn means a smaller potential market for the spring; there are few women "new" to slacks. But those who have worn them all winter must be persuaded that lighter weight materials will be needed for summer wear, and that trousers which have weathered a winter's ambulance driving are in no condition to appear in seaside sunshine.'[66] While this was sales talk, there was a clear message that trousers were now a wardrobe staple. The garments illustrated spanned from smart but casual daywear, featuring lightweight worsted flannels, through to the more sportif look of a Jaeger outfit with unusually high-waisted trousers, to the very tailored style of a lightweight summer suit in tweed. Well cut and very slim fitting, this suit could have been considered rather masculine at the time, particularly as it was styled with shirt collar and tie. This suggests that not only had the trouser become broadly accepted, but that fashion was now playing about with designing new and exciting variants. The story continued into April, when *Drapers'* predicted that 'basic sellers again will be slacks and dungarees' for the coming holiday season. Jackets were in general to be cut long to enhance acceptance of trousers. This was especially true for the more cautious, mature woman—also being encouraged into trousers—for whom a longer-line new smock top was recommended as the 'perfect answer'.[67] The smart fabrics being used and the choice of accessorizing sweaters, shirts and jackets all contributed to moving the trousered figure away from any taint of sloppiness or lazy dressing, and new season details like bust darts or shaped pattern pieces on dungaree bibs showed new design compromises with masculine lines.[68] There was no revolution overthrowing skirts and dresses. Trousers moved from practical workwear into both the formal and informal fashion wardrobe as their acceptance grew. In this way, fashion claimed and tamed a potentially rogue garment. Trousers remained, however, an essentially male garment no matter how commandeered they were by women at war. Battles to fully deconstruct their gender associations would continue to be played out, most notably during the 1960s.

Fashion was also coming to terms during the phoney war with the extent to which it was going to consciously accept elements of military influence in design or deliberately ignore it. At first, higher-class trade appeared to be moving away from it as part of a general distaste for the intrusion of uniform into civilian social spheres, while high street trade was happy to accommodate a limited number of military details. Aage Thaarup, well-known society milliner, reflected these tiers in the following comment about millinery to Mass Observation: 'I don't show any military styles at all. I don't like them. I object to anything to do with war, such as fashionable gas-mask carriers and so on.' When asked to comment on cheaper shops featuring them, he replied, 'Yes, there will always be a certain class who like that sort of thing, the kind of girl who goes out with her boyfriend in Balham and tries on his hat and puts on a soldier's cap.'[69] Ann Seymour also inferred a class divide, if obliquely, in discussing the same topic of millinery at fashion shows: 'Military fashion was nothing. I've been to practically every dress show and the minute anything military was shown people said, "I don't want to wear anything that looks like a military cap". The Glengarry etc. were being worn before the war by Society women, and I think this continuance of it by working-class women is just the tail-end.'[70] Two issues arise here. In the first place, sentimentality or emotional attachment to service or regiment seemed initially to belong to the high street rather than the loftier spirit of couture. This would not last. Secondly, there seemed to be a specific desire to keep the military influence on a very tight leash. While there was much to be said for keeping off-duty style quite separate from uniform, the fact that skirts and skirt suits for women often mirrored service uniform style made a level of comparison inevitable.

Certain uniforms, such as the Women's Royal Naval Service (WRNS) Standard Dress (or SD), had been conceived partly in imitation of the civilian dress fashionable at the time.[71] That the smart two-piece skirt suit very quickly established itself as a ubiquitous wartime style for the duration not only reflected a desire for relatively practical and durable clothes, but also for a smart look that, like uniform, signified a war-ready attitude. The authority and sense of purpose invested in a business suit or uniform now became a focus for women's civilian wear, emblematic of new responsibilities and a changing sense of status and role within society. Couturier Digby Morton, talking about his designs in spring 1940, acknowledged his ideas came 'of course from military influence' but 'I don't mean brass buttons and that sort of thing, but the simple smart line—spruce-like, slick, a general sort of trimness'.[72] These were the seminal elements of design that moulded the wartime aesthetic. Home-woven fabrics combined with quality tailoring in smart yet serviceable styles produced clothes that were not only war ready, but also in the tradition of British styling that had become iconic across the world.

Details on clothing did at times reflect the more superficial appeal of uniform, such as epaulettes on coats, larger pockets on coats and suits and some braiding and trimming. Regimental service badges had proved popular, with Peter Robinson's reporting in January 1940 that they were 'selling them all the time. They go as fast as they come in.'[73] Hats and head coverings, or lack of them, continued to reflect aspects of war, despite high-end disdain, with Priscilla Feare of Mass Observation summarizing, by spring 1940, that 'furs and fussy hats' had been put aside 'in favour of slacks, a length of material wound around the head to form a turban, or just no hat at all'.[74] The cold January of 1940, when the Thames froze over and Britain experienced the worst storm of the century,[75] had resulted in 'hand-knitted Pixie hoods', while 'interest in Finland encouraged hooded coats'.[76] There was also 'military influence' in the 'imitation forage caps, glengarries [and] peaked Service caps' that appeared to be increasing in the South of England.[77] But the hat style that had become most prevalent during this time was the pillbox cap, first made popular back in the early 1930s. There were two conflicting directions for hats, therefore, one war orientated, the other war resistant. For the latter, hat design and construction was also an avenue of escape from the bore war, with a range of imaginative styles retaining something of pre-war glamour and luxe.[78] By March 1940, *Picture Post* was at Aage Thaarup's Mayfair studio photographing the creation of an 'Easter Bonnet' featuring a black felt hat with mushroom crown and a 'fulsome bunch of snowdrops sprouting over the back. Beneath them [Thaarup] tucks a red and black velvet bow—"the red must always match the lips", he says.'[79] For the present, it was the Mayfair milliner's job to 'make women not in uniform more feminine than ever'.[80]

By the end of the phoney war, the types of clothing worn and the reasons behind the manufacture and retailing of a range of alternative styles and silhouettes all revealed a critical rethinking of the purpose and practice of dressing. By this time, elements of pre-war clothing had become inappropriate and redundant while others continued to prosper due to their serviceability and flexibility. Settle's less-is-more chic established before the war now became the focus for off-duty dressing, whilst a new, arguably tougher and more challenging aesthetic created the working clothes often required for war service. It would be these new elements added to the wardrobes of so many women that would reflect a significant renegotiation of the traditional imagery of femininity. Alternative forms of dress now spoke coherently for women's involvement in war, their changing identity within this culture of conflict and their practical patriotism.

# –7–

# Calls for Rationed Fashion

The preceding chapters have explored the issues affecting clothing both before and at the onset of war, looking in particular at the types of clothing being produced and worn, consideration of what constituted the fashionable and stylish and the changing social and economic climates in which clothing narratives operated. These revealed altering perspectives on established cultural constructions surrounding such problematics as class and gender. The nature of fashion and dress was clearly evolving to accommodate war, and as it did so, the clothing industry, manufacturers and retailers had to make adjustments to reflect the emerging priorities for everyday clothing. Manufacturers were also juggling the now-pressing need to produce the garments and equipment required by the armed forces and civil defence and were turning out uniforms in volume alongside new types of practical civilian wear. Pressure would soon be on to maintain war production, provide some level of export and continue to support the home market for civilian textiles. This chapter looks, therefore, at the economic factors that now began to affect manufacture and production of clothing. It will investigate why the price of clothing began to rise, how this could be controlled and the rationale that developed to justify the eventual implementation of clothes rationing. Given the social deprivation known to exist immediately prior to war, it was especially important that the government considered a range of economic strategies that could safeguard a democratic way of life. The population had to be provided with the essentials of everyday living, without which a war could not be successfully fought.

Historically there was some precedent for clothing control. During the First World War, there had been civilian shortages of boots and shoes owing to military needs being met at the expense of the home front. Scarcity had given rise to inflated prices, leaving those unable to afford the new costs lacking in essentials. Quality declined in civilian production. The government therefore implemented a scheme for 'producing boots and shoes of good standard quality at a price considerably lower than that of "non-standard" footwear'.[1] Manufacturers had to comply with 'specifications and prices approved by the Director of Leather',[2] and in this way a precedent was set to improve the existing home market via government intervention. A scheme for standard clothing followed in 1918 for hosiery, suits, skirts and standard blankets which had, however, an essential flaw because 'there was no compulsion behind it; manufacturers and distributors need not enter the line of business unless they wanted to', which not many did as the business was relatively unprofitable.[3] The whole issue of standard cloth production reflected 'the government's reluctance to interfere with the market'.[4]

The experience of severe inflation and fear of scarcity were legacies of the Great War. During the 1920s, numerous committees and subcommittees reported on different aspects of military and civilian defence in readiness for a future conflict. An important result of this was the recognition that a modern war demanded 'mobilisation of the total resources of the nation [and] the task of studying it and preparing for it, must involve investigations penetrating every sector of national life'.[5] Civilian life was unlikely to be immune to the effects of future military action. Another war might be characterized by massive air attack, and there were, therefore, limited attempts to define policy for civil defence and protection in the interwar years. The action prior to 1935 was relatively leisurely, but there was a clear awareness, as evinced from a Treasury memorandum of 1929,[6] that wages and prices must be controlled in relationship to one another and that the price of goods must be firmly maintained to avoid inflation. Imports needed to be strictly controlled and consumer goods rationed to limit capacity for spending and taxation increased to 'bridge the gap that yet remains between the national revenue *plus* national savings and the war expenditure'.[7] In 1932, another new subcommittee was formed to look into price and import control and whether rationing should be imposed on the outbreak of war or later. It reviewed delegating responsibility for these things to various government departments and established the notion that fair shares of a reduced number of consumer goods was no less important than keeping prices down. Efficiency in production and distribution would also be necessary.[8] Clothing and boots were to be almost entirely the domain of the Board of Trade. At the end of the meetings, rent control and fuel rationing had been agreed upon, and food control was well prepared for war. No scheme, however, had been agreed for clothes rationing of any kind, 'which was a significant item in the cost of living index'.[9] By September 1939, there had been 'no proposals . . . for controlling the prices of all those non-food consumer goods which formed an important part of the standard of living; nor had there been any discussion about the possibility of rationing such a fundamental necessity as clothing. . . . Government interference in civilian industry and trade on any appreciable scale was never envisaged.'[10]

The plentiful amounts of clothes in all consumer areas and good stocks of both raw and wholesale supplies suggested there was little need for immediate action, and only the way the war progressed would change this view. Steadily rising prices and the vulnerability of Britain's raw material stocks during the blitz endangered the government's capacity to confidently provide for civilian need so that towards the end of 1940, there began to be calls for some kind of rationing or standard clothing production. A number of different economic and social factors, acting cumulatively over the whole period, were finally responsible for the government's decision, in May 1941, to implement a full rationing scheme for clothing and household textiles, boots and shoes. These factors will now be explored in detail.

The cost-of-living index for 1939–1940 revealed that the price of clothing had risen by 18 per cent in the first four months of the phoney war. It would go on to rise by a total of 37 per cent by the following June of 1940.[11] The first import control measure in September 1939, to curtail expenditure abroad, required importers to hold a Board of Trade licence to ship much-reduced quotas of commodities from overseas. These included clothing, footwear, leather goods and jewellery. It was planned to reduce foreign currency on textiles from '£18 million to under £2 million' while 'imports of women's footwear amounting to about £1 million would be eliminated'.[12] Home production would have to make good these shortfalls, and, in the context of the growing need for war-related textiles, the high street would have to compete for resources. Even in the earliest stages of the war while stocks remained plentiful, prices rose in anticipation of harder times ahead.

Initial attempts to curb clothing prices resulted in the Price of Goods Act November 1939 that came into effect on 1 January 1940. It was the first order to refer to clothing, and the *Tailor and Cutter* clarified the legislation in their 22 December 1939 issue. In an article entitled 'Price Regulations from January 1st', it explained that it would become a criminal offence for price-regulated goods to be sold at above their cost on 21 August 1939, 'plus an increase representing the actual rise in costs and expenses'. Also a 'trader's net profit per article sold was not to exceed the net profit made on similar goods in August, 1939'.[13] 'Specified clothing' was covered within the act, including men's suits at £4 5s, overcoats at £3 13s 6d and youth's trousers at 10s 6d. These were 21 August prices to which tailors were allowed to add only the permitted increase. The article pointed out that it was the cheaper end of the market that was being controlled, to safeguard those on the lower incomes, but warned tailors that 'new orders are going to be made from time to time and it is obvious that the higher priced clothes will eventually be included'.[14] The act regulated the prices of 'clothing and boots and shoes for men, women, children and infants; piece-goods; protective clothing; household textiles; . . . and . . . knitting yarns'.[15] Interestingly, the order also included textiles and leather *used in the making* of 'regulated clothing, piece goods and household textiles' where such textiles had not already been controlled by other defence regulations.[16] Intending to close any loopholes, the order clearly signalled the beginning of an important change in the nature of control that would increasingly see government becoming involved with *all* levels of production from raw materials through to finished article. Such control was not yet considered necessary, but, as Sladen points out, 'without direct control over production and without specific definitions of the products, price control would always be ineffective'.[17] Given that commodities selling above the prices stipulated were 'free from control',[18] manufacturers soon recognized that they could sidestep the specified categories by simply making other types of higher-priced goods. As Hancock and Gowing pointed out, clothing prices continued to rise, and the Price of Goods Act unintentionally stimulated the production of 'uncontrolled, unessential clothing'.[19]

One suggestion for bringing about price reduction in clothing was put forward by Lord Woolton in October 1939. His scheme envisaged the mass production of certain standard clothes, such as men's suiting, which would apparently hold down the prices of the non-standard competition.[20] The scheme hinged on fixed cost margins to be applied to each stage of production, including the cost of retail, in order to secure a low price.[21] To manufacture clothing items even more cheaply than the successful volume production men's tailors, for example, called into question whether Woolton's standard garments could compete without some kind of subsidy and if the public did not like the standard lines, there would be 'wasted effort'.[22] Despite reservations and in order to safeguard the interests of the poorer sectors of the community, a scheme was finally agreed in March 1940 whereby a standard cloth—made to a standard or quality commensurate with reasonably durable final garments—would be made into men's suits. This was to be accompanied by standard-quality boots and shoes to be in production by October 1940.[23] However, the Ministry of Supply, who were asked to organize the enterprise, felt the scheme was unnecessary given the abundant existing raw material supplies and attempted to pass responsibility to the Board of Trade. With neither prepared to take it on, the scheme was sidelined and would not resurface until spring 1941. This hesitancy on the part of government ministries to get involved with the *processes* of industry, even given their desire to combat want at the lower end of the market place, meant that, according to Hargreaves and Gowing, 'much valuable time was lost in dealing with a major problem of civilian consumption and little done to check the rapid rise of the clothing component in the cost of living index'.[24]

On 29 April 1940, Alderman A. R. Bretherick of Yorkshire wrote to the Ministry of Supply, who passed his letter to the Board of Trade. Active in the textile industry for some years, he wrote of the now 'vicious spiral of ever increasing prices which is caused by the demand being greater than the supply at present'.[25] Bretherick spoke of this increased demand as a result not of 'the consumer requiring the goods for immediate consumption', but rather the perception that it was simply practical to buy before prices rose even more steeply, one point of view already borne out by Mass Observation. He noted that shopkeepers had been putting 'large stocks to reserve' in order to await the higher prices. This type of inflationary behaviour was exactly what the government had most wanted to avoid. Panic buying must not ensue, especially as there was more than enough stock of materials at this stage to provide for the nation on the basis of previous patterns of consumption. Some of these patterns were, of course, now changing, affecting the types of fabrics used and the type of clothing purchased, but neither of these factors was yet significantly affecting raw material stocks for the domestic market.[26]

Bretherick went on to suggest a scheme of rationing either 'by family or individual' which would create fairness within the community by limiting clothing by quantity rather than by quality. Production would remain variegated with a cheaper and higher end, and output would be regulated by the known factor of available raw material. By this method, not only would there be enough for all via the rationing of amount, but there would also be no need for 'standardization of cloth or garment which neither the trade nor the individual wishes to see and all the characteristics of any firm's clothing (which may have taken years to build up) would be preserved'.[27] In Bretherick's opinion, standardization threatened individuality by interfering with distinctive craft practices.

Such a system based initially on control of quantity rather than cost or quality would eventually form the foundation of the British clothing and textiles rationing scheme of June 1941. Clothing would be controlled by the amount of material in any item and not by its quality or price. The variegated production advocated by Bretherick would not, however, remain. As labour and, eventually, stock became ever scarcer, there would be an increasing need to concentrate production both of textiles and garments. The government acted by endorsing the manufacture of a *limited* number of specified fabrics that would help ensure controlled supplies of quality, value-for-money clothing in price ranges affordable by almost all. Known as the Utility scheme, this method of production finally accounted for over 85 per cent of cloth and clothing manufactured and will be returned to in greater detail in Chapter 9. At no time, however, was there a completely standardized output either of fabrics or garments, and while government did introduce production restrictions in due course, choice remained possible within them.[28]

Alderman Bretherick must have written again to the Board, this time to recommend the German scheme of rationing. Acknowledging receipt of this letter, via the Ministry of Supply, G. L. Watkinson for the Board of Trade[29] stated that 'the proposal that we should adopt the German system of rationing is, of course, regarded as undesirable at the present time'.[30] To what extent the general public in Britain knew that Germany had already implemented a clothes rationing scheme is hard at this distance to gauge, although there had clearly been some publicity about it. The *Tailor and Cutter* on 1 December 1939 had told readers that German civilians had now been issued with their clothing points. A writer from a German paper was quoted as believing that 'with all its disadvantages . . . the new method of rationing ensures that rich and poor will be equal in the matter of dress'.[31] By the week of 22 December 1939, the 'Continental Comment' section of the *Tailor and Cutter* was remarking, however, on the poor launch of clothes rationing in Germany and of the type of clothes being marketed there. The first story told of Nazis who, knowing of the advent of coupon restrictions, had led a 'veritable run' on Berlin shops that were now 'cleared of everything which could be had. . . . Not even the police warnings against unnecessary hoarding of clothing was able to stop this run.'[32] Obvious inequalities in the new rationing scheme in Germany appeared to exist from its inception. The *Tailor and Cutter* commented that German men were still able to 'buy clothes from their tailors *without coupons* while fur coats are also relieved of restriction if they are real fur'. They suggested that the 'much publicised equality between rich and poor does not exist'.[33] There were certainly lessons to be learnt here for any future scheme in Britain. Details were then given concerning a recent winter fashion show held in Cologne: 'The Nazi authorities had produced a whole series of new models of suits for men' with 'the peculiarity of the show [being that] no single suit was made of new material. All had been cut and tailored in old suits, partly worn out, which had fallen out of style.' The *Tailor and Cutter* saw this as part of 'an official campaign for saving textiles' which rather led to the view that textiles were already in short supply 'if one may judge by indications'.[34] The situation in Germany remained rather ambiguous, and later reports tended to endorse shortage of civilian clothing.[35] On reflection, the balance maintained between military and civilian need, consistently negotiated in Britain between members of the Board of Trade and the Ministry of Supply, would prove of profound significance in terms of adequately clothing the population, thereby promoting morale and unity on the home front.

On 9 April 1940, Hitler invaded Denmark and Norway. The Netherlands were already under martial law, and there was a tense recognition of a deteriorating situation across allied Europe. At home, and in response to the increasing need to fund military mobilization, there had been a flurry of activity to promote a healthy export drive. The Board of Trade as part of this concern had set up an Industrial Supplies Department with the brief of 'determining the competing claims upon raw materials advanced on behalf of the home civilian market and the export market'.[36] Their initial act was to launch the first of several Limitation of Supplies Orders on 16 April. This was a first warning of future austerity and curtailed the supply of cotton, rayon and linen piece and made-up goods by 25 per cent to wholesalers 'for resale to domestic retailers or makers-up'.[37] Supplies to retailers during the period from the date of the act to 30 September 1940 were, therefore, not to 'exceed 75% by quantity of supplies in the period from 30th April 1939 to 30th September 1939'.[38] These references back to previous trading dates were known as base periods and were used extensively to control percentage reductions in a fair and measured way that people could see was not merely arbitrary. Export supplies and government orders were not subject to these quotas, which were designed to limit domestic production only. These measures would restrict the amount of goods available to the home market, and there was a view that a kind of self-rationing by the population would allow the scheme to work.[39] However, there were already many exceptions to this 25 per cent quota in terms of goods like blackout material, overalls, hospital needs and the requirements of the Women's Voluntary Service so that in real terms the supply to the domestic market was 'a good deal less'.[40]

The Board of Trade had 'reject[ed] . . . control at the raw materials stage, choosing instead to limit the manufactured or semi-manufactured articles at the stage of wholesale distribution'.[41] Wholesalers and manufacturers needed to register, and there was 'no restriction over the supply from manufacturers of controlled goods to these registered wholesalers or to any other manufacturers of piece goods. The restrictions fell upon the supplies to all other classes of unregistered people.' Thus supplies 'from manufacturers or wholesalers to makers-up of piece-goods were limited, and so were supplies to retailers'.[42] The unrestricted supplies to wholesalers and manufacturers meant that they could respond to the call for exports, and makers-up were also invited to register for the same reason.[43]

By May 1940, the government had become 'the sole importer of 90% of all raw materials including wool' and the Cotton, Rayon and Wool Controls, as organizing industry-based bodies, allocated the various supplies to relevant firms for processing.[44] As the Dutch and Belgian people succumbed to blitzkrieg, Britain had already developed something of a siege mentality, having bought all the wool available in Australia, New Zealand and South Africa for buffer stock.[45] Later in 1941, Britain also entered into cooperation with the United States—prior to Pearl Harbor—in a joint raw materials allocation. When the United States bought heavily in Manila hemp, she reserved a part of it for Britain, and Britain secured a share of Egyptian cotton for the United States after buying the entire crop. Hancock and Gowing made the important point that 'the two countries acting together dominated the raw materials markets of the world'.[46]

The month of May also saw further controls put in place to limit 'supplies of civilian goods to 2/3rds the pre-war level'.[47] This Limitation of Supplies Order came into effect in June. Domestic quotas were made ever more vulnerable in September 1940, when the Woven Textiles Order of that month further reduced 'sales of cotton and linen goods between 1st October 1940 and 31st March 1941 to 37.5% of the trade in the equivalent period of the previous year'[48] and established a new list of '"essential consumers" to whom controlled goods might be freely supplied'.[49] This list included the police, hospitals, local authorities and the YMCA whose requirements would now be excluded from the domestic quota.[50]

On 28 May 1940, Belgium surrendered. The German army had taken Boulogne just the day before, cutting off British and French troops and trapping them on the beaches at Dunkirk. On 30 May, Operation Dynamo saw the navy rescuing the stranded troops assisted by a flotilla of small boats. France surrendered on 14 June, and Britain now stood alone. On 10 August, the Luftwaffe carried out its first aerial raid on South-East England, a prelude to the Battle of Britain. On 20 August, Winston Churchill announced that Britain now had two million soldiers to resist invasion. The need to continue mobilizing home defence had become ever more imperative as Germany began bombing raids, first on London on 25 August, and then night raids on twenty-one towns and cities on the 29. On 1 September, the RAF bombed Munich in a retaliative action just days ahead of Hitler's concerted bombing campaign of Britain. The Blitz began on 7 September when three hundred German bombers and six hundred fighters flew up the Thames and 'bombed Woolwich Arsenal, a power station, a gas works, the docks and the City'.[51] More bombers followed, and 'within minutes the Docks were ablaze. More than 400 people were killed . . . 1600 badly injured; thousands were made homeless.'[52] Now there was a concern to provide not only for the ongoing requirements of the home front but also emergency facilities for those losing homes in the bombing.

These people needed a whole range of essential supplies to begin again. There had to be mechanisms to dispense these necessities as well as temporary refuges, manned and supplied, to offer emergency accommodation and help. The Women's Voluntary Service, as an essential user, took on the role of dispensing clothing and other emergency supplies to bombees. September's Woven Textile Order also deregulated some previously restricted 'essential' goods such as 'adhesive anti-scatter fabric, blackout material, infants' wear, surgical bandages, boiler suits' as a response to the needs of the moment.[53] Certain manufacturers were now to be categorized as 'Special Producers'. These were possibly unregistered companies 'producing certain kinds of finished goods to whom controlled supplies might be freely given'.[54] These included many of the aforementioned 'essential' goods and such things as 'motor cars, batteries, books, fire hoses and tyres'.[55] By October, silk for civilian production was withdrawn as supplies were becoming more scarce,[56] and with increasing pressure on domestic textiles, a purchase tax was levied on clothing at the end of October that was 'equivalent to a three per cent rise in the cost-of-living index'.[57] The advent of the tax caused a pre-tax spree amongst shoppers which resulted in sales of clothing rising by 16 per cent above that of the previous month.[58]

In summary, then, as the blitz relentlessly bombarded industrial, civic and civilian buildings, stocks began to go down—some now as a result of fire-bombed warehouses—and prices continued to rise as only partially effective price regulations, combined with the added tax, raised the cost-of-living index. The need for emergency provisions also limited the vital task of recoupment of labour and space for munitions. It was out of all these conditions that during November there were two moves towards further control. The first was a rekindling interest in the validity of a rationing scheme that could ameliorate conditions prevailing in the home market. The second was a further Limitation Order (Miscellaneous) that came into operation at the end of November. Supplies of home front commodities were now further restricted to one-third of the base rate.[59] The result of this was estimated to free 'between 75,000–100,000 workers'[60] and would have two important effects on the home market: shortages of some essential goods which would need some kind of monitoring and a rather more streamlined civilian wholesale and retail industry. The first led to the setting up of various mechanisms to provide information on consumer needs, the second to the notion of industrial concentration.

The need to monitor the effect on the public of the rigorous restrictions introduced by the November Order led to the appointment in February 1941 of four area distribution officers followed in April by eight more, one for each civil defence region. They reported to a newly formed Consumer Needs Branch at Board of Trade headquarters, so establishing an intelligence network that would continue to be used after the advent of consumer rationing in June 1941.[61] The Board could now begin to get a better sense of the patterns of domestic consumption as well as develop a framework for explaining policy decisions to retailers dealing with shortages and blitz conditions.

Concentration was a government-promoted strategy for eliminating duplication of effort and output and rationalizing industries like textiles and clothing for maximum efficiency. The scheme, announced in March 1941, was voluntary and required firms to combine to create nucleus firms that would register as such in order to receive cloth allocations from the Board of Trade.[62] Concentration would, of course, limit capacity to supply, so specifying the types of commodities needed would become of increasing importance. Blitz conditions and the needs of hospitals, civil defence and other essential users were already creating urgent requirements for a range of essential commodities, and as clothing prices continued to rise through the winter, adequate appropriately priced clothing for all became imperative. The best solution to this lay not in governmental interference in clothing production itself with the creation of standardized clothing and textiles, but rather with the inauguration of some kind of rationing system that could respond to the population's needs.

The *Manchester Guardian* for Saturday, 16 November warned its readers of the impact of the new Limitation Order that would come into effect on

1 December. 'After 15 months of war the civilian consumer will begin to feel the pinch in earnest [when] . . . supplies of a large range of goods . . . will be reduced to the kind of short commons on which the Germans have been living for years.'[63] While this clearly demonstrated a patriotic sideswipe against the inadequacy of German organization, it also implied that if the German population could manage then so could the British, particularly given the comparatively higher standard of living that had so far been enjoyed. The *Manchester Guardian* went on to explain to readers that losses at sea and the ever-necessary demands of war munitions made the sacrifices imperative and that even these new stringencies were 'still not comparable to those in force in Nazi Germany'. The shopper would find shelves 'rather emptier than they have been, but within fairly wide limits he still has a free choice in spending his money'. This was a positive spin on a worsening situation designed to boost morale through recognition that variety still did exist, if in more restricted measure, and that 'rather emptier' by implication did not exactly mean shortage. The article stressed one very important point about this downturn in availability and that was that the 'success of this system (of Limitation Orders) relies on self-rationing by all members of the public, so that the poor shall not find the shops cleared by those who can afford to buy more than their fair share'.[64]

Appealing to the better nature of the population at large would not prove an adequate solution. Even at this stage, however, rationing was seen as the final threat because it would bring about 'a much more severe restriction of civil consumption than anything so far visualised in this country'.[65] The *Manchester Guardian* reminded its readers that 'if those with money to spend should be shown to obtain an undue share of the available goods, the Government is keeping in the background a plan for compulsory rationing that would cover the whole range of the limited goods. That is the system in force in Germany.'[66] In an article entitled 'More Restriction Next Month—Self-Denial Call', the paper quoted Oliver Lyttleton, President of the Board of Trade, as saying, 'It is important to realise that there is no shortage of consumer goods and that one of the objects of the new Order is to conserve our stocks and to make them last as long as we can in order that the effort which would be devoted towards their replacement may be released for the direct production of munitions.'[67] In a talk with the Federation of British Industry and Press at about the same time, Lyttelton 'expressed a hope that with the co-operation of all those concerned in distribution it would be possible to avoid rationing'. If this could not be done then 'he would face any difficulties and introduce a scheme'.[68] No valid plan yet existed.

The *Financial News* had already called for greater strategic planning that might need to go beyond self-rationing. In its 11 November issue, just three days before the catastrophic bombing of Coventry, it called for action while stating the situation remained 'favourable',[69] possibly referring to the fact that even at this stage in the war, cotton stocks were good and wool supplies still plentiful. Rightly cautious, however, the article foresaw that a less auspicious time might arise when planning would already be too late.[70] The government was urged to take action specifically to control two things—a system of fair shares and distribution for all and the right to warmth and cleanliness, 'two of the greatest necessities in coping with the situation created by air raids'.[71] The paper expressed concern that the wealthier sections of the population would be 'able to buy up the stocks, so that the shops will be empty and a substantial proportion of the community will be unable to satisfy their elementary needs on that account. . . . For these elementary essentials, rationing of some kind is necessary just as for the elementary essentials of food, rationing is necessary.'[72]

That rationing was clearly beginning to be seen as the only way to safeguard not only fairness but also the health and well-being of the nation rather changed the way in which it was viewed. Fear of poverty, disease and unsanitary conditions were felt especially keenly as people herded together in underground shelters during air attacks, enduring a public and communal existence rarely experienced before. The enforced togetherness of service life necessitated new health, hygiene and clothing protocols, but no such requirements were made of the civilian population. The fear of disease that had surfaced through the clothing practices of the poor and the lack of enough clothing to facilitate changing and appropriate laundering were reminders that a lowering of personal dress and hygiene standards could quickly lead to a drop in morale and a lack of common cause on the domestic front.

The *Financial News* believed a 'plan for clothes rationing' to be 'highly desirable' in order to combat the inequality that would arise through predictable scarcity.[73] The government too had become uncertain enough about the economic outlook to decide on the need for greater intervention in production, distribution and consumption. Late in November 1940, therefore, they started to consider a scheme of rationing, should it become necessary. The Board of Trade had to 'think out the problem on their own'.[74] The Ministry of Food had control over all their rationed foodstuffs in a way the Board did not have over the manufacturers and wholesalers of the textiles and clothing industries. An initial plan emerged by the end of November 1940 which was to be the first of several possible rationing schemes discussed as the months went by.[75] In the end it was decided to ration clothing, boots and shoes on the German model of a quantity system based on points. This was officially adopted by the end of January 1941 as the most sensible, simple and straightforward scheme and one which the public would quickly come to understand. Under this final scheme, all items were to be given coupon values, and an annual ration of coupons would be allocated to each individual. This calculation was based on some limited pre-war consumption statistics and a good deal of inspired guesswork as to what clothing and footwear an average man or woman would require in the course of a year. The exact nature of how the ration was finally arrived at is explored in the following chapter. It is important to remember here that in the final few months before rationing came into operation, the Board of Trade worked hard both on the scheme itself and to justify what might be seen as an unwarranted intrusion into people's lives. Circumstances now made state intervention unavoidable if equality of opportunity on the home front was to be safeguarded.

Concentration from March would significantly reduce the numbers working in textiles to the extent that after 1941 it would be impossible to use all stocks of cotton because of a manpower shortage.[76] Also in March, the cost-of-living index revealed that the price of clothing had escalated at a quite 'alarming' rate,[77] and by May, the index revealed that clothing was 75 per cent more expensive than at the outset of the war.[78] With a general cost-of-living rise estimated at between 25 and 30 per cent,[79] clothes clearly remained problematic.

During spring 1941, the Board of Trade had attempted to come to terms with all the disadvantages of rationing. In May, the President of the Board of Trade put the completed scheme before the Lord President's Committee suggesting a 1 June commencement. Yet even at this stage there were concerns expressed about what were to be called rationing's '"un" criticisms';[80] Churchill also 'in particular doubted the wisdom of the scheme. Could not sufficient clothing be made available for civilians to avoid rationing?'[81] The then President of the Board of Trade, Oliver Lyttelton, later claimed that 'clothes rationing had only slipped past Churchill when the latter was absorbed in the hunt for the Bismarck'.[82] In an anonymous Board of Trade memo[83] responding to the doubts about the scheme raised by the Lord President's Committee, the writer explored what he saw as the three main criticisms and the resolutions to these difficulties. His arguments will serve as a fitting conclusion to this chapter on the background to rationing and calls for clothing controls during the early war years.

In 'Notes for Lord President's Committee Meeting', the concerns that rationing would be 'unnecessary, unpopular and unworkable' were reviewed.[84] The writer proposed that there were now too many variables affecting the supply of new clothes to accurately predict how long stocks and suitable manufacture could continue to provide enough for all. It was necessary, therefore, to operate a new level of control over consumer spending. Any further reduction in goods in the light of rising prices favoured the wealthier and threatened shortages to others. There could be no guarantees about the outcome of conflicts such as the Battle for the Atlantic on which to base plans for future imports and realistically no calls could be made on shipping for civilian needs. Rationing was therefore necessary.

Unpopularity was easily dispensed with on the basis that any system that led to want and lowering of standards for any section of the population would be far more unpopular than the system put in place to guard against it. The writer further expressed the view that the Minister of Food, who had already introduced a scheme of rationing, would 'confirm that what the public wants is *fair sharing*, and that the pressure on him is *not* to discontinue rationing but to extend it to other things'.[85] In conclusion, regarding the scheme being unworkable, the writer was hopeful that good organization would see the Board through the initial stages of the scheme's launch. Thereafter, the coupon-accounting system underpinning the passing back of coupons along the supply chain would eliminate opportunities for fraud and also work to the advantage of smaller shopkeepers now no longer in unfair competition for supplies with larger chain stores. Coupon custom would entitle any retailer to the coupon equivalent in supplies. The relatively speedy launch of the scheme would be helped by additional manpower anticipated from '60 or more Dons during the long vacation—an experiment tried with success last year when the Limitation of Supplies Scheme was extended'.[86]

By May 1941, retail stocks were only 'about 2/3rds to 3/4 of their pre-war volume. Wholesale stocks were, by volume probably under half the peacetime average. If . . . rationing and shortage alike were to be avoided at least 200,000 additional tons of cotton and wool a year and at least 350,000 additional workers would have to be provided for civilian clothing.'[87] These facts were 'strong enough to win the day',[88] and permission was granted for a points-based system of clothing control to begin on 1 June, Whit Sunday.

In summary, the basic needs of the nation had to be met. The government now had a much greater awareness of both the level of suffering that had been exposed through the evacuation process and the needs emerging from the destruction and homelessness caused by the blitz. Without adequate clothing and the means to maintain cleanliness, there was the risk of distress, disease and low morale. While the towns and cities coped with bomb damage and devastation that created an unprecedented drain on resources, it became essential for the government to act. Alongside food rationing, clothes rationing now sought to provide enough for all and more for those left with none.

# –8–

# Setting the Ration

On 1 June 1941, clothes rationing was officially launched with every man, woman and child receiving sixty-six coupons to last for a year. Newspapers and radio broadcasts carried essential information, and over the bank holiday weekend there were carefully phased announcements that both prepared people for the new procedures ahead and gave them time, while the shops were closed, to think how the restrictions were going to affect them. The first announcement[1] clarified why rationing was being introduced, how the scheme would work and the rationale for 'special cases' entitling certain people to additional coupons. Clothes rationing would address the need for fair shares across all classes, curtail the capacity of spenders to spend and allow for a continuing overview and control of the clothing and textile resources of the nation. The more obvious signs of privilege would now be further muted as the needs of the many were put before the wants of the few.

The public were told that the scheme was 'as much a surprise to your retailer as it is to you', with the explanation that 'of course it had to be kept secret, or some people might have tried to get in first'.[2] The wish to circumvent panic buying or, possibly, black-market stockpiling were possible justifications for secrecy and there was also the memory prehaps of the rush for the high street that had been seen in Germany just before rationing. In a 'Notice to the Public'[3] from the Board of Trade, issuing from the Pine Court Hotel Bournemouth where the Board had taken up administrative residency, not only was the 'fair distribution of available supplies' discussed but also the important function of rationing to 'assist people to secure their essential needs by preventing others from buying too much'. The statement went on to suggest that those with 'well-filled wardrobes . . . help by making-do with their existing clothes as far as possible'. The public were further brought to attention by the exhortation—in capital letters—'DO NOT BUY MORE THAN YOU NEED, NOR BEFORE YOU MUST.'[4] Those for whom hardship had long been a way of life needed little guidance on this path of restraint.

The broadening reaches of the middle, lower middle, and salaried working classes that had enjoyed widening consumer opportunities on the high streets of the later 1930s now experienced a slow but relentless reversal of these in line with new wartime stringencies. The higher echelons of society would also experience a new sense of consumer control out of kilter with the privileged lifestyle, although here the size and variation that already existed in terms of established wardrobes much offset the effect of restrictions. Government intervention in public spending through rationing would not only alter the mechanisms of purchase but also bring about a reconsideration of the quality and value for money of what remained available to buy. People would want value for their coupons, particularly at the lower end of the market, where, historically, the shoddy and cheap did not provide adequate standards of clothing and footwear, as evacuation had revealed. If the same number of coupons were going to be surrendered for an item, its quality had to be guaranteed, no matter at what price point it was bought. Without such a guarantee, the system would be unfair. Out of considerations of durability and quality would come new government ventures in quality control and fabric specification. Under the auspices of a textile production and making-up regime, known subsequently as Utility, cloth and clothing would meet new benchmark standards that would especially benefit those buying at the cheapest end of the market. Utility products would later account for most high street manufacture and retail.

The initial announcement regarding rationing warned people that ‘things may be a little confused for a few days’ and reminded shoppers that they would ‘lose nothing by postponing . . . purchase[s], because from today it is illegal, as well as against his own interest, for any retailer to sell rationed goods except against coupons’.[5] There was no rush to panic buy. Retailers were informed that their replacement stocks would now depend ‘not on what you can extract from your wholesaler, but on the number of coupons you are able to turn-in’.[6] Thus smaller shops could compete fairly with larger for supplies providing they attracted customers. The changing patterns of demand, in line with newly shifting populations, could be accommodated by this mechanism for supply. Thus the ‘goods pass[ed] forward as the coupons pass[ed] back’.[7] This system, as a Board of Trade clothes rationing manual pointed out, provided ‘an automatic control of the flow of goods from the maker to the wholesaler and from the wholesaler to the retailer’.[8] The number of coupons was ‘calculated to correspond with the raw material available for clothing manufacture’, and the manufacturers—who were still to be regulated by quotas or proportions of what they had sold before—had ample fabric for the controlled output. The Board of Trade stated confidently that ‘the total amount of clothing produced will be sufficient to meet the total demand of the public’.[9] Throughout the war, the Board of Trade had to constantly adjust this equation between coupons and raw materials depending on fluctuating resources. Board papers and memoranda over the period clearly indicated the arguments and debates that surrounded the setting, each year, of a new coupon number in line with available resources and the minimum amount of clothing that people needed in order to survive.

The first set of sixty-six coupons was arrived at by estimating how many items of clothing people might be expected to need, as opposed to desire, in a year.[10] Sufficiency was the guiding principle along with a fair allocation of the resources that could be made available. Margery Spring Rice had pointed out how many families on very low incomes had suffered from 'lack of sufficient food and clothes and warmth and comfort',[11] and providing warm and comfortable clothing became key elements of Board of Trade thinking. A memoranda marked 'Secret' and entitled 'Cut the Clothing Ration?' began with the following remark: 'There no doubt comes a point when a man has so few clothes that he cannot keep himself warm or clean, and on washing day has to stay in bed. No doubt when this point is reached there is a real threat to health.'[12] This observation was being made just over a year *after* the advent of clothes rationing in July 1942 and reflected the concern that basic needs *still* had to be met. Spring Rice had already identified such things as no boots resulting in no school and no outdoor clothes confining an individual to the house,[13]

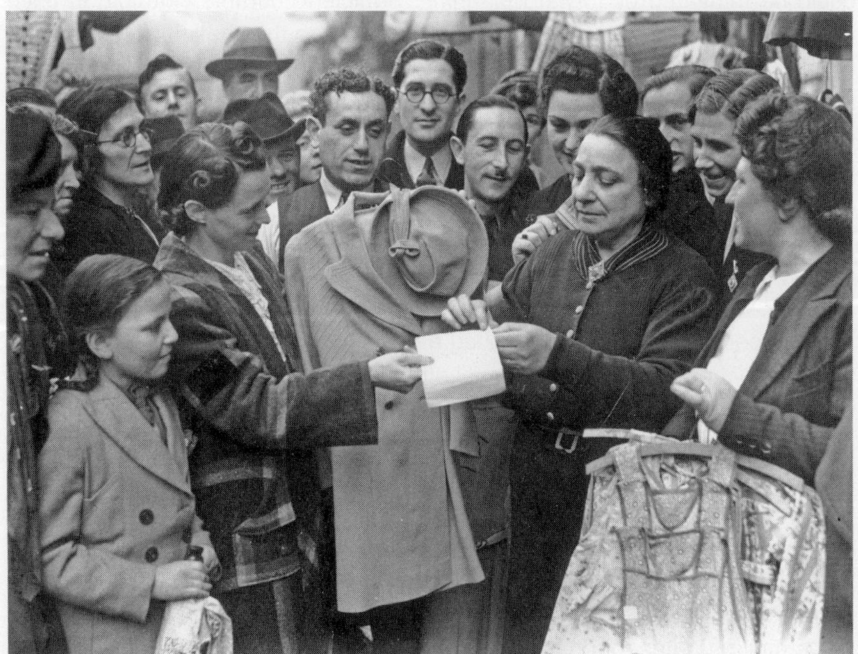

**Figure 10** The first day of clothes rationing in Petticoat Lane market, 1 June 1941. A shopper takes a coupon from her ration book. Reg Spiller/Stringer. Getty Images (3094572).

but there had been neither the will nor the time, with the advent of war, for her recommendations regarding the alleviation of poverty to be acted upon.[14] The later publication of *Our Towns* in 1943 by the Women's Group on Public Welfare[15] would also set forth a number of important welfare recommendations[16] and was another reminder of the iniquitous and exploitative system for obtaining clothing that had led to the poverty of dress revealed through evacuation. Any policy that affected the purchase of clothing, particularly at the most disadvantaged end of the market, should have the longer-term purpose of establishing sufficiency via provision of suitably priced, durable, fit-for-purpose garments.

Conversely, as we have seen, there had been wider opportunities to purchase cheap fashion than ever before. But the lower middle and blue collar classes who had enjoyed this greater purchasing power were now vulnerable in the face of rising prices and scarcity. While the capacity of the moneyed to buy what they wanted remained largely unaffected, those on more limited incomes, perhaps overstretched by domestic responsibilities and/or house payments, might be exposed to financial hardships they were powerless to allay. This could threaten living standards. Government intervention in clothing production and retail needed, therefore, to be reactive to specific social and economic conditions and proactive in foreseeing economic hardship ahead that could be mitigated by forward planning. Sufficient, durable clothing, in price ranges that reflected the buying capacity of all, was the challenge. Setting the ration entailed calculating need, guaranteeing quality and securing manageable prices. Clothing also needed to be appropriate for a lifestyle conditioned by war. This complex series of requirements would result in the Board of Trade not only establishing the coupon purchase system but also developing Utility cloth and clothing.[17] This required more rigorous quality control of textiles and would be accompanied by the introduction of a series of austerity regulations setting specific parameters for design and make. These measures, taken altogether, would complete the process of clothing control.

The Board of Trade finally reached a decision to restrict clothing consumption to two-thirds of the pre-war level although it was 'not possible to assume a reduction of two-thirds—no more, no less—in the consumption of every single item'.[18] Outerwear might be more easily manageable, but underwear and certainly footwear were much less so. In the end, 'common sense came to the rescue and a schedule of the average war-time consumption of each item of men's and women's clothing was drawn up'.[19] This course of action was based on a good deal of 'inspired guesswork'[20] by a limited group of civil servants, without the help of any panel of experts or other outside body.

Details regarding rationing were not disclosed until shortly before its inception on 1 June, when it became necessary to disseminate information to selected parties. On 27 May, the agenda for a meeting of the Board of Trade's

Publicity Committee referred to the President's meeting the following day with Lady Denman representing the Women's Institute (WI), Lady Reading for the WVS, Miss Keeling for the Citizens Advice Bureau, Miss Thorley for the Women's Co-Operative Guild as well as the Chairman and Secretary of the Association of British Chambers of Commerce and National Chamber of Trade. It noted also that the Committee anticipated trade associations and the Trades Union Congress (TUC) becoming involved.[21] Female support was now clearly being enlisted to introduce rationing nationwide, particularly to other women who, it might be supposed, would have a good deal to do with it. The meeting on 28 May gave details in a document marked 'Most Secret' of a further meeting to take place between the President and Lady Reading and Lady Denman, where each would be given 'a draft of a letter to send to their branches arranging meetings with our envoys in the following week'.[22] One hundred and fifty 'envoys' were now ready to impart information to traders 'throughout the country',[23] and explanatory leaflets were also produced in quantity. The official history view, looking back on the period from 1952, was that 'although the Board of Trade had been working so much in the dark and had been unable to enlist the advice of any outside bodies the scheme had obviously been soundly planned. It proved workable and flexible and was to last with little major change for nearly eight years.'[24]

The ration was, therefore, based on an assumed 'average' wartime consumption. Oliver Lyttleton, who had become President of the Board of Trade in October 1940, remarked retrospectively that 'the most difficult part of the scheme on which to form a judgement was, of course, the total number of coupons which each person should have and, within this, the weighting to be given to each coupon. . . . This in turn posed the question how much, in terms of our tentative number of coupons, did the lowest paid people in the country spend each year on clothes and shoes? They should in principle be able to buy rather more than they were accustomed to, because they had no stocks to come and go on'.[25] The problem of adequately assessing need was considerable given the general lack of knowledge about the living conditions of the poorest. Lyttleton was fortunate, however, to tap into an hitherto unknown source of information on which the subsequent scheme appears to have been based. A colleague at the Board[26] suggested that an estimate of sufficiency could be given but only with a margin of error of around 10 per cent. Lyttleton was happy with this but enquired how the figures were to be calculated: 'It came out that for eleven years he and a lady in the Statistical Department of the Bank of England had been compiling and exchanging statistics on this very subject. Their researches proved invaluable and we could count on our scheme resting on a sure foundation.'[27]

The official history does not mention this source about which no more appears to be known. It cites the use of the 1935 and 1937 Censuses of

Production figures and some other figures 'collected from wholesalers under the limitations Orders'.[28] It also mentioned rather vaguely 'some figures of clothing purchases by different samples of people in 1938'.[29] This may refer to the Ministry of Labour's budget enquiry carried out across 1937–1938 and mentioned in a Board of Trade secret memorandum in July 1942. This informed Sir Thomas Barlow, Director General of Civilian Clothing from 1941 to 1945, that 'roughly a fifth of the families . . . reported less than 50 coupons' worth of clothes', a proportion that would be 'much higher if the poorest section were taken separately'.[30] It was clear there already existed a 'bottom end' of the population with less clothing than was desirable even though this sector had appeared to manage.[31] Such figures are a reminder that need *was* recognized and could be factored in to any subsequent ration. It remains difficult to assess exactly how good the statistical bases for rationing were although the relative success of the scheme might suggest less guesswork than history has subsequently related.

The next step was to allocate a number of points for every item of clothing that matched, as near as possible, the amount of material used in their making-up. A yard of woollen cloth thirty-six inches wide would be worth three coupons, a yard of any other material two coupons. Woollen goods were more durable and therefore claimed the higher points value. On this basis, the rest of the points were allocated. For knitted hosiery goods such as socks or stockings, where yardage was not a good starting point, and goods like footwear, it was again common sense that set the ration points at a manageable level in line with likely need. A series of calculations then ensued to add up the average supposed consumption of points to get a figure for total coupon allocation. This figure was then subjected to a 'rough cross-check' to see if 'the ration seemed roughly comparable with the scale of the current restrictions on supply'[32] under the Limitation Orders. Hargreaves and Gowing noted that while there must have been a 'considerable margin of error in the calculation . . . the two sets of figures fitted together miraculously well'.[33]

On the Whit Monday bank holiday, a second notice appeared in the press outlining the points scheme for adults and children. Children would be given additional coupons to reflect their growth, and children under four years of age were able to get their clothing coupon free. Many other additional coupons were given out as the system found its feet, particularly for work-specific clothing, boots and shoes. A full list of all these additions and changes appeared in the Board of Trade's *Clothing Quiz* booklets,[34] issued each year and giving the latest pointing for all cloth and clothing. They also included a question-and-answer section that provided full explanations on how the scheme might operate in specific circumstances. Examples of likely questions included: Did receiving unsolicited clothes from abroad require the handing over of coupons? Would dressmaking take the coupons at the cloth stage or the made-up stage? Were coupons needed to obtain clothing from charitable bazaars? By this mechanism a comprehensive understanding of the rationing scheme was created that covered all situations.

While certain cloths and clothing underwent minor point changes, and some items were added to the ration while others were derationed, there were more significant changes in the amount of coupons issued over the period from June 1941 through to the end of rationing in March 1949. The first year of rationing awarded everyone sixty-six coupons. As stocks depleted, the ration had to change, and even the sixty-six coupons could only be honoured by using up some reserves. In brief, the gradual diminution of supplies and labour created stringencies in the textile industries that had an inevitable effect on the size of the ration. This, in turn, had its impact on the general public. Across the period of rationing there was a slow but necessary retrenchment in the number of coupons allocated as the 'general' ration, although where need was especially great—such as for growing children or industrial workers—the supplementary coupon system worked well.

In the initial year of rationing (1941–1942), the year was effectively managed by not issuing clothing coupons in their own booklet until the twenty-six margarine coupons that first acted for clothes were spent. Then the board regulated the remaining forty by requiring the final twenty to be spent only after 1 January 1942. Ration books for 1942–1943 were printed with sixty coupons but ministers agreed that a number nearer fifty coupons would be more manageable. However, the rationing year actually went from June 1942 to the end of August 1943—a fifteen-month period that effectively reduced the ration to forty-eight coupons a year. The reduction in available cloth and clothing was estimated to have released more than half a million men and women from the textile industries for war work elsewhere during the first two years of rationing. The saving of shipping space for alternative imports was also of paramount importance, and people learnt to manage with less.

Coupons had to be effectively managed to get the best use out of them. To restrict spending too many coupons at one time and risking need later, the Board of Trade devised a system of colours that divided up the coupon allocation into sets or series. For example, in June 1942, three different coloured sets each worth twenty coupons appeared in the ration book: green, that could be used immediately; brown, not to be used until 12 October 1942; and red, which were to be held on to. The green coupons were to last for the first four and a half months. From October to 31 March 1943, the brown and any remaining green coupons could be used while the red coupons would not be valid until 1 April. These final twenty red coupons had to last until 31 August. In deciding when new colours could be used, the Board of Trade effectively controlled coupon expenditure in line with available supplies as well as manipulated how long the rationing 'year' actually was. The 1942–1943 rationing year thus proved to be fifteen months long so that the sixty allocated coupons in fact created a real ration of forty-eight coupons. Viewed in this way, the limitation on clothing becomes much more real and the increasing stringencies more recognizable. The ration was reassessed over three four-month periods, and extensions to the ration year effectively reduced the original ration as required. In later ration books, in addition to the main batches of coupons, there were also small allocations of tokens whose value could be set by the Board depending on the industrial climate. These tokens generally worked out as the equivalent of one, two or three coupons and were another mechanism of controlling the overall ration. For example, the next rationing year ran from 1 September 1943 until 31 July 1944. The clothing ration booklet had thirty-two 'real' coupons but now had a further sixteen coupons each valued at one-quarter, making a batch of thirty-six, or three per month. These were again divided into three sets: yellow coupons marked A1–16, purple coupons marked B1–B8 and including the sixteen quarter coupons, and black/grey coupons marked C1–C8. Of the four additional green tokens lettered *W*, *X*, *Y* and *Z*, *W* and *X* were worth one coupon each while *Y* and *Z* subsequently became worth three each, giving forty-four coupons in total across the eleven-month period. Over twelve months, this again sustained a ration of forty-eight coupons, below which the government had no wish to go if at all possible.[35] A forty-eight-coupon ration 'provided ordinary adults who received no supplementary coupons with something like half their pre-war consumption in terms of quantity'.[36] Raw material stocks, however, continued to fall during 1944, and the new ration year that began on 1 August 1944 and ran until 31 August 1945 (thirteen months) had an overall average of less than the desired forty-eight coupons a year. Thirty-six coupons were again issued in the same format as the previous year (*D, F* and *H coupons*), with four additional tokens—*A, B, C* and *E*. Eighteen brown *D*-series coupons, combined with tokens *A* and *B* valued at three coupons each, gave the ration for the first half of the year as twenty-four—in line with a forty-eight ration again. Over the thirteen months, however, Hargreaves and Gowing stated that the ration for the year had fallen to just over forty-one coupons, which suggests that given the first six months were in line with a forty-eight-year ration, the second seven months lowered the ration to something like seventeen coupons, or less than three coupons a month.[37]

The reasons for this were clear. A 'crisis of production' occurred. There was much to be made—demobilization suits, jungle warfare outfits, relief clothing, as well as clothing for the civilian ration—and the industry was simply too short on labour, and in some sectors cloth, to be able to meet all these requirements.[38] The first part of the next ration year extended from 1 September 1945 to 30 April 1946, a period of eight months. Twenty-four coupons were issued for this period, or a yearly ration of thirty-six coupons, three coupons a month. This decision to cut the ration again was 'impelled by fall of stocks at all stages beyond danger level'.[39] The 'outfits and additional coupons for demobilised members of forces' were cited as particular drains on resources. On 1 May, however, the ration rose to about three and a half coupons a month, or fourteen coupons which were to last until 31 July 1946. This effectively reduced the rationing year to eleven months, raising the ration in the second part of the year to just over fifty-five coupons. From 1 August 1946 until 28 February 1947, there were thirty coupons,[40] or just over four a month, which raised the yearly total to a little over fifty coupons, and from 1 March 1947 up until 31 August, thirty-four coupons were allocated, nearly six coupons a month.[41] This gave a new annual ration of over sixty-seven coupons just a little higher than the original allocation of sixty-six back in 1941.

Imposing new strictures on clothing rationing anticipated certain responses. It required new levels of household management; it endorsed traditional skills such as home sewing and the alteration and repair of clothing; and it promoted new standards of hygiene in the care of clothing and textiles. The impact of rationing across the population at large, and the ability to adjust to it, was varied. At one end of the scale, Conservative MP Sir Henry (Chips) Channon commented: 'Oliver Lyttelton is only going to allow us 66 coupons per annum. A suit takes 26. Luckily I have 40 or more [suits]. Socks will be the shortage. Apart from those, if I am not bombed, I have enough clothes to last me for years.'[42] For the wealthy, the hardship of rationing was likely to be limited. For them, changes in dress protocols as a result of war would have arguably greater impact. The early demise of evening dress and then other occasion-based types of clothing, for example, reflected a less formal aesthetic of restraint and practicality far more in keeping with current life.

A quantity ration could not, on its own, keep down the actual price of clothing. As Sladen points out, 'As the coupon value was fixed according to the amount of cloth in the garment, both manufacturers and consumers were encouraged to spend more by concentrating on the more durable—and more expensive—types of clothing.'[43] It was this factor that led to the inauguration of far tighter controls over the *types* of cloth and clothing manufactured. Rationing had to go hand in hand with new initiatives in textile production. If poverty was to be ameliorated and the needs of all the population were to be met, the manufacture of reasonable quality, durable clothing across a manageable price range had to be the focus. Only then would production be truly fair. The false economy that underpinned the very cheap and exploitative end of the market had to go as it undermined one of the first principles of rationing—maintaining longevity in both new and existing clothing. The Utility scheme was the answer to this heightened demand for quality control over textiles, and it was to be the key factor in maximizing coupon value. With rationing, and the soon-to-emerge Utility range of textiles and clothing, the Board of Trade embarked on a new level of governmental control over the clothing industry and clothing retail on the high street. Based on a growing recognition of the way people really lived, particularly the most disadvantaged, it set about creating a more democratic, egalitarian system of manufacture and distribution that would improve the welfare of all.

During rationing, 'personal expenditure on clothing . . . was about sixty per cent of the pre-war level',[44] a figure higher than might be expected and possibly accounted for by full employment and higher wages. This allowed those elements of the population who had been highly restricted in their buying practices before the war to start spending, particularly on commodities like boots and shoes which replaced poorer quality footwear or plimsolls. Capacity to buy was limited, nevertheless, and thus stocks were made to go round. Styles changed to reflect the stringencies of the ration, and streamlining of design was both a response to, and a reflection of, economic necessity. As people learnt new craft skills and harboured resources in an ever more inventive way, so new fashion narratives arose, each with their own meaning and message. A specific change took place during the war years in the way many people had to plan and operate their clothing requirements. The consumer boom that has been described as affecting a significant proportion of the population in the later 1930s was effectively reversed. Emphasis now lay on making do with what you had rather than buying new and planning out yearly expenditure in line with specific need. The general public was exhorted to foster a new sense of patriotic thrift that would reorientate style and fashionability and place them both at the service of the nation at war.

# –9–

# The Utility Clothing Scheme

Question 39 in the second edition of the *Clothing Quiz* booklet for 1941–1942, undated but probably issued later on in 1941, asked the question, 'What has been done to ensure that the price of clothing does not increase unduly?'[1] The answer was, 'Special releases of cloth are made for the production of clothing of general utility. The cloth and the clothes which are made from it will bear the official mark CC41. The prices at which they can be sold will be controlled and the public will thus find on sale an adequate supply of clothing in the lower range of prices.'[2] The initial concern of the Board of Trade, as this answer makes clear, was that rationing had unintentionally fostered a practice of 'trading-up' whereby both manufacturer and consumer were seeking the best value per coupon with better quality but more expensive goods. The clothing index had risen from 175 in May 1941 to 191 by December 1941. In order to keep the total cost-of-living index stable, 'the price of sugar then had to be reduced by 1d. a pound'.[3] By December, however, the Board of Trade had already come up with solutions to curbing prices and maintaining supplies of lower-priced clothing goods. The production of those goods just took time to accomplish. Given that limiting the capacity to buy had not, on its own, restricted rising prices, the government, via the Board of Trade, introduced a new scheme that sought to control the manufacture and production of a large part of the domestic textile and clothing supply so that prices of this production could be fixed. The first step was an enabling act of July 1941 which created a new industrial structure whereby 'price policy and production policy' became 'closely intertwined'.[4] The Goods and Services (Price Control) Act combined various powers, the most important of which was to 'fix maximum prices and margins', and this was impossible, as the original failings of the Price of Goods Acts had already demonstrated, 'without clear specifications of the goods concerned', which implied 'control over production'.[5] The Board of Trade would also have the power to fix service charges and to control trade in second-hand goods via a new scheme to register dealers and to cut out unnecessary middlemen in the supply chain that pushed up prices. Inspectors would be appointed to carry out these tasks.[6] If control was to extend over production, then defining exactly what was required in terms of serviceable fabrics for specific types of clothing would now become the basis for policy. Garment manufacture under these new requirements would, in the first instance, make good the shortfall in the cheaper ranges. As Hancock and Gowing confirmed, 'a plan emerged to encourage manufacturers to produce particular garments from particular cloths at prices to be clearly specified at each stage of production and distribution'.[7] This was to be the Utility system.

The difficulty in getting Utility up and running was that of 'forcing a large number of people to make something they did not want to make'[8]—the cheaper and longer runs of more economic fabric. The Board of Trade decided to offer an inducement system for producing Utility fabric and clothing by significantly increasing manufacturing quotas for these commodities over non-Utility goods. In August 1941, therefore, in a Woven Textiles (Cloth and Apparel) Order, the Board of Trade 'extended the system of quota control for a further nine months and introduced a quota for Utility goods roughly double the non-Utility quota'.[9] The importance of this lay in the 'guarantee of raw material supplies, these being uncertain for the remaining percentage of permitted non-Utility production'.[10] There was also a promise of protected labour for Utility—that was labour not available for relocation to other war industries. These 'inducements' were crucial, Ady explains, because 'the other details of the scheme tended to reduce the financial stimulus, and it was by these measures that adequate supplies were secured'.[11] This sustained the capacity for future business. By the end of the first period of Utility from 1 November 1941 until 31 May 1942, 'supplies of cheaper clothing' had been 'assured' and the clothing factor in the cost-of-living index had been stabilized.[12] Utility prices also remained stable from October 1941 until a fall in August 1942 whereas the 'prices of non-Utility clothing continued to rise' until August 1942, when they were controlled under the General Apparel and Cloth (Max. Prices and Charges) Order.[13] With firms selected or 'designated'[14] to undertake Utility production and with the Board of Trade issuing key certificates for obtaining raw material and fabric in line with honouring the ration, the Utility system was complete.[15] Utility wear was made even more cost effective in August 1942 when, under another government order,[16] purchase tax was removed from almost all Utility goods. Only fully fashioned stockings, expensively high on labour, and fur clothing remained taxed. In due course, a broader range of better-quality fabrics 'within reasonable limits' began to be produced under the auspices of the scheme, so avoiding the fear that Utility would be only associated with something 'cheap and nasty'.[17]

The first range of cloths to be specified for production as Utility were for cheaper clothing to ensure an adequate provision of garments for those on limited incomes. Forty cloths were introduced in September 1941 under Limitation of Supplies (Cloth and Apparel) Order SR & O 1281, which also introduced the Utility CC41 mark. The sixteen cottons, nineteen wools, four woven rayons and one lock-knit were all given three-figure codes, such as flannelette

301, and a brief description.[18] As an example of the type of quality these cloths provided, Wadsworth gave the relative prices in 1939 of shirts made up from flannelette, selling for 6d, and fine two-fold quality cotton poplin selling for 10s 6d. The price variants illustrated that Utility was being sold initially at the lower end of the cloth scale.[19] The first stage of planned production therefore created a limited range of value-for-money textiles.

This first tier of Utility met with varying success dependent on the nature of the industry it encountered. The case of wool reflects the difficulties inherent in superimposing a level of external regulation on a highly diverse industry. Wool manufacturers often had strong and established trading links with clothiers for more expensive cloths, which now conflicted with the Board of Trade's requirement for cheaper weaves.[20] Utility cloths were numbered, briefly described—for example, number 208 referred to 'Woollen Tweed, other Woollen cloth, Woollen and Worsted Mixture cloth'—and given a maximum price that could be charged both wholesale and retail. Wool types spanned tweeds, meltons and serges in a range of middle to higher costs to a cheaper flannel and a cheap Union shirting. The cheapest of the retailers' prices was 3s 1d per yard net measure for union shirting, the most expensive 18s 8d for a woollen tweed.[21] Wool numbers ran from 201 to 222, and different numbers and prices were often given for the same simple description indicating that there were generic differences in construction. Price reflected this variegated offering but was not necessarily an indication of quality.[22] The Wool Control felt unable to produce an exact register of cloths 'because of the wide variation in types of raw material—there were upwards of 7,000 grades of raw wool. . . . Two pieces of wool cloth manufactured in the same way from the same raw material would not result in the same article.'[23] The loose control over specification resulted in some cloths of dubious quality from an industry that seemed reluctant to change its working practice despite new perspectives on civilian need. Hargreaves and Gowing were ambivalent as to the effectiveness of quality control over wool in the absence of close specifications and noted that some woollen mills, in resisting the ceiling prices required for Utility cloth, economized by 'spinning to lower counts [and] using fewer picks per yard'. The wool controller acknowledged that 'the cheaper Utility cloths . . . were undoubtedly not durable [but] they were not worse and were probably rather better than comparable cloths before the war'.[24] Utility shoddy cloths—the cheapest of the wool lines with the lowest cost—were scrutinized especially closely to ensure a baseline quality in this poorest of fabrics, and the Wool Control 'enforced certain precautions' on the production of shoddy, including making manufactures declare 'the ingredients from which it was made'. Wool Textile Research Association tests confirmed there had been 'no detectable adulteration of these cloths',[25] but that such monitoring was necessary might infer the price-driven priorities of the industry further endorsed by its bias towards more expensive products. Hargreaves and Gowing believed that 'serious deterioration' never occurred as adequate raw material supplies rendered undue cheapening of the product unnecessary. Flexibility in maximum prices also allowed for a limited move towards higher-end trade.[26] The industry's unease with Utility resulted in a fall in production between 1942 until 1944, however, as manufacturers increasingly turned to non-Utility wool stocks of higher quality that could be sold accordingly. Even though purchase tax remained in place on non-Utility wear from August 1942, the wool industry continued to discriminate against Utility and its generally lower quality. Only the advent of more expensive Utility wool cloths introduced by the Board of Trade in January 1945 ameliorated this.[27] It is important to emphasize that cloths like shoddy were *not eliminated* from the industry, but rather the *standards* to which they were produced under the auspices of the Utility scheme were kept under surveillance to maintain the necessary improvement on the pre-war product. Without precise specifications for comparison, proof that this was so could not be provided.

Specifications for cotton and rayon were more successful. The first range of cotton cloths were numbered from 301 to 309 and ran from pyjama cloths to cotton shirtings and dress fabrics in plain, gingham and other woven designs and also included a range of work-style fabrics, including overall cloths and fustians, and special application cottons such as corset drills and coutils, calico and linings.[28] Retailers' maximum prices per yard (net measure) ranged from 1s 5d for calico, 1s 9d for overall cloth and 1s 11d for cambric shirting with the highest costs for cotton gabardine at 5s 5d and plain or cord velveteens at 6s 2d. The far fewer rayon cloths numbering from 401 to 404 with lining fabric 409 provided a dress and blouse fabric at 7s 3d, lingerie cloth at 5s 2d, a lock-knit fabric at 3s 7d and corset cloths under one number at 4s 8d. These medium to lower prices reflected that rayon was more expensive than the cheaper cotton dress cloths at 2s 7d but provided stylish and popular clothes in various weights.[29]

During the early summer of 1942, the Board of Trade in conjunction with the British Standards Institute were able to produce a much-wider series of cloth specifications for rayon and cotton which not only clarified their precise manufacture but also married up the different cloths to the clothing for which they were best suited. These did not affect the print or colour so that a wide variety of fabrics could now exist under the aegis of the specification system. This offset the idea that Utility was somehow a standardized product with little style or variety. Initially, the number specification had not appeared on the Utility fabric or garment because garments marked with the same fabric number and therefore assumed to be of the same quality could be sold at different shops for different prices, so confusing the shopper. The selling prices between the multiple or chain stores and that of the small independent retailer were likely to be different,[30] and the trade had opposed making this disparity more obvious via a number. While the Board of Trade 'Draft Minute' outlining this debate[31] does not press the point, it seems likely that the trade were unwilling to render their commercial methods more transparent to the public. It seems reasonable to suppose that the different mechanisms via which Marks and Spencer could sell a similar product for less than a small retailer tended to lead the shopper to assume the more expensive garment to be somehow better quality than the volume-produced item. That this was not necessarily so, or where the chain store product was in fact better, the small retailer's business was at risk, and thus the hosiery trade and various trade associations had expressed concern.[32] By July 1942, the Board of Trade believed that differential pricing would not, however, be especially noticeable given the widely different treatments individual fabrics could reflect and the style variations between garments made up in fabrics of the same number: 'It seems unlikely that the public will assume that a blouse with Marks and Spencer No. 209A is the same as a blouse with another retailer of the same number but with an entirely different colour, finish, cut, make-up and trimming. We know of no case in which the same blouses sold both direct to the retail and through the wholesaler have been noticed by the public in different shops at different prices.'[33] The Board therefore pressed for the addition of the numbers in order to firmly control price and to render infringements of maximum prices or margins a more provable offence. Numbers finally appeared on cloth and clothing in August 1942 with the newer four-figure numbers for cotton and rayon and the old three figures for wool cloth. At the end of August 1942, there were '102 cotton and 69 rayon specifications . . . for apparel cloth'[34] with rayons numbered from 1000 to 1206 and divided into categories such as spun rayon, acetate and viscose crepes, jacquards, cuprammonium crepes and taffetas. Cottons ranged from four-figure versions of older three-figure fabrics like flannelette pyjama cloths 3010 and cambric shirtings 3021, through various types of dress cloths from dobby cambrics to striped zephyrs at 3042 and 3053, respectively, to heavy overall cloths starting at 3110 and eight corset cloths beginning at 9000. In every case, the weight of the fabric and any percentage of foreign matter to be included were registered, as well as the minimum number per inch of threads in the warp and weft, the actual number of threads, the dye type and the maximum washing shrinkage per warp and weft. Yarn counts were given for cotton, and rayon warp and weft threads were specified, ground ends numbered and minimum selvedge ends specified. The number of picks in the loom state cloth were recorded and the minimum finishing shrinkage set down with the weave types and finish required.[35] Unlike wool there was no specification by price. The type of fabric resulted in the price given. The Utility Fabrics Exhibition held in Manchester in early 1943 revealed the huge range of fabric choice now deriving from the specifications,[36] and the various requirements on finishes that appeared in the British Standards Institution (BSI) documents—fastness to washing, fastness to light and perspiration and, for some cotton cloths, waterproofing—were evidence of the application of technology to fabric production that had been pioneered by the industry during the 1930s.[37]

A good example of this use of modern technology in fabric construction can be found in the laboratory set up by Marks and Spencer in 1935. With quality control as its central purpose, the laboratory analysed materials and then 'reported back on them so that improvements could be made on the factory floor'. Israel Sieff believed that 'the more we did this . . . the more manufacturers decided they had better do the same thing for themselves'.[38] In 1936, Marks and Spencer introduced a Merchandise Development Department run by German chemist Dr Eric Kann[39] to test 'for colour fastness and shrinkage . . . the character of yarns and dyeing processes' and other 'problems' associated with volume production. This move led to a 'very close relationship' between Marks and Spencer and 'the great firm of Imperial Chemical Industries'.[40] Thus the clothing industry had already begun to create new paradigms for cloth and clothing production that would be made standard requirements of Utility production during the war. The creation of Utility fabric 1005, a spun rayon, appears to have come from a collaboration between Marks and Spencer and the BSI via the Board of Trade.[41]

While Utility fabrics were carefully specified so that quality and durability could be maintained in clothing production, there were still savings in terms of labour that could be made during the *process* of production. Long runs of fabric were encouraged as economically time saving, and in line with this the Board of Trade decided to introduce a series of simplifications into garment construction that would save on fabric and increase the speed of production by reducing the work involved in pattern cutting, making-up and finishing. These came into being through a series of Making of Civilian Clothing (Restrictions) Orders from May 1942, with minor changes into 1943. Known as the 'austerity' regulations, they applied to *both* Utility and non-Utility clothing. Any commercially made garment had to abide by these restrictions, although home dressmaking did not. The precise visual details of these regulations will be looked at more closely in Chapter 14 as part of a discussion on the aesthetics of fashionable dress during rationing. Here the type of regulations imposed can be examined as progressive exercises in curbing and constraining clothing production, both in terms of labour and use of raw material.

Hargreaves and Gowing divided the restrictions up into various types, each of which would have ramifications for the appearance of clothing.[42] There were regulations that affected 'the style and design of garments'[43]—for example, women's outerwear was to have a limited number of seams, pleats, and buttonholes and a maximum width set for sleeves, belts and collars.

Hem allowances were limited and the number of buttons was regulated—only four for a coat, for example. These would make savings in both labour and resources. For men's clothes there were new regulations that cut the length of shirts, eliminated trousers turn-ups and double shirt cuffs and limited buttonholes and buttons. Pocket flaps, cuff buttons and double-breasted jackets disappeared.[44] The demise of the turn-up proved surprisingly unpopular, so much so that Sir High Dalton, President of the Board of Trade, in a press statement in March 1943 nearly a year after the initial regulations had come into force, had a 'final word on turn-ups': 'Permanent turn-ups on trousers have been prohibited since May 1942. This was done to save an entirely justifiable waste of cloth. In making this and other clothing regulations I was advised by the trade. The economy of materials due to the prohibition of turn-ups runs into the millions of square feet per year. Even if the saving were less than it is, it would still be our duty to make it.'[45] The word *permanent* could have referred to the practice of some men having their trousers made too long and then turning them up later.[46] Dalton did not leave it there, such was the feeling regarding the importance of this austerity regulation. 'There is no serious case at all for restoring turn-ups whilst the need for war economy lasts. There are no turn-ups to the trousers of officers or other ranks in either the Army, Navy or Air Force, and I should have thought a style good enough for the Fighting Forces should have been good enough for the civilian population. Nor do the police and other wearers of uniform have turn-ups. Nor, as I am glad to see the "Daily Mail" points out this morning, did many men who take a special pride in their appearance, wear turn-ups in pre-war days.'[47] The two inches removed from the bottom of a man's shirt and the elimination of double cuffs together 'saved about 4 million square yards of cotton annually, and about 1,000 operatives in the cloth manufacture alone'.[48] Small things were not as insignificant or petty as they might seem.

A little after the initial style regulations were introduced for woven goods, hosiery too became subject to austerity restrictions. In September 1942, similar simplifications arrived for knitted goods including shorter sock lengths for men, again unpopular; limitation on buttons and pockets; and the demise of button openings on men's vests and pants.[49] These design restrictions were made in conjunction with a second tier of regulations that looked more to the surface decoration of a garment. Here, too, the additional labour and time needed to add detail was considered expendable in the name of efficiency and durability. Thus embroidery and appliqué finishing was eliminated for outerwear together with fur or leather trimming, and decorative stitching on underwear was abolished.[50] A number of new methods of cut and construction were implemented in line with the austerity drive to save on fabric and labour, such as cutting a collar, shoulder and front yoke all in one piece and using a selvedge edge without a seam allowance in a finished garment.[51] The clothing produced therefore became plainer than the fashion offerings of the pre-war years but could still provide variety of print, colour and overall design within the limitations imposed. Good-quality tailoring of Utility fabric was also possible, and wartime style consolidated around the compromises of austerity. As Hardy Amies wrote in his memoirs, the restrictions were not problematic as 'I had settled down to an extreme sobriety of design'.[52]

A third type of austerity restriction, arguably the most stringent, was the implementation of style templates. Where manufacturers were largely concerned with fashion clothing and producing seasonal collections, the number of basic designs was now to be limited. This was intended to save on labour and increase longer production runs of fewer garments. Women's underwear producers were to work on only six templates for each article manufactured, such as petticoats or knickers,[53] while producers of ladies dresses were restricted to fifty sets of templates per year.[54] These could be changed each year. Infants' wear was also fiercely reduced in variety to one template each for 'buster suits, buster rompers, rompers', two templates for 'blouses up to 14 inches long' and only fifteen templates for infant' and girls' 'dresses, day gowns, robes and tunic shorts up to size 38 in'.[55] While this might seem severe by today's standards, there had long been encouragement throughout the 1930s for young mothers and mothers-to-be to make their children's layettes and early clothing themselves at home. Books like Agnes Mialls's *Making Clothes for Children*, first published in 1934, suggested that there was 'no task more appealing to all that is best in a woman than the preparing of the tiny garments for the little one who is to come'.[56] Limitations on style now gave the home dressmaker something of an advantage in terms of variety, and all women were encouraged to rekindle home crafting skills for both choice and economy. With the advent of various media campaigns such as 'Mrs. Sew-and-Sew' and 'Make-Do and Mend', women who lacked experience or confidence in these areas now had easy and free access to information and tuition, and a new emphasis on the home-made and refurbished emerged as a result.[57]

The last restrictions were those limiting certain fabrics that were in short supply. Elastic could now only be used very selectively, in women's corsets and knickers, infant's wear and some industrial use, for example, and steel and rubber were much reduced to the home market.[58] The *Clothing Quiz* booklets informed people each year of the scarcity of individual commodities, reflected in higher rationing points or, in the case of rubber or synthetic rubber boots, the need to acquire a special permit prior to buying to endorse genuine need. With buttons in short supply, one solution for home-made garments was the use of 'wooden button-moulds covered over with a knitted square or crocheted circle using machine yarn. . . . If no moulds were available, crocheted buttons could be stuffed with oddments of left-over wool. . . . A clever idea was to paint old buttons with coloured enamels, (while Lucy Rie, the distinguished potter, made wonderful ceramic buttons as part of her war effort). The easiest solution . . . was to knit garments that required no buttons at all.'[59]

Austerity and Utility combined clearly created a new dynamic for the designer to work with. To facilitate ever-better coupon value—a now-intrinsic combination of quality and durability—the Board of Trade also introduced safeguards to the whole process of production and manufacture. These were in the form of new controls over the final garment that required minimum standards of making-up and sizing.[60] If there were to be ever-fewer garments and fewer purchases of new clothes, then these clothes had to be a good fit as well as fit for purpose. For dresses and overalls, there were to be 'minimum measurements for each size of garment', and for women's underwear and nightwear a required standard of sewing had to be met, together with sizing regulations, that complied with the 'width, type and finishing' necessary for all seams.[61] Overalls and underwear were the only garments to have a maximum yardage of material laid down for each size.[62]

In summary, fabrics and finishes were selected for specific garments consonant with their intended use, such as a wool gabardine coat's 'waterproofness' or rayon's crease resistance.[63] This process allied to the fixed prices for specific fabrics and maximum retail selling prices, all made Utility unique in terms of the planned and controlled economy it represented. Better standards resulted for the textile industry *as a whole*. The Utility scheme built on the sure foundations of the British mass-produced ready-to-wear clothing industry that had been so impressively established during the interwar years. Consumers on limited incomes had been able to buy cheap fashion on the high street, elements of which had taken advantage of improvements in fabric technology such as those notably pioneered by Marks and Spencer in the mid-1930s. Utility, in much the same way, sought to produce value-for-money textile and clothing ranges retailing across a broad spectrum of price points to cater to the public at large. Its specific achievements, however, were to ensure reasonable quality *within each tier* of production and by so doing effectively outlaw the very poorest and most exploitative sector of the industry. With unemployment falling and wages becoming more stable, poorer families were no longer tied to the iniquitous trading practices of the past and might now look forward to greater material comfort exemplified by better quality and more serviceable clothing and footwear. The Board sought to eliminate those wool fabrics that might bring the scheme into disrepute, and, in general, the scheme maintained a restricted, carefully specified range of cloths across the industry to produce durable, fit-for-purpose clothing. While in the case of wool durability could not always be guaranteed, there was not enough negative feedback to suggest this altered the overall balance of success achieved by the scheme as a whole.

While some of the austerity regulations were relaxed in 1944, notably for men's outer clothes on the run up to demobilization, men's sock lengths in November of 1945 and men's hosiery in January of 1946, most of the restrictions on women's wear remained in place until March and April of 1946.[64] For between three to four years, depending on gender, Utility style predetermined the keynotes of the wartime look of the nation as the average output in total for Utility cloth, and thus clothing, was 80 per cent of the market.[65] Non-Utility clothing—hats, for example—did exist in small quantities but was expensive and had little effect on the high street. While Utility restricted choice, particularly at the more moneyed end of the market, it ensured that sufficient amounts of essential clothing could be made available. By careful regulation and specification of the design, manufacture and distribution of civilian textiles and clothing, the Board of Trade created an economically viable and sustainable system that addressed the clothing needs of the nation across all classes.

# –10–

# Assessing the Impact of Clothes Rationing

The policy of fair shares enshrined within clothes rationing now had to be monitored to assess the degree to which the coupon allocation was indeed sufficient for the health and well-being of the whole population. Asked by Churchill what his policy for clothes rationing was now to be, Lyttleton replied waspishly, 'Strength through misery'. Churchill enjoyed the joke and 'repeated it under his breath once or twice with apparent relish'.[1] A number of fact-finding mechanisms now arose to assess the impact of rationing, and these facilitated access to the experience of both the consumer and the retailer. The results afforded the Board the opportunity to tune and refine the scheme as war progressed so that rationing could continue to provide the civilian population with adequate and appropriate clothing despite war demands on the textile and garment manufacturing industries.

Churchill had warned the Board not to 'strip the poor people to the buff',[2] and the Board of Trade were keen to develop their own intelligence-gathering channels represented by a consumer panel, wardrobe checks and reports from area distribution officers. In this way, data essential for reviewing the ration each year could be collected.

Alongside the Board's own mechanisms, there were other means available to survey the impact of consumer control. Trade papers like the *Tailor and Cutter* and the *Drapers' Record* commented on industry response to rationing with retail figures and news from the high street, while the work of the Mass Observation organization reflected the views of the ordinary individual on the street. Between all the different elements of news gathering, the story of wartime clothing unfolded in some detail.

The first moves to assess the impact of restriction on domestic economy had begun a year earlier, in June 1940, when Francis Meynall had been asked to conduct a survey into the effects of the Limitation of Supplies Orders. While this revealed no cause for concern, the principle was laid down that the Board needed a 'moving picture of equally moving events'.[3] Sufficiency needed to be monitored not just as a result of particular legislation but also because of movements in the population as a condition of war. These had begun to cause new problems of distribution and supply that needed action.[4] The stringencies arising from the Limitation of Supplies Order of November 1940 had caused concern, and this had led to the Board appointing four area distribution officers in February 1941, followed by eight more in April, as described in Chapter 7. These officers, representing the twelve civil defence regions, formed the basis of an information-gathering service that would continue to grow over the next two years. The area officers reported weekly to the Consumer Needs Branch of the Board on retail and industry points of view and provided any additional information that might affect the successful continuance of trade. Just after the inception of rationing, a new retail panel was created with about 1,500–1,600 member retailers who all contributed information regarding their stocks. From this information, the Board could gauge any likelihood of shortage or glut. The British Market Research Bureau took over this work in May 1943.[5]

These mechanisms for retrieving information from the field did not directly consult the consumer. In order to engage with the shopper on the high street, the Board set up a special consumer panel that would be its most important mechanism for monitoring feeling on the ground. Begun in August 1941, this panel was run from the start by the British Market Research Bureau, who compiled lists of items bought and prices paid from all panel members.[6] This information, in conjunction with irregular wardrobe checks on members of the consumer panel,[7] provided a mass of information on how coupons were being used and what garments were becoming scarce or needed in greater numbers than the ration would allow. While the panel gave information on purchases, the wardrobe checks reviewed stocks of clothing, both rationed and unrationed, held across different sectors of the population. This gave a good idea of those living largely off pre-war supplies and those living much nearer to the extent of the ration during any one year. Combining trade and consumer information provided the Board with an overview on clothes rationing that could be built on as war progressed and as access to further data became available. This subsequently included trade figures from different sections of the textile industry, feedback from trade unions, results of consumer surveys and the findings of Mass Observation investigations. Closer exploration of a representative selection of these review methods reveals the type of information the Board now became party to and the discussion and action to which this gave rise. The Board's own feedback mechanisms are a good place to start.

The Slough Borough Survey conducted in September of 1941 was one of the earliest surveys to review consumer reaction to clothes rationing for the Board.[8] Conducted during the week ending 6 September 1941, 161 private families, totalling 560 individuals, were interviewed on how the first three months of clothes rationing had affected them. Housewives provided the primary level of information, confirming what the Board had foreseen—that housewives would be the main organizers of the coupons for the family, with pooling of resources likely to occur. The survey was also compiled under two headings according to the estimated earnings of the family. Five pounds a week was taken as a dividing line. Below this, families were grouped as working class; on or above this, middle class. The findings showed more shared concerns than differences, irrespective of income, and the questionnaire revealed a number of problem areas, such as the need for robust shoes. These would become more troublesome as time went on. The survey was indicative of the type of thing that could cause public anxiety and what the reaction was likely to be. Differences were seen in how pooled coupons were used. In middle-class homes, the adults tended to provide coupons for growing children, the report concluding that this was most likely due to the 'better "clothing stock" position' of the adults and also the requirement for school uniform within this group.[9] In working-class homes, the adult females' and infants' cards provided for the men and boys. This could be partly accounted for by the fact that men in this group were more likely to have manual jobs which were heavier on clothing. Across both classes, there was a 'tendency for men, boys and girls, to take from the books of women and infants'.[10] Heaviest purchases across the survey as a whole were on footwear at 19.1 per cent, followed by stockings and socks at 17.7 per cent. Next came underwear at 13.2 per cent, with few coupons yet being used for 'cloth, overalls or aprons', although criticism of putting overalls on the ration at all was a feature of the questionnaire.[11]

Several things emerge from these findings. Footwear was already a sensitive area. For working-class families, shoes were serious items of expenditure if hard-wearing leather was to be bought. Cheap alternatives did not wear well and had been a false, if necessary, economy. With the advent of war work and with many family incomes now on the rise, new pressure for better-quality footwear arose. Children's shoes were singled out for comment in the questionnaire with the second-highest number of respondents. There were complaints that they wore out 'so quickly . . . a child needs new shoes once a fortnight; new shoes needed every three weeks; infants' shoes cannot be mended', and shoes could not be 'cut-down'.[12] Even for middle-class families, shoes were potentially problematic. While adults might have spare pairs, children's feet grew, and new shoes were a necessity. By August 1943, shoe leather was in very short supply, and shoes had to be up pointed, although children with larger feet might be eligible for a supplementary award of coupons if buying adult sizes. The Slough survey was an early warning that shoes were one of a small number of key wardrobe items that would have to be monitored carefully. Enough had to be made at appropriate price levels to accommodate all sectors of society, with a product at the lower end of the scale considerably more durable than currently existed.[13]

Stockings were another source of almost constant concern for the duration of the war. A pair of stockings was valued in June 1941 at two coupons a pair. This was irrespective of the fabric. In October of the previous year under a Woven Textiles Order (Supplemental), silk had been controlled, as we have seen, and no more was to be used in products for the civilian market. This meant that stockings other than those from stocks in silk were now being made up largely in either rayon fibre or lisle, a hard-twisted cotton yarn, or wool. Complaints about stockings from the Slough survey centred on the fragility of the more popular fashion sheers, which could be in silk or rayon, and the need to replace them regularly. Heavier-gauge stockings were clearly considered less stylish, although they were more durable and available. There was specific concern over this issue of stocking quality given the need to surrender two coupons per pair, irrespective of weight and thread, and this resulted in the section on stockings in the questionnaire having the fourth-highest number of respondents. Fully fashioned stockings would be up pointed in October 1942 from two to three coupons per pair in deference to the additional labour expended on their making-up, while the less stylish seamless stockings remained at two.[14] Being offered practicality rather than 'fashion' was not popular from the outset.

The first rationing order had placed overalls, dungarees and like garments for men, women and children at six coupons for adults and four coupons for children. A concession was made for the working person in that boiler suits and workmen's bib-and-brace overalls were left unrationed, as were clogs. These unrationed goods proved equally useful for purposes other than the manual labour for which they had been intended so that in November 1941, the bib-and-brace overall and boiler suit were rationed with new, but low, pointings.[15] This was to stop these garments being used for such things as housework or gardening, despite the saving to other clothing that had resulted. The main concern expressed by respondents on the Slough survey was that if war work needed overalls, they should be available without coupons. The issue of whether government should provide what amounted to a working uniform was a continuing source of debate. Some employers did provide workwear but claimed back the coupons, not always easily. By October 1941, however, specified services were allowed uniform, including overalls, at a concessionary coupon rate. These included 'the Civil Defence Service, Fire Service, Police Force, uniformed staff of Government departments, local authorities, N.A.A.F.I. and such undertakings as transport, gas, water and electricity and such classes of nurses as the Board might specify'.[16]

The biggest response to an individual item in the Slough survey questionnaire was on working trousers.[17] Not only were trousers not durable enough for hard work, but there was already a downturn perceived in the second-hand market that had clearly supported working men previously. Without this and hand-me-downs from relatives, the trouser situation was of real concern. Second-hand goods had originally been unrationed, but there had been a hasty adjustment to this ruling a month later so that only cheaper garments could now be obtained without the ordinary number of coupons.[18] In due course, the Board would directly address the issue of working clothing through supplementary coupons called the Industrial Ten, to which we shall return later. Where feedback suggested the rise of genuine need, the Board attempted to ameliorate it via increased production or additional coupons. Meeting additional need was not always easy, and protocols for qualifying were stringent. The usefulness and importance of feedback from surveys, such as Slough's family review, allowed the Board to develop a broad overview of trends and needs that they could then assess and integrate as necessary into their forward clothing policy.

On 3 July 1942, a Board of Trade circular entitled 'The Clothes Ration' referred to figures currently held by the Consumer Needs Branch on the first rationing year. These identified that the year had ended with 'a couple of coupons in each average hand (aggregating and including the supplementary issues in the average)'.[19] The supplements referred to were for children who, depending on their age, now received additional coupons to take continued growth into consideration. From November 1941, children aged fifteen years ten months to sixteen years five months had received twenty extra coupons, children aged thirteen years eight months to fifteen years ten months, forty, and children below thirteen years eight months and above-average height or weight were also given forty coupons. These last children were considered 'outsize' and were eligible for the coupons after being weighed and measured at school or, for those not at school (as were an unknown number especially in blitzed areas), on receipt of a special form initially to be signed by a Justice of the Peace (JP) or similar.[20] Supplementary coupons had also been allocated in August 1941 to expectant mothers at a rate of an additional fifty as infant clothing, initially unrationed, now became part of the scheme.[21] With these supplements in mind, and with a full set of figures not yet available, the Board of Trade circular was as yet unsure whether to interpret the leftover coupons as evidence of an 'ample ration or the borderline of hardship' given that three coupons were not enough to buy anything substantial.[22] The circular drew the Board's attention to the results of the first wardrobe check, which had been carried out in March 1942. These checks focused on what people actually had and were revealing of sufficiency or the reverse. The circular explained that for this check, '1600 homes of all classes' were reviewed. Of these, between 40 to 50 per cent believed they had fewer clothes than at the same time the previous year, and in terms of occupations, 50 per cent of 'light factory and building operatives' felt they had less, while 75 per cent of miners believed they had the same.[23] The survey reported little difference between classes, although this phrase is unclear. Given the relative distance between a well-stocked middle- or upper-class wardrobe, or even a well-maintained working-class wardrobe, and that of a family on a very low income or unemployed, this statement would appear to refer to the fact that the *same things* were being bought now, reflecting the same needs and priorities across the classes. The Slough survey had already born this out.

Youths appeared to have suffered most in terms of wardrobe stock, and 'condition of clothes . . . in this group was found to be bad to a higher degree than elsewhere, (20%–30% in bad condition in the lower-middle and working classes)'. Footwear for boys was also cited as of primary need. Again, this had already surfaced as a potential problem through Slough and would need some amelioration. For girls, too, shoes were a concern, and for women and young girls, stockings were beginning to become difficult 'particularly among factory workers'.[24] Stockings of a more durable nature were now necessary or recourse to either bare legs or trousers. Trying to inculcate new dress practices more appropriate in the face of rationing would be on future agendas at the Board as clothing stringencies became more marked.

Lack of shoes was used to indicate relative levels of need. Those family members owning only one pair revealed a level of clothing ownership 'one-quarter to one-third lower than the average for men and at least one-third lower for women'. These facts were underlined and the conclusion reached that such people 'look to be on the border of destitution'. Further research revealed that such a level of need and the inability to buy more shoes was more than '"normal" e-class destitution'.[25] This designation referred to a class below the A–B higher classes and C–D lower classes including not just the pre-war unemployed but the lowest-paid manual workers who, prior to rationing, would have survived on the cheapest goods and second-hand markets. With further investigation and information from social workers operating in Deptford and Greenwich, it appeared that there was certainly 'hardship in working class homes', primarily created by three interlocking problems.[26] To some extent these were caused by rationing: lack of money, coupons and second-hand clothing. With the cheapest goods no longer in production, there had initially been no option but to buy pricier clothes. These were of inferior (pre-Utility) quality and had not lasted. Coupons had been used up, and with the curtailment of the second-hand markets there had been little opportunity to supplement clothing. E-class rates of spending were 'consistently higher than the other classes', partly due to the higher proportion of heavy industry workers and labourers and the likely need to replace working clothes more often. Both men and women here had 'topped the 66 coupon mark by 28th March', or four months prior to the end of the rationing period.[27] A new type of poverty had arisen across the first year of rationing at the lower end of the social scale, and the Board was swift to recognize that 'our ration policy is likely to drive into this class numbers who have never been in difficulty before and that we are thereby putting extra strain on the social services'. While inferior goods were still being sold, the 'poor get poorer'.[28] Various solutions to this impending crisis were suggested, including having clothing reserves, later to become well known as clothing exchanges; additional coupon assistance for the needy (a system already in operation, if quietly, as other Board of Trade memoranda reveal; see below); and the need to promote Utility further in the marketplace. As Utility clothing finally came to represent 85 per cent of home market production, this would be achieved.

Surveys like the wardrobe check were, therefore, important. In conjunction with information from retailers on buying habits, from social workers on home needs, and from area distribution officers on trade and stock positions and consumer reaction, the Board was able to stay in reasonably close touch with ordinary people on the home front. A paper by H.J.B. Lintott for the Board of Trade, circulated on 17 July 1942, put forward a variety of viewpoints as to whether the next year's ration could be cut to save further labour, shipping and factory space. He took up the concern about destitution raised the previous fortnight. An investigation of the numbers who had applied for assistance revealed that there had been two hundred applications a month of which 75 per cent had been agreed.[29] This was not a large number in the overall scheme of things but brought to the fore the condition of the poorest and how they should be helped. Industrial workers requiring additional clothing had been allowed supplementary coupons during this first year of rationing, which, with additional children's coupons, helped provide for the needs of poorer families.[30] Lintott acknowledged that 'opinions differ as to the scale of the problem presented by the wardrobe-less class' while advisor on consumer needs Francis Meynall felt some cushion against hardship was required if the ration were to be cut. Monitoring the situation was essential, and another wardrobe check looking particularly at a wide swathe of the lower income groups was scheduled and took place in December 1942.[31]

The next ration year saw a new supplement, therefore, known as the Industrial Ten. Introduced to the public by Sir Hugh Dalton, new President of the Board of Trade, on 18 September 1942, this supplement would now give a much-larger number of workers a flat rate of ten additional coupons per year. The list covered 'many millions of workers in a great variety of trades—more than twice as many workers as were granted extra coupons for the first rationing period'. Employers were to make a 'collective application' to the Board 'on behalf of the claimants', distributing the additional coupons received amongst employees.[32] This action, in conjunction with the continuing down pointing of industrial overalls and other work clothes, including heavy-weight fustian and corduroy trousers, and coupon subsidies for certain civilian workwear/uniform, created a package of extra coupon support for those sectors of the population most likely to encounter need under the rationing scheme. It was hoped this would offset destitution and that new plans to regenerate the second-hand market together with continuing access to the Board for specific hardship would create economic stability for all.[33]

During 1942, the panel of consumers consisted of 'about 2,500 families of varied ages and incomes which reported regularly on their coupon expenditure'.[34] The results from the panel suggested that buying patterns did not vary a great deal over time, findings which were subsequently checked in other ways such as 'production statistics, special consumer surveys and statistics of retail shortages collected by area distribution officers'.[35] The consumer panel was divided up according to coupon allocation: men and women without supplements, men and women with supplements and children and infants. Returns revealed how many garments had been bought per head across the groups, and by multiplying these figures with the known numbers in each group nationally and taking other extra coupons into account and 'contingencies such as bomb damage, and a small amount to cover black market activities, the Board possessed a summary of the clothing needs of the population for one year expressed broadly in terms of garment categories'.[36] From this a ration could be calculated. A Board of Trade memo dated 1 June 1943 entitled 'Some Facts about Coupon Expenditure' related that in both years older people had been subsidizing younger adult family members, with fourteen- to sixteen-year-olds being the highest spenders, including their supplements. In general, spending on the different types of clothes across the two years, whether for men or women, had hardly changed, and there was little sign of 'the extravagant use of coupons . . . on average people appear to keep very close to the ration. The reduction in the ration from the first to the second year seems to be fairly faithfully and equitably shared by all groups.'[37]

In a Board of Trade draft for a speech to celebrate the second anniversary of clothes rationing, the public were congratulated on the sacrifices they had made and the gains that had accrued to the war effort because of them. In the course of the draft, the writer referred to the fact that the Board of Trade had been receiving five thousand letters a week with enquiries about coupons, 'mostly from young wives anxious to do their best by their homes and men folk. Nearly all the letters are good natured and all are replied to individually.'[38] Such a wealth of correspondence told the Board what people still did not know or were anxious about. The fact that the enquiries were 'good-natured' also further revealed the 'honesty and play-the-game attitude of the British people' that the writer felt was 'clearly revealed in the use of the coupons'.[39]

There were minor variations both in the provision of garments and footwear on the ration and the points required for various items as resources became scarce or need was recognized. In the 1943–1944 ration, for example, new categories of overalls came into being for women and children—two new pyjamas categories appeared and also two new stocking categories, one providing a non-wool seamless stocking at the economic rate of one and a half coupons a pair for a woman and one for a child.[40] Coupon value for rubber footwear went up this year in line with shrinking stocks, as it did for other forms of day and sportswear shoes needing leather. Boots were also up pointed. Industrial and related rubber footwear were only obtainable through buying permits which also required the surrendering of coupons.[41] From this date until the end of the war and beyond, there were few changes to the pointing scheme. One further wardrobe check was made in April 1944 with no findings appreciably altering the next year's ration. Difficulties in re-establishing the textile trades in the immediate post-war period caused supply shortages that made the continuance of the rationing scheme necessary to avoid inflation. But after the war, controls were applied as a component of a new series of economic concerns that no longer had winning the war as a central feature. The story of rationing beyond 1945 therefore took on a different set of rationales and operated under new criteria.

The Board's policy of information gathering lay at the heart of the success of clothes rationing because it kept a fair scheme fair. Keeping abreast of the domestic economy they were changing and the type of public reaction they were causing were key. As Hargreaves and Gowing concluded, 'the administrator found himself compelled to take an interest in the consumer and his needs to an extent unparalleled in peace-time . . . when war-time controls had interfered with the market mechanisms and when the principle of "fair shares", unknown in peace, had been introduced, the Government had in effect to assume a broad measure of responsibility for seeing that the basic requirements of all sections of the population were covered'.[42]

Other organizations and bodies had a specific interest in reporting on the impact of clothes rationing to the parties they represented. Trade papers like the *Drapers' Record* offered guidance and advice to high street retailers on the likely effect of the coupon system while topical magazines like *Picture Post* and fashion magazines such as *Vogue* were swift to reassure readers that rationing did not mean the end of fashion. There would instead be a whole new approach to the buying and wearing of clothes. This material will be returned to in Chapter 12. The members of the Christian Contemplatives Community saw the advent of rationing as a potential beginning to a whole new way of life as people turned their backs on industrial life, made their own clothes, grew their own food and so embraced a new ideological landscape of rural innocence.[43]

Mass Observation was quick to publish their findings, shortly after the inauguration of the scheme, providing further information for both official and general use. They surveyed nine hundred people from three parts of Britain loosely representing the country as a whole: Bolton, for the Industrial North; Worcester, a western county town; and an area from Hammersmith to Kentish Town reflecting London. People across all classes took part, comprising the class bands A and B for the upper and middle classes and C and D for artisan and unskilled working classes. Respondents were asked a total of fifteen questions on all aspects of the impact of rationing, from changing buying habits to altered perspectives on domestic economy and wardrobe management. The survey was conducted in mid- to late June in Bolton and Worcester and early July in London. Coming so soon after the beginning of the scheme, the most important finding of the survey was how little people felt rationing would affect them, irrespective of background. Researchers believed that existing trends in clothes buying were continuing normally. These could be summarized as a slight retrenchment in purchases for both men and women due to limited supplies and a move away from elegant, more sophisticated clothing, particularly evening wear, in favour of less formal, practical clothing. Such differences from pre-war style had a higher visibility amongst the higher classes, while emphasis on more practical and simple lines united all sections of society. Clothes rationing appeared to have inspired no knee-jerk reaction from the public at all. Harrison reported, 'There is no sensational swing in any direction, and a great many people do not think they will have to give up anything much, though a good many think they will have to cut down in a number of smaller ways . . . we never remember to have done research and a report on such a negative subject.'[44]

This could partly be explained, he believed, by the fact that people had rarely planned clothing purchases with any rigour before and were therefore not used to doing it now. People were unprepared to look ahead to the future for a whole range of psychologically understandable reasons. The future was insecure. During the warm, sunny days of June, people were, as yet, unaffected by rationing. In terms of evaluating the answers Mass Observation received, some broad indicators for the future were noticeable, however. On a positive note, a large majority of replies favoured rationing. One-fifth of interviewees also currently held stocks of clothes large enough to offset the effect of rationing. These covered all the locations, although, predictably, there were far more A and B class respondents in this fifth than C and D class.[45] The lack of well-stocked wardrobes in the lower income sector was compounded by figures that seemed to suggest that the lower down the economic scale one went the less likelihood there was of any sense of planning. While there was a high incidence of rejecting any notion of planning across all sectors of society, it was most marked by those arguably most in need of it through meagre wardrobe provision. Never having had the resources to plan ahead before might well have accounted for this point of view. Pooling coupons, and the idea that sixty-six coupons seemed plenty, both mitigated against looking to the future and facing up to the real limitations now being imposed. Harrison thought some kind of 'suitable propaganda' might be one outcome of this finding, to assist people in the careful allocation of their coupons.[46]

In terms of the pointing system itself, the survey did reveal early anxiety, as would the Slough survey, regarding both stockings and boots and shoes. Given that 'what people say they intend to do' is not always what they actually do, the survey suggested that 55 per cent of women and 56 per cent of men intended to spend at least ten coupons on shoes. As men's shoes took seven coupons and women's five, this meant that men were thinking in terms of at least one pair of new shoes, and women, potentially two. The need for durable, good-quality shoes was flagged up, particularly for workwear and children, as well as concern at surrendering the same number of coupons for poor- as good-quality shoes.[47] Stockings were at the top of the list when it came to concern. Unlike shoes, which were essential clothing requirements by anybody's estimation, silk stockings—the variety so heavily prized—were merely a fashion item. Harrison noted that what was 'striking' was the assumption 'which appears in innumerable answers (July): that present-day inessential fashions such as collars, ties, silk stockings, are permanent and immutable'. He went on to hypothesize that with all women sharing the same dearth of silk stockings, fashions might change and that 'in a few months' time anyone wearing silk stockings may look not smart, but peculiar'. The problem was specifically with society's apparent demand for silk stockings. They lasted a shorter time yet women were loath to buy the less fashionable, more durable alternatives in wool, cotton or rayon. Women would continue to spend 'more on thin ones . . . thinking out ways of wearing them on fewer occasions, wearing them in a more ragged state, mending them more'.[48] It was an issue to which the Board would return when setting the ration in 1942. The rules of fashion, the protocols of what garments had to go together, what must be worn on certain occasions and why, would set them thinking about how to undermine this powerful etiquette of dress as it increasingly conflicted with the economies required by clothes rationing. This theme will be returned to in Chapter 12. The Board continued to hold firm on the matter of stockings, and women had to find their own ways of managing the tyranny of fashion in this respect.

The survey also made some interesting observations on the take-up of trousers in the female wardrobe. Women were asked whether they ever wore trousers and whether rationing would bring about more or less recourse to trousers. Figures suggested that outside of London, the wearing of trousers had not been that great. Younger women wore them much more than those over thirty, particularly young women living in London, and there was a noticeable conservatism in the C- and D-classes over thirty in wearing trousers at all. Better-off women wore them far more than any other group.[49] Given the ambiguity surrounding the place of trousers in the fashion world, their general acceptance, whether in terms of practical workwear or as play clothes, seemed to have affected only the better-off. Other sectors still regarded them with mild distaste as either too masculine or only for working in. Respondents who owned trousers felt the need to justify why they had bought them, linking them with new patterns of work and thereby disassociating them from more traditionally feminine patterns of dress. As Harrison summarized, 'slacks, which are the only new female garment of the war mentioned as in

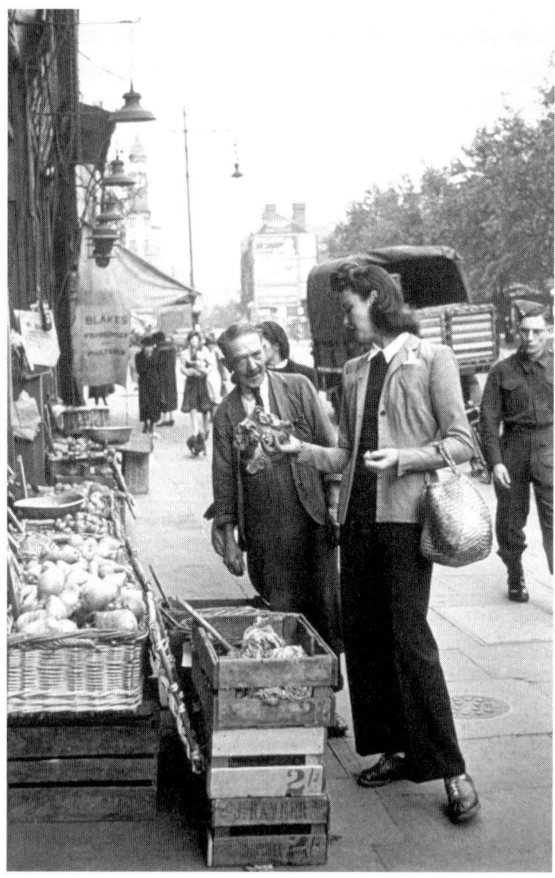

**Figure 11** 'Should Women Wear Trousers?' *Picture Post* posed this question on 1 November 1941 using an image of a smartly dressed woman out shopping wearing trousers. Bert Hardy/*Picture Post*/Getty Images (3314247).

fairly general use, do not yet appear to be quite accepted as normal wear by those who have acquired them at all recently'.[50] No run on trousers could be expected, and the survey confirmed that in accommodating the ration to early war trends, the Board of Trade was making accurate assumptions about both fashion and broader-based dress practice.

This early survey revealed two other things of specific interest to forward planning on clothes rationing. The first was the current unfair treatment of smaller children who were not rationed if they wore clothing suitable for infants of four and under. This seemed inequitable for bigger children of this age range. There was also the concern about fast-growing children of all ages and the unfairness of cloth being rationed even if it were to make things for infants. This, as we have seen, would be almost immediately addressed by the Board of Trade, who repealed their original ruling on children in November. Reaction from both men and women on this aspect of unfairness was the only time, as Harrison points out, that criticism on any of the broader issues was considerable.[51] The second element was the noticeable lack of any real thought on how to make coupons last. As most people were still thinking that rationing would not really affect them, it was unlikely that they would have thought through contingencies for shortage. Of the solutions that did arise, altering clothes was more popular in the A and B class, while mending and use of second-hand clothing (never mentioned by A and B) came as suggestions from the C and D sectors, who were no doubt only continuing what they had always done.[52] The Board of Trade recognized the need for clothing maintenance on a much-greater scale than had previously existed and began work, shortly after the inception of rationing and in conjunction with the Ministry of Information, to develop a publicity campaign that would promote craft, thrift and forward planning. The many different approaches taken both centrally and locally to extend understanding of the care and maintenance of civilian clothing will be returned to in Chapter 11.

Such social and consumer surveys, together with regular trade and industry returns, established the mechanisms via which the Board of Trade was able to assess the reaction to rationing. Feedback confirmed the importance of supplementary allowances while small fine-tunings to coupon pointing controlled over- or undersupply in line with consumer requirements. Oliver Lyttleton, looking back in his *Memoirs*, felt that subsequent refinements to the system had at times been stringent. He cites that Hugh Dalton's motto was, 'If Lyttleton chastised you with whips, I will chastise you with scorpions.'[53] His criticism reflected that some aspects of the scheme were considered overly harsh. The decision to abolish the turn-ups on men's trousers is specifically mentioned. The longer-term objectives of rationing did, however, achieve parity and sufficiency across an often-beleaguered population while managing to retain the public consensus that rationing was right. In his annual Board of Trade message introducing the rationing points for 1944–1945, Dalton made it clear that the country could be congratulated on the results of clothes rationing. 'More than half a million men and women have been released from making cloth and clothing for civilians and have gone into the Services or on to War-production. . . . 250,000 tons per annum of valuable shipping space has been saved for essential war cargoes. And yet prices have been kept under control and everybody has had his fair share.'[54] The Board had been at the centre of a complex system of information gathering, utilizing broad-based cooperation between trade organizations, research bureaux and survey networks. The outcome was a just set of controls that successfully upheld commonality of interest and unanimity of purpose by providing clothing of reasonable quality in sufficient quantity for all.

# –11–

# Home Front Clothing Initiatives

Looking through magazines of all types from the period, one is struck by the enormous number of inducements to keep busy. Women on the home front were encouraged to take up some form of work, very often in addition to specific paid employment or civil defence volunteering, that could be done in off-duty hours as a form of useful relaxation. Knitting and sewing were especially promoted alongside other craft- or food-based projects to extend household efficiency and contribute to the war effort. Knitting wool companies produced brochures with patterns for the forces, including the Merchant Navy, the trawler men, and the Red Cross, while people who could sew were encouraged to make a variety of articles from simple bandages to the home necessities no longer so available.

The initial need to keep busy in the absence of loved ones was soon superseded by a real need for the home front to create additional supplies over and above the necessities produced by the textile and clothing industries. These had been endeavouring to keep pace with Ministry of Supply requirements for uniform and equipment from before the war. With new production priorities limiting domestic consumption, home knitters and sewers were soon recognized as holding especially valuable skills. To what extent they supplemented shortfalls in official supplies to places like hospitals, children's homes, shelters and other refuges will never be known. Not only were knitting and sewing making a real difference in this way, but they were also increasingly to supplement home wardrobes. As the price of clothing within the cost-of-living index rose, so shoppers looked to greater home economy, and, after rationing, there was little choice but to continue to save rather than spend, make-do and mend.

There was a great deal of spontaneous voluntary activity throughout the country, and in due course the government would support a 'Make-Do and Mend' campaign designed to steer the population towards new practices in household and wardrobe management. Initiated by the Women's Group on Public Welfare and the National Council of Social Services, the campaign acknowledged the stringencies of limitation and rationing policies and sought to encourage people to address their needs by making, altering or mending rather than buying. People needed to be educated in dressmaking and tailoring skills, knitting and other home crafts if maximum value was to be obtained from the supplies of clothing and textiles people already had. In this way, the individual ration would go a great deal further. Care of clothing became central to a developing culture of patriotic thrift, all the more necessary in the context of continuing conflict and increasing shortage.

There were well-documented precedents for early group action much before the inception of rationing. On 17 February 1940, *Picture Post*, for example, ran an article entitled 'Happy Knitters'. It featured a group of women from Keswick in Cumberland who had come together in October 1939 to form a knitting party. They started to produce comforts for those on active service from the local area. The Women's Work Guild of Keswick at that time had a four-hundred-strong membership and had created over twenty-five hundred garments. The youngest member of the group was nine years old. Meeting in the dining room of the Keswick Hotel, their mission was to provide a box of comforts for every man and woman hailing from the Keswick area currently away on active service. Each comfort box contained 'a pullover, scarf, helmet, mitts, socks, book, soap, towel, cigarettes, toffee and a pot of their local delicacy, rum butter'.[1] Several things are interesting about this story: the desire to group together so early in the war despite the lack of actual conflict, the wish to reassure those in the services of the continuing thought and well wishes of their own community and a readiness to be organized, meet regularly and work to a common goal. Community craft projects clearly had much to contribute, and *Picture Post* reminded readers that while this was just a local effort, 'it could well be a pattern for thousands of willing knitters all over the country'.[2]

For those serving in the ranks, uniform was provided. Garments were durable and of reasonable quality but, unlike bespoke officer's service uniform, standard issue and not always well fitting. Hand-knitted items in quality wools added comfort as well as something more personal to the experience of wearing uniform. They became enormously popular. The services of home comforts knitters emerged in large, though unknown, numbers. As knitting parties gathered momentum, articles were sent from across Britain to locations both at home and abroad, land and sea. Knitters would often include their signature or a personal message with the clothes. A booklet entitled *Knitting for the Merchant Navy* (undated, as are so many pattern booklets and knitting patterns of the period) referred to the fact that during 1941, the knitters connected with the Merchant Navy Comforts Service had sent a set of six garments to 'approximately 60,000 men [who] each received . . . a sweater, a scarf, a helmet [balaclava style], a pair of gloves and two pairs of socks; sea boot stockings were added for the deck crew'.[3] The booklet went on to inform readers that another sixty thousand knitted garments had been made for 'Emergency Rescue Kits' in the first year of the service and reproduced an extract from a merchant seaman's correspondence considered representative of 'hundreds

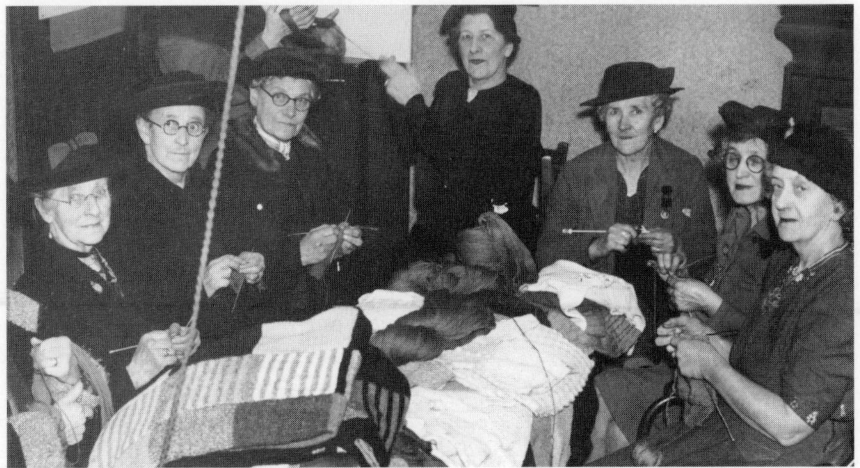

**Figure 12** A knitting club creating garments for the Merchant Navy in Northampton, c. 1940. Popperfoto/Getty Images (78966571).

received: "words are inadequate for me to describe the pleasure on the men's faces when they collected their woollies for use on Board their ships. It means *so* much to the men to be warmly clothed, makes *all* the difference to their cold hours of duty."'[4]

With special skills in sewing and needlework, Mass Observation diarist Nella Last spent a great deal of the war making everything from hospital comforts, to soft toys and interior furnishings. An entry from her diary for 16 November 1940 is indicative of how people could make a real contribution. A parcel of items for the local Barrow hospital comprised 'fifteen dolls and soft toys, sixteen bed-coats, nine night-dresses ranging from those to fit a child of two to large ones for ten or twelve year olds, six face-cloths made from scraps of new towelling, two good dressing gowns cut from larger ones, and a big bundle of linen—old "real" linen for dressings'. The head sister received them, commenting, 'Oh, I've heard of you, Mrs. Last—you are the Salvage Queen, I believe!' Requests came to Nella for a variety of blankets and night wear or '"anything your ingenious mind can plan!"'[5] Thus *before* any official campaign for thrift was launched there was already a flourishing collection of people and organizations contributing to the war effort.

Sirdar wools suggested that 'If you can knit—you can "do your bit"', and the Royal Air Force Comforts Committee (RAFCC) in their 'official' book of instructions, *Knitting for the RAF*, included an exhortation from the Secretary of State for Air (the Rt. Hon. Sir Archibald Sinclair, BT, KT, CMG, MP) to 'carry on knitting'.[6] This type of organization professionalized the services of the home knitter to some degree. The RAFCC is a good example of how service committees worked. Knitters formed into working parties that then registered with the RAFCC. After the introduction of rationing, when balls of wool were pointed at one coupon per two ounces, knitting parties could obtain RAF wool, coupon free, under certain schemes. Supplies of wool might come direct from the RAFCC and charged for at wholesale rates or, alternatively, could be obtained from local retailers against coupons issued by the RAFCC. Instructions for making were clear. All unnecessary trimmings were to be avoided, and knitters were asked to concentrate on the provision of 'mittens, pullovers (preferably polo-necked), helmets and gun-boot stockings' as socks and gloves were already provided.[7] A formal knitters' working party had to have ten or more members and be prepared to give a 'guarantee that all wool obtained coupon free from any source for knitting for the RAF will be used in its entirety in the making of garments for that service and that the garments made will be sent direct to the official Depot of the RAFCC, 20 Berkeley Square . . . and in no circumstances disposed of in any other manner'.[8] To complete the sense of performing official business for the RAF and as an outward sign of loyalty, voluntary workers' badges, in chromium and enamel, could be earned by registered parties. The heads of parties were urged to 'maintain a high standard for qualification. It is suggested that this might be taken as one hundred hours for the RAFCC (not total work performed for all services), with a suitable reduction for children under 14 years.' Each registered work party was entitled to one badge free, and applications for further badges had to certify that 'the badges ordered are for issue to duly qualified members only'.[9] In this way, the work of a new type of auxiliary force was recognized both by the service and the broader community—through seeing the badge—and, perhaps most importantly, the knitter herself was commended.

A broad range of knitted articles was needed. Hospitals, for example, as reflected in Weldon's knitting leaflet 'Hospital Woollens', required the following: water-bottle covers, knee-cap pieces, woollies and slip-ons, balaclavas, slippers, bed-socks, operation stockings, helmets, convalescent woollen comfy bed-jackets and pullovers.[10] *Vogue,* in their *20th Knitting Book* (undated),[11] impressed upon readers the importance of getting the tension right as wool quality varied, and the wool companies advocated using the precise wools mentioned in the patterns for best results. Weldon's published a number of *'Go to It' Win-the-War* booklets for the home front, where they rallied women to 'help your country—your men folk—your family—yourself, by knitting, sewing, by food gardening, by economy cooking'.[12] Using private time wisely was a common theme and gave justification to a plethora of advertising from yarn and craft companies eager to take advantage of the propitious circumstances now favouring home skills. Many of the booklets produced were attractively laid out and an enticement to even the less proficient to have a go. People knitted everywhere, in shelters, in cinemas, at work in lunch hours, as well as at home, and the stylish home-knit product, when successfully achieved, became a part of the signature style of the period particularly in terms of the knitted sweater from plain twinset to Fair Isle.

In September 1940, the magazine *Stitchcraft* carried an advertisement for Old Glamis Fabrics: 'Women's part in wartime . . . is often the most difficult of all—that of waiting. She must keep the home together, keep it cheerful and normal through difficult times. The wise housewife turns leisure hours and long evenings to good account, making new things of use and beauty for her home.'[13] Here crafting connoted domestic loyalty and duty, woman as steadfast ally, quietly safeguarding home and hearth. These qualities were also associated with home crafting in a similar advertisement for P and B Knitting wools which used traditional cottage imagery of an open fire and ladder-back chair as the setting for a woman knitter who 'sits alone and serves . . . waiting'.[14] In both cases, a woman's role knitting or sewing was described by a rhetoric of service and resilience. Many editorials and advertisements of the period expressed similar sentiments so that the ethos of sustaining the home front in this way was well established by the time of clothes rationing and provided a ready-made vocabulary to hand for the subsequent promotion of 'Make-Do and Mend'.

In the same way as with knitting, sewing groups quickly began to form to provide essential war articles. *Picture Post* carried a story in February 1940 about a rather distinctive group known as 'Mayfair's Own Sewing-Bee'. Comprising the wives and daughters of foreign diplomats, the war comforts sewing-bee took place every Wednesday afternoon in the Mayfair home of the Hon. Mrs. Ronald Greville,[15] the only other British member being Lady Halifax, wife of the foreign secretary. Known as the Dip Work Party, the group put on 'white overalls and caps', covering their 'Paris frocks and pearl necklaces', and got to work with hand sewing or using the sewing machines provided. The Diplomatic Corps wives paid for the material themselves but worked on official patterns. At half past four, 'exhausted by its labours, the Dip Work-Party, like any other work-party, rejoices at the entrance of tea, which Mrs Greville understandingly provides'. The writer comments on the business-like nature of the venture: 'You must not run away with the idea that this is . . . an amateurish affair.' The women themselves apparently sewed to a high standard (if we can believe this from the at times deferential tone of the article) due, the writer suggests, to many members having been in convent schools 'where fine needlework is a tradition'. The illustrations showed participants from South America and the neutral countries of central Europe, as well as Mme Lelong, wife of the head of the French Military Mission in London, and Mme Prytz, wife of the Swedish foreign minister.

The work to be done was generally supplied from the Lord Mayor's Red Cross Fund, and the pieces arrived from the clearing house already cut out by experts. Work was graded according to ability, and no scrap of material was wasted, even selvedge edge strips being saved and 'knitted into squares for blankets'. Such demonstrations of thrift which underlay groups like this reflected the need to harbour resources, plan with vision and be well organized. The stringent economy with all materials was all the more praiseworthy in the context of the phoney war and clearly established the principle of careful management some time *before* rationing enforced it. The party was 'one of the thousands . . . officially recognised' throughout Great Britain, run by the Central Hospital Supply Service Committee (CHSSC), the London and greater London groups of which were under the control of Lady Gordon Finlayson. This committee, the 'joint effort' of the Red Cross, Order of St. John and the WVS, carefully deployed administrative units across twelve national regions. Each unit operated separately with their own clearing houses. Lady Gordon had control of fifteen of these clearing houses, '365 work-parties and 12,000 individual workers'. The operation of the units was meticulously organized using indexing systems so that Lady Gordon could see what each work-party was producing and could match this up with the hospitals' known requirements. In this way, 'matron does not receive a hundred operation stockings when she wants a hundred open-backed shirts'.[16] The capacity for large-scale organization that the CHSSC revealed, still within the first six months of war, reflected the level of

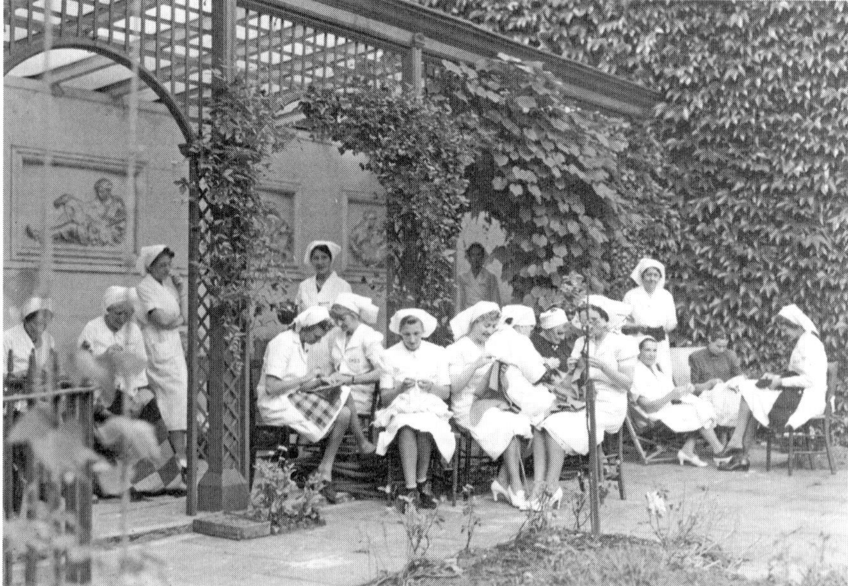

**Figure 13** Women working for the Central Hospital Supply Service, 1 January 1940. Tunbridge-Sedgwick Pictorial Press/Getty Images (3333690).

thought and planning that had *already* become established for the provision of additional and supplemental supplies in Britain, and while the article focused on a collection of privileged ladies, it ended by emphasizing that people from all backgrounds and occupations were part of this vast, nationwide organization.

In a British Movietone Newsreel of 1940 entitled *Britannia Is a Woman*, the WVS was seen distributing warmer winter clothing to evacuated children living in the countryside. Cinema audiences were informed that clothing supply depots 'had been set up in every district', establishing the type of organized assistance now in place. Lady Reading, at the helm of the WVS, was spearheading a 'concerted drive' to coordinate voluntary work across the country.[17] This work clearly progressed as another cinema short produced by Verity Film in 1941 for the Ministry of Information entitled *WVS (Women's Voluntary Services)* showed how the WVS had successfully systematized the processing and distribution of large stocks of clothing received from 'all over the Empire [and] from America'. Gifts of 'coats, dresses, shoes, underwear, all this is given into the keeping of the WVS. Their workers sort, check and catalogue these clothes and give them out. They've handled nearly three and a half million pounds' worth of clothes at their depots; eight hundred thousand dresses, three hundred and twenty three thousand shirts; one million jerseys.'[18] The clothing needs of the evacuated or bombed out were clearly being addressed. Another role for the WVS was to supervise the small children sent to one of the seventy-three reception nurseries established for the under-fives as part of the continuation of evacuation. On their way to permanent homes from these nurseries, each child received clothing amounting to a whole new wardrobe if necessary, including 'sleeping suits, warm under things, socks, suits, dresses', many of which had come as gifts from overseas. In a similar vein, WVS women also ran third-line rest centres offering respite for bomb victims when larger rest centres were full. Here clothes were given to those who had lost everything in the blitz. A family with twelve children was featured who received 'one of everything', and women might also be given a 'housekeeping satchel' from the American Red Cross' which contained important 'simple tools for combing your hair, washing, mending torn clothes', a toothbrush and a torch.[19] By 1944, when World Wide Pictures produced the film short *Willing Hands* for the Ministry of Information, there was a view that the WVS clothing collections had 'caught the imagination of the world'. Donations of gift clothing were arriving in Britain from 'the Dominions, Colonies, America and other friends' and being made accessible as quickly as possible via twenty-four regional storehouses. The 'great wooden crates' were unpacked and arranged by the WVS 'rather like that of a large shop'. The film reported the main duty of the WVS at this stage was to 'keep the two thousand clothing depots throughout the country well stocked' because 'in a period of heavy raids the WVS gave out five million garments, shoes and boots and seven

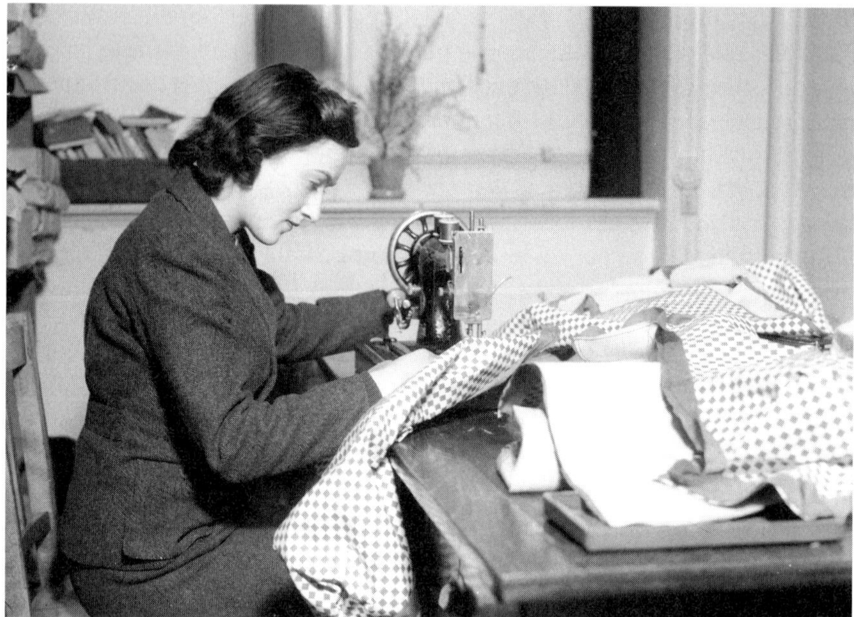

**Figure 14** 'Lady Seamstress': Lady Reading, head of the Women's Voluntary Service at service headquarters, c. 1940. Tunbridge-Sedgwick Pictorial Press/Getty Images (3333194).

hundred thousand blankets'.[20] These films give a particularly vivid account of the way in which the need for clothing was seen as an essential component of home front defence and morale. They also highlight that from 1940 onwards, voluntary services associated with the organization of textile-based supplies escalated in scope and administration as war demanded. The voluntary mobilization and management of women by women on this scale was a powerful indicator of the resources to hand on the home front. An invaluable infrastructure of operational control and support clearly already existed, therefore, from an early stage in the war and could be utilized after rationing to help implement the important making-do and renovation initiatives that would begin to surface in the summer of 1941.

On 2 July 1941, a paper entitled 'Extension of the Life of Clothing—A Preliminary Investigation into Possibilities', written by one of the Board of Trade area distribution officers, stated that 'the need for such a campaign is already in the minds of many of those organisations which cater for the practical and social needs of middle and lower class women and girls'. Contact had already been made with the Women's Group on Public Welfare affiliated to the National Council of Social Services, the Women's Institute, the Townswomen's Guild and Lintas, the publicity organization of Lever Brothers, and all were keen to be associated with promoting care of clothing. It only remained now

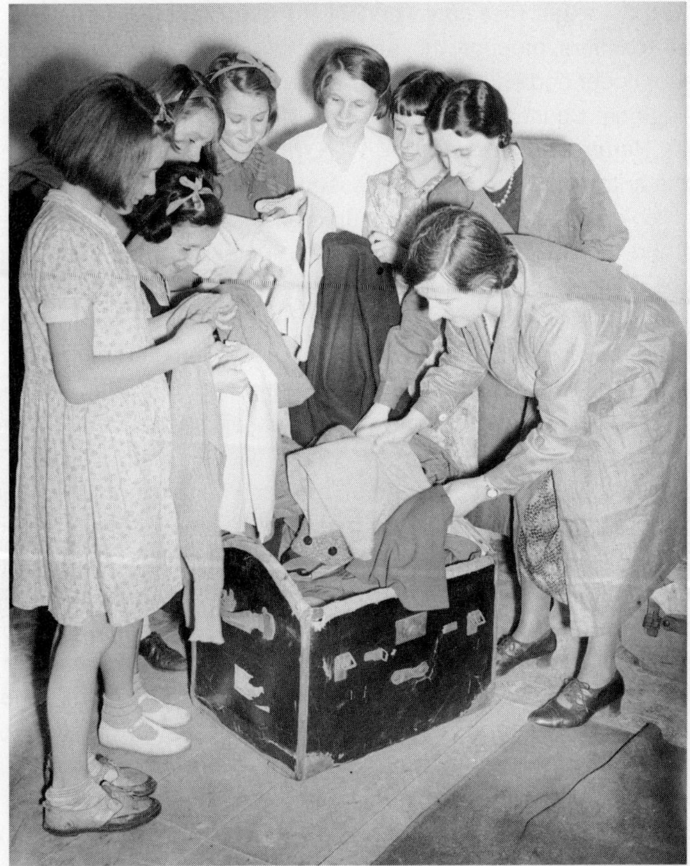

**Figure 15** Evacuees from the Channel Islands now living in Marple, Cheshire, England, investigate a chest of gift clothing from the United States, 1940. Ministry of Information Second World War Official Collection. © Imperial War Museum (D741).

to 'find a means of co-ordinating and organizing their activities on a sound basis capable of infinite extension in the interests of the nation as a whole'.[21] The resolution to this question would eventually materialize as the 'Make-Do and Mend' campaign. There was a need for proper teaching particularly in the context that 'renovation and mending is a much-neglected subject, and only a few of the "handi-craft" teachers have specialized in it, or even taught it at all' so that there was also a need to teach teachers as well. Working in parallel with the need for skills classes was the need to coordinate activities connected with clothing, such as 'exchanges of material or skilled services'.[22] Publicity was the vital third strand. A response to this report, also dated 2 July 1941, acknowledged the need to 'organise the mending groups as they form' so that they could benefit from the 'existing panels of trained handicraft teachers, most of whom come under either the Local Education Authorities, or under bodies affiliated with the Women's Group on Public Welfare, (of the National Council of Social Services)'.[23] Referring to a memorandum from Miss Harford, secretary of the WGPW, the paper summarized the need for '"Make and Mend" groups and classes . . . provision of technical instruction' and 'co-operation between consumers, the Local Authorities, the Board of Trade and the Board of Education'.[24] The outcome of all these coordinating factors would finally result—a year later—in a comprehensively organized clothing scheme promoting mending and making as a moral obligation for all. There would be various debates on organizational structure and responsibilities in the ensuing year, but the scheme made continuous headway, and initial interest was quickly registered as a summary of agenda item 5, 'Organisation of Clothes Renovation Groups', from the twelfth Board of Trade Publicity Meeting on 9 July 1941, makes clear. The 'maintenance and renovation' of personal clothing was considered 'a most important side-issue of consumer rationing' particularly for those on incomes of 'between . . . £3–£4 a week' who would 'be forced' into such activities.[25] Any rise in the spending capacity of the poorer sectors of the community through better employment opportunities would only be curtailed by rationing so that those with already limited wardrobes were likely to remain at a disadvantage. Revisiting the whole area of the care and management of clothing was felt to be worthwhile. Promoting renovation would encourage the public to get the most use out of the clothes *they already had* and those they would use precious coupons buying.

The Board did not want to get directly involved with the operation of a clothing care campaign but wanted to provide an 'authoritative lead',[26] a position it largely maintained given the organizational skill of the participatory voluntary organizations. It was well informed about the number of activities already connected with clothing as both craft and commodity. In the first place were the 'thrift crafts' as 'promoted by the W.I. and the National Council of Social Services and affiliated councils—700 clubs composed largely of wives of low wage earners—which already have renovation and dressmaking classes'.[27] This category was interesting as it established that women on a lower income were clearly happy to join a craft group despite mending and alteration being a necessary part of everyday life. That they existed in good numbers suggested that there was no evidence the women felt patronized by organizers or teachers. The opportunity for society beyond the house was, arguably, as important to these women as any skills they might learn, as we have seen elsewhere.

The second category was of groups involved in the exchange of clothing. The WVS, for example, was experienced at handling gifts of clothing for the homeless and clothing aid for evacuees and in due course would also spearhead the organization of children's clothing exchanges. Where the first exchange was set up, or on precisely what date, is unknown. The Board was referring to their existence by July 1942 and expressing the desire that they be turned into a 'nationwide movement', which at that stage they clearly weren't.[28] The view was that they should be only for children as it was 'not the function of the Board of Trade to be a Moss Brothers for grown ups', and this is what they remained. Clothes and shoes had to be outgrown, but not outworn, and could be exchanged without money or coupons.[29] While the Board had allowed all children additional coupons depending on age, this was an extra mechanism to allow for the adequate clothing of children when coupons would no longer go round. These later exchanges, while dealing with second-hand goods, must

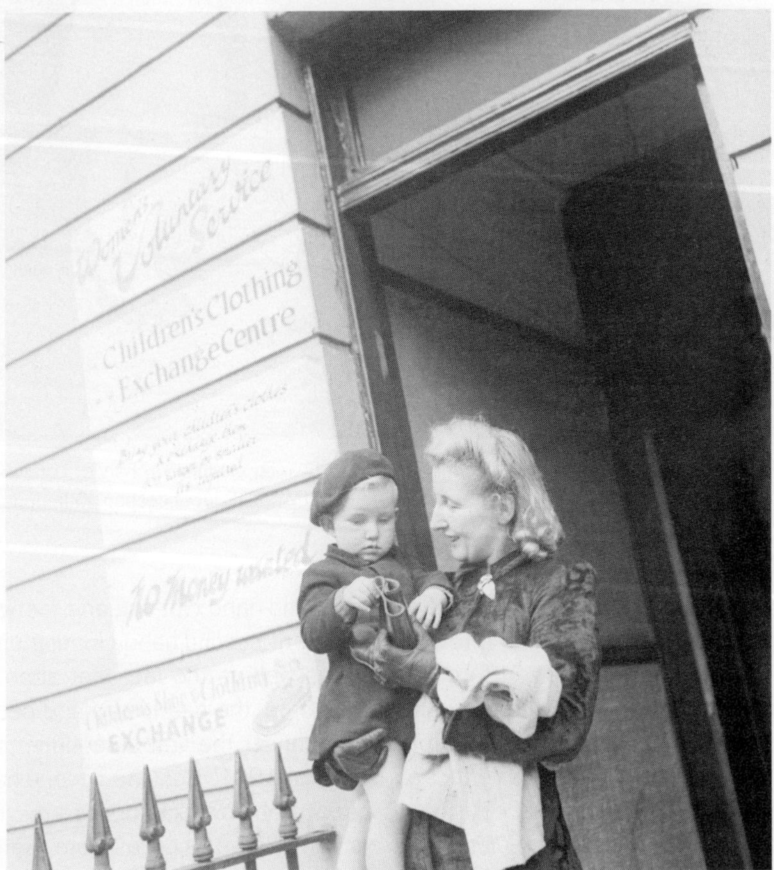


**Figure 16** A childrens' clothing exchange run by the Women's Voluntary Service, Norwood, London, England, 1943. This mother and her son have exchanged 'a pile of baby woollies and some of his outgrown shoes for a thick overcoat and a pair of Wellington boots'. Ministry of Information Second World War Official Collection. © Imperial War Museum (D15091).

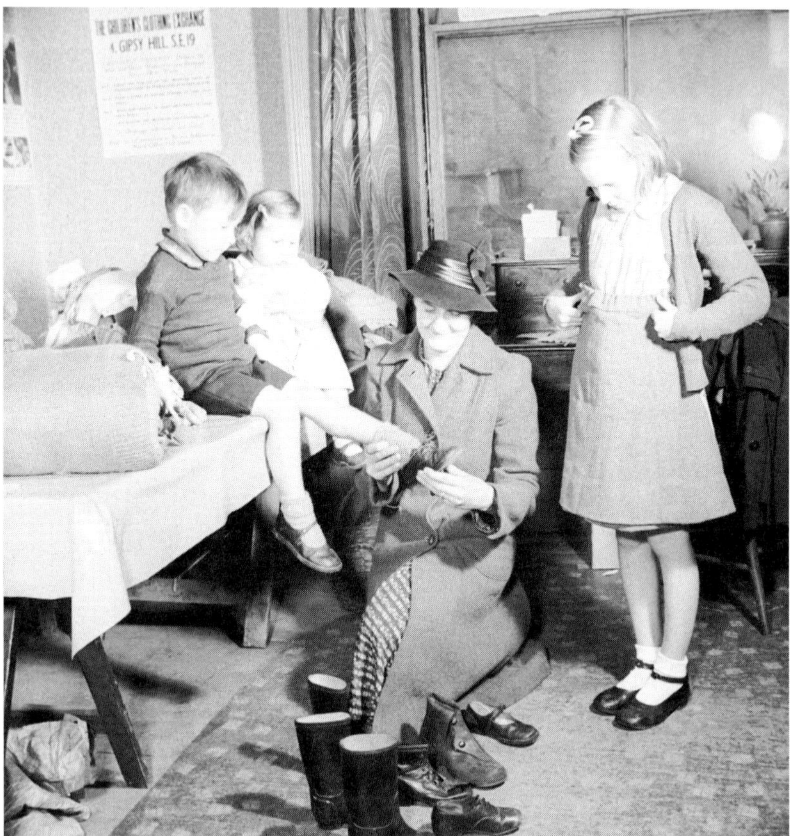


**Figure 17** Trying on clothes and shoes at the Norwood clothing exchange, London, England, 1943. Ministry of Information Second World War Official Collection. © Imperial War Museum (D16857).

not be confused with the open market for second-hand clothing and footwear which operated differently. The relative demise of second-hand clothing up to this point has been referred to elsewhere, as well as the fact that although second-hand garments were originally coupon free, the nearly new and better-quality garments became subject to rationing under the first amendments to the scheme which came into effect on 5 August 1941. Genuine second-hand clothing still did not require coupons if sold at or below fixed prices specified in the rationing leaflets and *Clothing Quiz* summaries. The prices were fixed by multiplying the number of coupons that would be required for the article if new by the prices as quoted. For all rationed goods, other than underwear, boots and shoes, the fixed price from 1941 through to 1946 was two shillings.[30] If a new rayon dress was seven coupons, a second-hand version could only be coupon free if sold for fourteen shillings or less. Second-hand garments selling at higher than the fixed price incurred the exchange of coupons. These rules had to apply to all such purchases including school uniform, goods sold at charity bazaars, sales of work and jumble sales. Coupons collected from these sales were sent by organizers to Area Collection Centres for the Board of Trade.[31]

The third category comprised the 'various sewing parties' already functioning and '"make and mend parties"'.[32] A Ministry of Health circular from 24 September 1941 reported that the WVS had started operating 'make-and-mend parties in the reception areas' alongside of their other roles in connection with evacuation, clerical and community work,[33] and it was clear that before the official launch of the campaign in the late summer of 1942, making and renovation groups were already being rebranded with this name. These 'parties' were, strictly speaking, interchangeable with category one, the difference being that they were not clubs as such. The Central Hospital Supply Service Committee's work parties would have fitted within this category. Overall, the Board was keen to 'supervise' all these activities to 'demonstrate the official desire to help people to overcome the hardship occasioned by Consumer Rationing and . . . to provide a useful channel for sampling public opinion and morale in a direct way'.[34]

The minutes of the sixteenth meeting of the Board of Trade Publicity Committee on 10 September 1941 gave 'unofficial backing' to a care-of-clothing campaign which would be 'best carried out by voluntary organisations, such as the W.I. or WVS'. The 'immediate need' was for 'practical advice on clothing economy' and expert guidance. Assuming that the 'new economy technique will take some time to evolve . . . the campaign cannot be instituted now, or in the future, at a moment's notice'.[35] At the 'Joint Meeting of the Standing Conference of Voluntary Organisations and Women's Group on Public Welfare to discuss the promotion of "Make-and-Mend" Classes' on 25 September 1941, it was 'unanimously agreed "that the Woman's Group on Public Welfare should be asked to set up a committee to take the necessary steps in launching a nation-wide 'Make-and-Mend' Campaign"'.[36] A memo summarizing aspects of the joint conference referred to the two million women already 'organised' into groups and the desire to draw in an estimated further 'unorganised' six million. The Board of Education had agreed to 'promote classes through local education authorities, and provide skilled instructors, one of whose function would be to train leaders of local groups and teachers for small classes'.[37]

The WGPW set up a committee comprising 'experts in homecrafts, representatives of women's organisations and advisers from Government departments' and proceeded to launch classes amongst their own membership. They also enlisted the support of the Citizen's Advice Bureaux to supply information 'to women who are in difficulties through too rapid use of clothing coupons and need the help of the "make and mend" class'.[38] A paper entitled 'Make and Mend Campaign' issued by the WGPW also gave details of activity across the winter of 1941 into spring of 1942, including reviewing existing classes, working with the Board of Education to pass on information via Local Education Authorities (LEAs) about women's groups and the courses available for teachers and leaders and considering appropriate publicity.[39] Articles had appeared in journals of the organizations involved, and a publicity subcommittee had been created. The BBC had been approached about radio talks, and the idea of a film was raised, although the director of the Film Publicity Department at the Ministry of Information was disinclined to support this unless there was 'some nationwide organization . . . formed to interest the public in applied clothes sense'.[40] At this stage, and as an advisory committee to the Board of Trade, the paper stated the WGPW's serious misgiving that the public were still not fully apprised of the need for clothing salvage and that a 'decline in clothing standards may be accompanied by a decline in self-respect and a consequent slackness of the mind'.[41] The paper ended by making a fulsome appeal to the new President of the Board of Trade, Hugh Dalton, for a 'nationwide campaign on the lines of the Food Front' to meet shortages that would 'begin to be felt in the second year of clothes rationing'.[42]

During July, there were various publicity ideas planned to promote the clothing campaign, including 'Make-Do and Mend' displays in gas and electricity showrooms for three weeks starting 10 October, films and other exhibitions

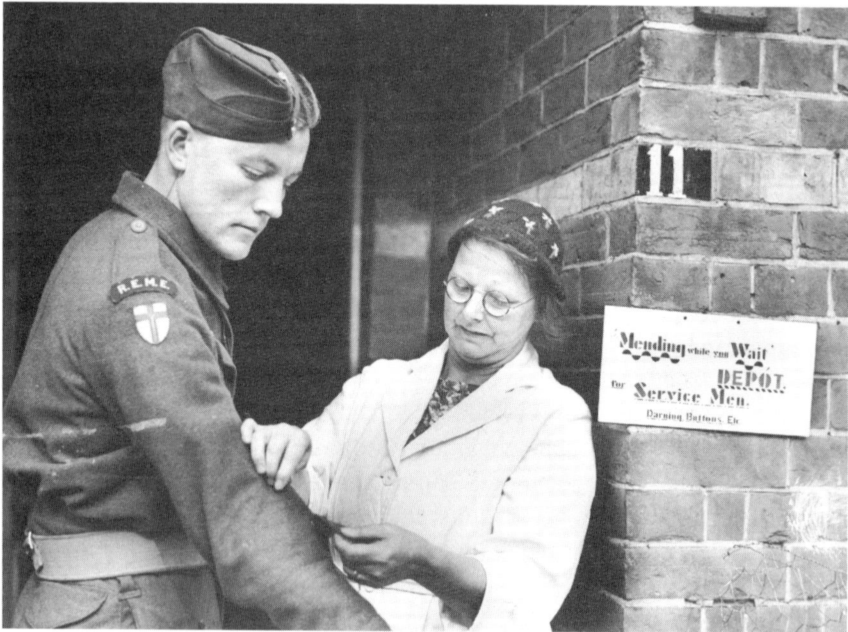


**Figure 18** 'Mending While You Wait': Mrs G Baker from Tonbridge, a member of the Women's Voluntary Service, mends a soldier's uniform at her door, 13 October 1943. Fox Photos/Getty Images (3288664).

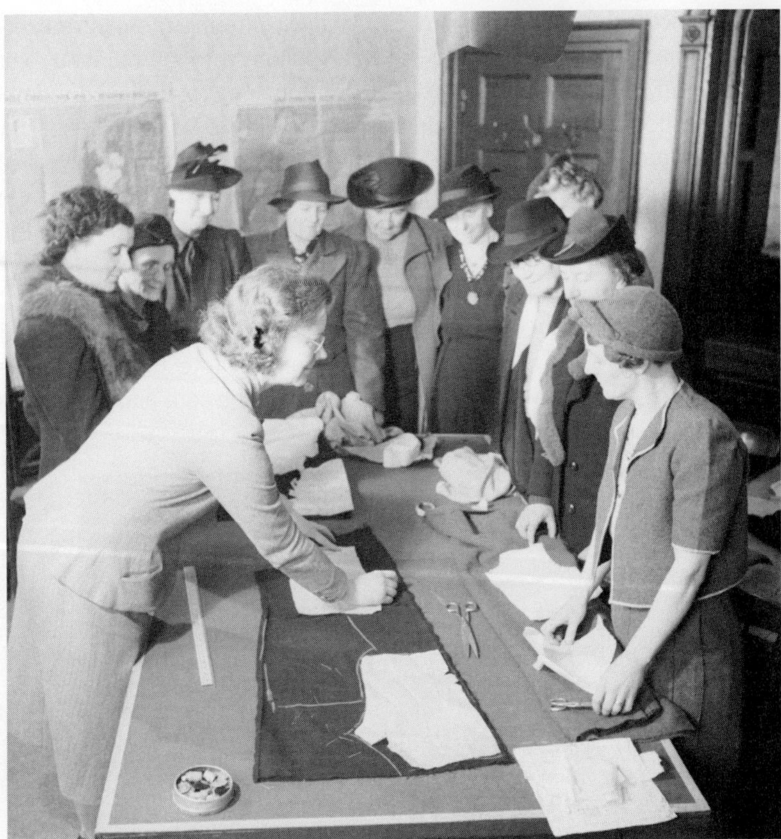

**Figure 19** A Make-Do and Mend class, London, 1943. Housewives watch a London County Council teacher demonstrating pattern cutting techniques. The term fee for the classes was 1s and included tuition in Keep Fit and First Aid instruction. Ministry of Information Second World War Official Collection. © Imperial War Museum (D12882).

in key sites across the country.[43] The scheme was obviously gaining momentum, and by early September an advisory panel of experts had finally come into being.[44] 'Make-Do and Mend' was given the ultimate seal of approval in a letter to the women's organizations from Hugh Dalton on 16 September 1942 stating that it was necessary to 'do all in our power to make the whole nation conscious of the need to Mend and Make-do'. He applauded the work being done, describing it as 'absolutely invaluable, and . . . essential to the success of our efforts'.[45] Thus the campaign finally achieved the scale the voluntary organizations had hoped for and the practice of thrift became an intrinsic part of wardrobe management for the remainder of the war.

*Pathe News Reels* produced a short advertisement for wardrobe management in December 1942 which featured a family of four with two growing children.[46] Clothes in the cupboard came alive, offering themselves for re-modeling projects for all the family. The well-spoken mother professed to have never sewn anything in her life, presumably reassuring to audience members in the same position. The film ended at a local 'Make-Do and Mend' class, where a welcoming organizer turned to invite the audience to join in—after all, thrift was also fun. The tone and language of the film was unhesitatingly middle, even upper class, as was so much media of the day, whether to target the better off, who might also now be feeling the pinch, or simply in the belief that this style would appeal.[47]

In 1943, the Ministry of Information prepared a booklet for the Board of Trade entitled *Make Do and Mend.*[48] Hugh Dalton wrote the Foreword and thanked the Advisory Panel for their input. Advice on the care and management

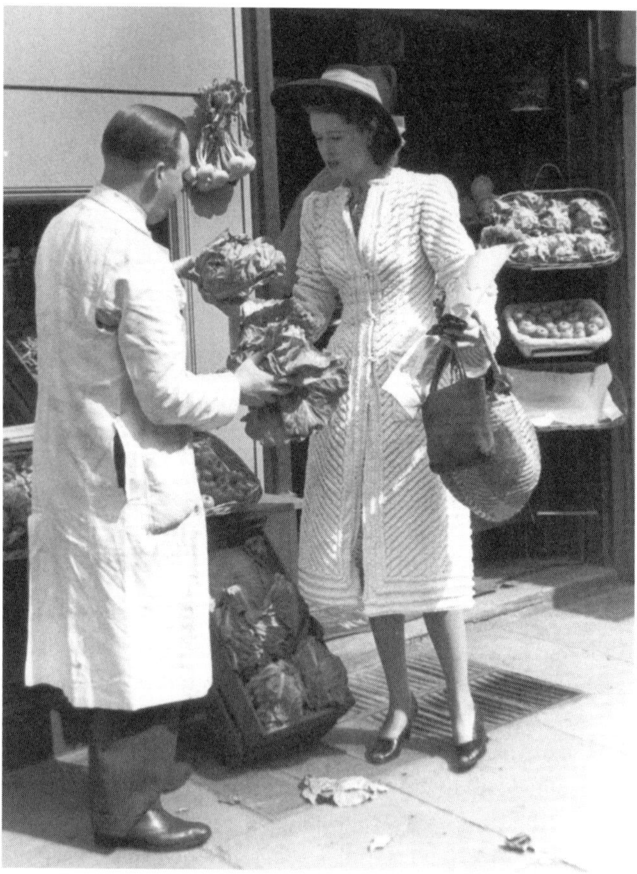

**Figure 20** 'Old Clothes Make News': Promoting recycling, *Picture Post* photographed a woman wearing a coat made from a white candlewick bedspread, 26 July 1941. Sultan Glass/Getty Images (2696570).

of clothing ranged from how to launder, patch and darn, to both simple and more sophisticated alterations. The Board were keen to reiterate some key facts: careful laundering was essential to the longer life of clothing; day-to-day management of the storing, airing and upkeep of clothing also extended life and kept clothing more wearable for longer; skills like patching, darning, and turning collars might look complicated but were relatively easy ways of rehabilitating and strengthening clothing; every ounce of fabric in a household could be used. Much could be done with care and some level of supervision for the inexperienced. The number of projects undertaken, blankets converted to coats or nightgowns out of old bed valances, for example, are legion. What is more to the point is that a spirit of giving something a go prevailed, with systems in place to increase the likelihood of success. The cartoon character Mrs. Sew-and-Sew, a strange rather pincushion-like doll with wide staring eyes, along with another unnamed character made from a needle case, cotton reels, buttons and a thimble, were also used in posters to remind the public to keep home crafting and salvage always in mind.

As everyone was subject to the stringencies of clothes rationing, looking to what you already had was common to all, and even those with plenty were now far more aware of it. Skills of home sewing and domestic ingenuity now grew in status, and people with the creative ability of Nella Last were much applauded. For others, the constant need to mend and alter was no doubt tedious drudgery, no matter how well promoted by the upbeat, 'go-to-it' bravura of the advertising. It is difficult to assess to what extent the essentially middle-class tone of getting on with things in a good spirit was either conducive or detrimental to the cause, although the wide range *and* constituencies of the craft groups might have gone some way to prove that the establishment tone inherent in much publicity rhetoric did not matter.[49] The appeal of the friendship and company that classes and clubs offered, alongside the skills they sought to promote, were arguably more important.

Reynolds points out that the number of sewing and needlework teachers increased over the war years. The new Education Act of 1944 promoted 'practical dressmaking skills' and '[a]ll girls in state schools were required to do some needlework'[50] While this suggested the burgeoning social value placed on home sewing, it could also be seen as an element of social demarcation that located women at home pursuing traditional domestic skills. In the short-term, as war drew to a close, many women longed for the chance to return to a normality centred on home and family. Here, home craft skills would be at a premium in the austerity of the post-war period. But these constructions of femininity, with their lingering associations of Victorian virtue and angel-of-the-hearth imagery, did not represent that component of womanhood who had significantly redefined the sexual boundaries of working life and outlook through the context of their wartime lives. While the 'Make-Do and Mend' campaign did encourage boys to sew on buttons and darn socks, its philosophy was unapologetically aimed at women.[51] In just the same way as immobile men were never encouraged to take on housework even while their wives juggled home, family and jobs,[52] so 'making-do' reflected a society still deeply sexually stratified where women, far from finding domestic work boring and repetitive, were expected to respond gracefully and enthusiastically to their country's call to craft.

–12–

# Clothes for Coupons

Clothes rationing was introduced on June bank holiday weekend 1941. The first broadcast and press release on bank holiday Sunday gave a general summary of the need for rationing and emphasized that it was 'not the same as shortage: rationing, or *fair shares*, is the way to prevent a shortage without interfering with full war production'.[1] The scheme was launched on a largely unsuspecting public in hope of their compliance on the basis of fairness first. The total expenditure of sixty-six coupons across the rationing year was estimated to be 'just about half the quantity bought by the average civilian in a year in normal times. A man's ration was enough to enable him to buy little more than he stood up in',[2] and there was a similar story for women. The *Times* reported all the main aspects of the new rationing order as well as providing details about dressmaking practices and the coupon allocations for different widths of cloth. For wool, these ranged from exemption for cloths under 3 inches wide, to three coupons for cloth 33–39 inches wide and four and a half coupons for the widest cloth at 54–57 inches. For non-wool cloth other than jute, all pointings were lower, ranging from exemption again at the narrowest end, to two and three coupons respectively.

The *Times* also carried extracts from Oliver Lyttelton's nine o'clock radio broadcast from the previous morning, when he had introduced the idea of changing dress protocols in line with the war effort. In what signalled an important departure from previous codes of smartness and job-specific clothing, the President of the Board of Trade had suggested that while he knew all the women would look smart, 'we men may look shabby. If we do we must not be ashamed. In war the term "battle-stained" is an honourable one.' When people felt tired of their old clothes, they were to be reassured that by making do they were 'contributing some part of an aeroplane or a gun or a tank or, perhaps even more simply, an overcoat to one of our fighting men'.[3] The confident assumption that women would remain smart reflects an unquestioned acceptance from Lyttleton that women would place some premium on continuing to look good.

The various magazine editorials that followed provided encouraging rhetoric on the management of coupons and rallied women to step up to the challenges ahead. *Woman* reached a quite wide cross-section of the population living on more modest incomes and on 28 June provided a careful analysis of the common clothing concerns that would affect everyone. These included what type of styles and fabrics to buy and how coupon effective certain types of clothing would now be. For dresses, the advice was to buy 'simple, tailored' designs in plain colours or with a small pattern that could be worn in various ways with different accessories. Coats at fourteen coupons were significant purchases out of the annual allowance, and women were directed to ensure 'freedom at shoulders and arms, that the sleeves are really long enough . . . [and] that the skirt wrap is generous'.[4] Suits requiring eighteen coupons (a fully lined woollen jacket was twelve coupons and a woollen skirt six)[5] were also acknowledged as costly in terms of coupons, but 'a good suit outlasts many a little frock' and a classic style without details that would date was best. Comfort and durability were essential features allied to styles that could be flexible and interchangeable. If a reader were average in size and chose an economical pattern, making garments rather than buying ready-made might save on coupons. This depended on the price of fabric per yard and the amount of material needed. Thus the average woman might get a 'short-sleeved dress in wool material out of 2 1/4 yards of 54" [wide] material equal to 10 coupons (not 11 required for a ready-made). A short-sleeved dress in any other material 36" wide takes 3 yards (6 coupons instead of 7)'.[6] Back in the summer of 1939, *Vogue*'s pattern book was suggesting that a 'standard day dress of slightly more intricate design and some fullness in the skirt' would take four and a half or four yards, some less.[7] Armed with information on fabric widths and prices, readers would decide how best to work their ration. The same calculations needed to be made for knitted items. *Woman* suggested that an 'average jumper takes 8ozs of knitting wool', which if home-made on the basis of one coupon for every two ounces would take four coupons. This was rather better than buying sweaters from either the eight- or five-coupon category listed under rationing. On the other hand, knitting a 'long-sleeved cardigan may take 10–12ozs' worth between five and six coupons, which could make the lower-pointed sweater category equal in coupon terms.[8]

While allocating coupons across family needs now had to be addressed, prices of clothing still continued to rise, as we have seen. Utility cloth and clothing which would control prices in due course would not appear in any quantity until the following spring, and for those living on more modest incomes, coupon value in relation to price was an important consideration. It is useful to remember at this stage—with coupons now a reality and high prices affecting all clothing purchases—that Utility was being inaugurated initially to ensure good quality commodities at the lower end of the market. Given that industrial workers represented 65 per cent of the population (D class) and the poorest-paid workers another 15 per cent (E class), a significant proportion of the country could be anticipated to be feeling the pinch.[9] Spending on clothing across the population had reduced considerably,[10] and the working-class cost-of-living index would show by December 1941 an inflation rate of 91 per cent on base prices at the onset of war.[11] To illustrate how prices had risen, at the most economic end of the market, Marks and Spencer had kept to a maximum price for commodities of five shillings throughout the 1930s. Bookbinder suggests that in early 1939, a long wool dress would have been five shillings, and a short-sleeved dress 2s 11d.[12] At the same time, Flora and Edith Hodson were using wholesale firms such as Wilkinson and Riddell who were retailing ladies long-sleeved art silk frocks at 12s 11d each and short-sleeved summer frocks at 11s 6d. Goods to be sold in the shop were marked up by 20 per cent or more,[13] so final prices were a good deal higher than those of Marks and Spencer. Wilkinson and Riddell were also advertising the popular swagger coat at prices ranging from 15s 11d to 23s 11d and a two-piece flannel suit for 12s 6d. Their three-piece flannel suit with swagger coat cost £1 12s 11d.[14] *Vogue,* in contrast, in an article entitled 'Smart Fashions for Limited Incomes' in January 1939, described a generously cut swagger coat retailing at six guineas from Gooch's and a trouser suit for seven and a half guineas from Dickens and Jones.[15] Such were the disparities in prices from the cheapest mass-produced clothing to high-end department store. Bespoke prices would have been higher again. With an increase in the cost of clothing of 75 per cent on prices at the outset of war,[16] all these prices rose accordingly. Marks and Spencer had had to abandon their nothing-more-than-five-shilling policy,[17] and in April 1941 Wilkinson and Riddell were sending the Hodson sisters an invoice for a woven rayon frock wholesale price 22s 11d.[18] This reflects the 75 per cent increase in the price of clothing, and similar rises would have been commensurate across the clothing retail market. Prices would continue to rise until maximum price restrictions were implemented the following year, and this level of inflation combined with the coupon restrictions created the desired downturn in consumer spending. Thus every penny parted with during this time, particularly for those on the lowest incomes, had to be carefully considered and achieve the best value for money possible. Once Utility wear became more established, the price capping it created worked for all the Utility output across the fabric-quality spectrum from the cheapest cotton dress fabrics with a maximum selling price of 2s 7d to much more expensive Utility wool tweeds. As an example of these different Utility markets, the *Drapers' Record* later recorded in February 1942 that Norman Hartnell in association with Berker-Banner, the well-known high street fashion brand, was creating a Utility range that would enable clients to obtain a 'Hartnell designed dress for about 35s. . . . Mr Hartnell's designs, however, will be represented in each of the controlled price groups ranging from 18s 9d to 62s 10d.'[19]

In the third week in June and with rationing well underway, *Picture Post* featured an article in its 'Practical Living' section on 'How to Run Your Dress

Allowance'.[20] Written for a broad reach of the public, including those on both limited and more comfortable incomes, columnist Anne Scott-James declared in her opening paragraph, 'Now that clothes are rationed, we shall all be better dressed!' The rationale for this was clear: 'Just as food coupons have raised the standard of English cooking so dress coupons ought to teach us to pick our clothes with keener discrimination.' What followed tried to forewarn readers of how the apparently generous allowance of sixty-six coupons would not, in reality, go that far and emphasized that readers could only buy one major item, such as a coat or suit, per year or they would leave themselves very short for other things. The thrifty woman making her own clothes was recommended certain styles that were more economic, both in terms of fabric and time. Thus, 'narrow skirts, single-breasted fastenings, collarless necklines and short sleeves' were all promoted as appropriate components of a wartime look. Trimmings were especially important, illustrated in the article by a series of images where the same model in the same dress created six different outfits by the careful use of a variety of cotton and lace collars and themed hats. Thrift required simple chic on the one hand and an imaginative use of accessories on the other. Together, unremarkable clothing, such as the plain black dress featured, could be made to accommodate a range of social occasions for little extra cost or coupon outlay. For readers of Alison Settle, the advice had a clear continuity with the conception of good taste operating in the years before the war, suggesting that a classic sense of style remained secure. Alongside of thrift features, Anne Scott-James pointed out the importance of a good fit. This not only made an outfit more attractive to look at, as well as to wear, but would also improve its longevity: 'No dress will stay smart or even wear well that isn't a first class fit. The skirt will go out of shape, the seams will wear, or the sleeves go thin. If you buy one that isn't quite your size, have it altered straight away; or, if you do the job yourself, do it at once, before your resolution wears thin.'[21] Anne Seymour, editor of *Women and Beauty*, later suggested, in an interview on Utility wear for Mass Observation in March 1942, that she would buy a Utility garment 'one size too big for me . . . and then take it to my tailor and let him make it to fit me for a guinea or two.'[22] Money still had its advantages where dressmakers and tailors were still available for this type of work.

In July, *Picture Post*'s 'Practical Living' section offered a variety of practical dress tips for a 'Coupon Summer'.[23] With the British climate in mind, Anne Scott-James was quick to remind readers to buy clothes that would give service throughout the year. Buying for the three of four months when warmer temperatures might arise was a false economy which a bad summer could make even worse. Cotton dresses were dependable with various weights of cardigans, jumpers and jackets depending on the time of year, and cotton trousers continued to be useful in cooler months for housework and gardening. Thicker cottons, such as corduroy, were durable and already year-round fabrics. Made into hard-wearing trousers and dungarees as well as the ubiquitous boiler suit cotton fabrics were not only practical but also washable and easy care.

The ankle-length trousers and just-below-the-knee dresses and skirts featured in the accompanying photographs confirmed a staple wartime look that would so often combine slightly zany printed fabrics, checks or tweed patterns with a slender, graceful, if rather practical, silhouette. Outfits were already beginning to adopt a mildly eccentric edge as waistcoats, collars and cuffs were cut in contrasting fabrics, paving the way for the more challenging

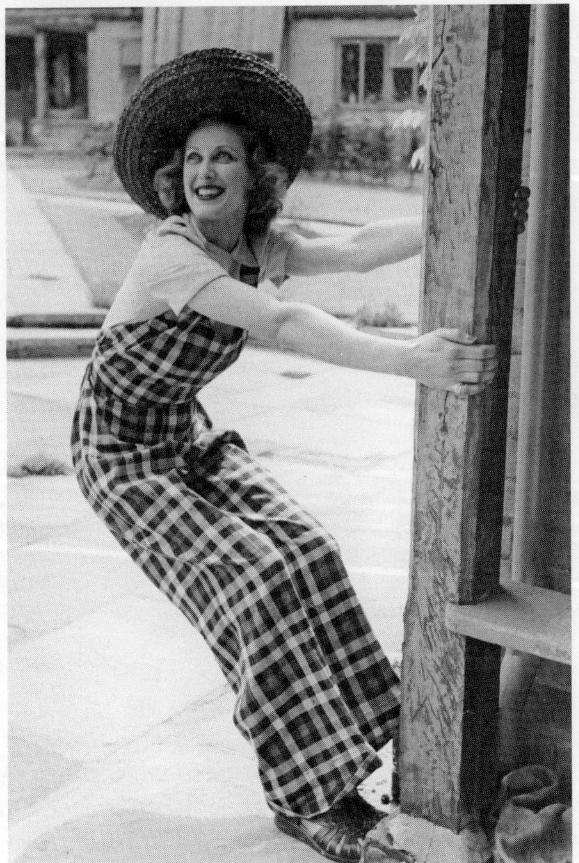

**Figure 21** 'Clothes for a Coupon Summer', 5 July 1941. *Picture Post* featured these ankle-length dungarees with wide sunhat as part of a range of less formal outfits for more relaxed summer living. Zoltan Glass/*Picture Post*/Getty Images (3251397).

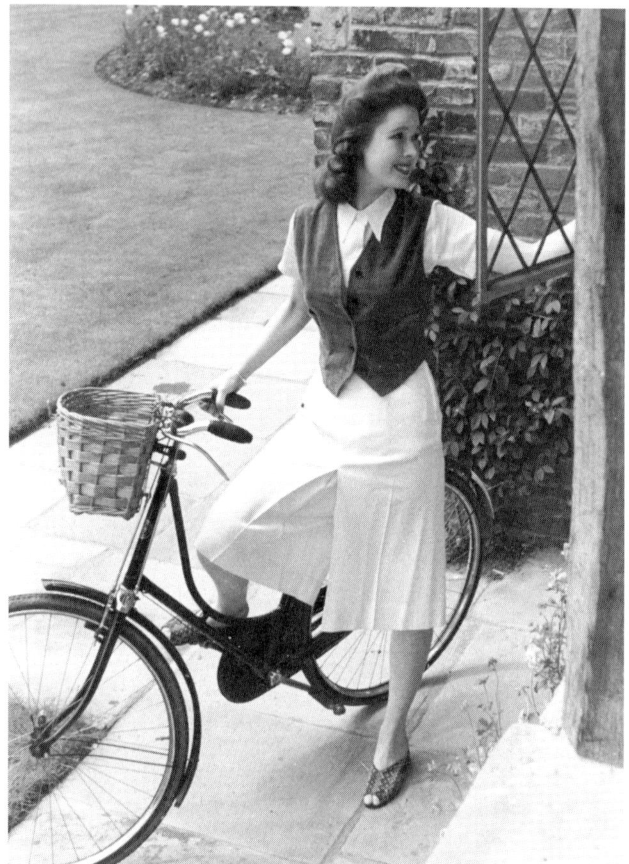

**Figure 22** 'Clothes for a Coupon Summer', 5 July 1941. This red corduroy waistcoat cost 33s 11d from Bourne and Hollingsworth. It also required five coupons. The divided skirt for cycling may have offered a style compromise for those still resistant to trousers. Zoltan Glass/*Picture Post*/Getty Images (3252439).

collages that would result from patching and making-do. The bold and often distinctive accessories that also became a key part of the wartime aesthetic were clearly visible here in bright summer items ranging from straw sombreros to fresh wild flower posies. To finish the look, sturdy footwear was recommended rather than seasonal 'play' sandals, which would take up coupons but give little real wearability beyond a single season. Despite the trousers and pinafores, the cycling skirts and baggy print trousers, the look remained beguilingly feminine, partly because of an ingénue, girlish feel to the clothes. In dropping sophistication and adopting practicality, it was hard to avoid a younger, more active look for summer, unencumbered as it was by the tweed skirts and knitted twinsets of the colder months. While men might have some leeway for looking a little shabbier, women began to take advantage of an evolving sense of aesthetic freedom within dress, where new combinations and configurations were justifiable in the name of austerity. Busy lives juggling more elements than ever before were reflected by a practical simplicity of dress that would continue to feature for the remainder of the war. Coupon clothing for civilian life became, therefore, an amalgam of all the things it had to be. It had practical wearability, was increasingly inventive in the way it was conceived and styled and yet remained true to a traditional spirit of femininity in the soft silhouettes, seasonal colour shifts and quirky accessories that bore little comparison with anything male.

The wealthier readers of *Vogue* could arguably embrace a more philosophical rhetoric about rationing. In an article entitled 'We Re-Affirm Our Faith in Fashion' that appeared in July, the new approaches to the buying and wearing of clothes were seen as reflecting fashion's flexible nature, its changing psychological and social purpose. Just because seasonal variations might be less and traditional influences no longer as evident did not mean that a sense of fashion was any less vibrant than it had been before the war. Then, times had been easier in terms of the free rein for glamour and luxury. Now these things were seen as hollow and trivial in the face of more important ways to spend both one's time and money. The 'airy playtime fantasies' of 1939 had gone 'unmourned by a world awake—at last—to stern realities'.[24] Clothes rationing was the indication, if any were still needed, that for fashion, business as usual was no longer the message.

*Vogue* reminded its readers that it had long advocated spending less and planning more and that lavish outlay hardly guaranteed style. War only emphasized these maxims. Rationing could not affect 'a sense of style'[25] because this was ingrained into a way of doing things that put care and quality first. The impulsive, unstructured dresser, without a coherent strategy for putting pieces and items together, would not survive the new wartime test for coupon-conscious chic. To be well dressed would now take a lot more than just money.

Women were greatly encouraged to become 'self-reliant, self-expressive and self-conscious, in the best sense'.[26] Rather than look elsewhere for trends to imitate, the smart woman would be finding her own 'formula' for dress success, playing a 'lone hand' in contriving a sense of style. Focus would now fall on the thoughtful use of an existing wardrobe rather than on future purchases, fostering a more timeless elegance. Looking at the situation optimistically, *Vogue*, like *Picture Post*, anticipated that even with all the restrictions, indeed because of them, British women would become even better dressed. The fashion astute would adopt new trends, such as 'interchangeable outfits, dual and even treble-purpose dresses . . . [and] the short-skirted, tubular silhouette'.[27] Ingenuity was given its own drama as *Vogue* conjured up a vision of the 'many Scarlett O'Haras, who snatch curtains from windows, to cut a dash in something new',[28] recalling the 1939 film *Gone with the Wind.*[29] While the historical parallel was undoubtedly tongue in cheek, the image of the Southern beauty ripping a pair of green velvet curtains from the great windows of her colonial plantation mansion during the American Civil War captured something of the dynamism and flourish that *Vogue* sought to associate with their heroic, if unskilled, readers making-do.

Rationing and increasingly high prices continued to reverse the spend trends of the pre-war years, whether in the chain stores or the more expensive department stores and independent fashion retailers. The increasing need for uniforms and other war-related textile products meant fashion garments were no longer the mainstay of textile production, and both shops and shoppers now coped with less. For some of the larger retailers, areas of the shop floor could no longer be filled. By February 1942, nine months after the introduction of rationing, Mass Observation was reporting that D.H. Evans had closed a large portion of their third and fourth floors to regroup stock more effectively. A member of staff explained, 'we haven't got the stuff to sell. If it was spread out it would look nothing. So they have closed some of it down, and pushed things together more.'[30] By March 1942, the lack of ordinary fashion stock was noticeable even though Utility fashions were being produced in larger quantities and entering retailers in time for the new spring season. Mass Observation made a comparative study of a variety of West End London stores, looking into stock, shopping habits and the take-up of the new Utility wear, and noted a generally low stock of ordinary lines, which also affected size and colour. The fact that limited stock was evident in one of the major shopping districts of the capital reinforced not only the stringencies that would have been felt across the country, but also reassured provincial buyers that London was not being given special treatment. Mass Observation reported that 'shoe shops have well filled windows, but inside it is a different story. In varying degrees this is true of most things. A good show is made to suggest that the department is well stocked, but this illusion is seen through when any particular colour or size is required. Thus heavyweight coats are very scarce . . . or anything of a heavier weight than brushed wool or tweed, or a few cheaper fluffy coats.'[31] The writer went on to confirm that the same story was also true for shoes, with 'even ordinary walking shoes . . . difficult to obtain in anything but large sizes, and windows are filled with high heeled or flat heeled crepe-soled shoes for which there is less demand'.[32]

With less choice of styles and limited availability, the reality of shopping on the local high street or in one of the larger towns or cities was much the same; it was harder to find things, it often took longer and there was no guarantee of success. Just as buying Utility wear was, for some, already a compromise in terms of restricted choice if not necessarily of style or quality, so other compromises had to be made throughout the remainder of the war. Favoured brands disappeared, whether of cosmetics or corsets, stockings or silk lingerie, and where replacements did appear the product might, arguably, be similar but without the signature image, branding appeal or quality of the original. In the process, the 'paraphernalia of the mending-box'[33] that had been, to a degree, rendered less attractive by the artefacts of mass-production, was retrieved and reinstated.

The clothing anxiety that surfaced soonest and was least easy to assuage as war progressed was about the need for stockings in larger quantities than the ration could allow for by a wide margin. As we have seen earlier, women's desire to wear stockings and of the best quality they could afford was a hard dress protocol to undermine. The *Draper's Record* made enquiries concerning the extent to which some major employers and institutions *required* women to wear stockings and found a mixed response. With various brands still being available in late June 1941, when the survey was undertaken, Barclays Bank was sympathetic to coming difficulties but was not anticipating changing their dress codes yet, while Leeds University saw no reason at present to relax their ruling on women students being required to wear stockings. In fact, the Pro-Vice Chancellor bullishly expressed the view that 'there is a strong feeling that women students should not be permitted to attend the University without stockings'.[34] On the other hand, the London County Council had never had a dress ruling, leaving their staff to dress as they saw fit, and the Prudential Assurance Company thought that codes must relax with the coming stringencies. In October, after four months of rationing, official authority was given for women in the Civil Service to go without stockings,[35] a move which acted in parallel with other relaxations in dress codes taken up by employers, so allowing a range of available mix-and-match clothing to be worn instead of suits. This kept down the numbers of new garments needed and continued to undermine previous dress rules that worked against the thrift principles of the ration.

As rationing became a way of life, older traditions surrounding the buying and wearing of clothing inevitably began to break down. In broad terms, the necessary economies caused by rationing alongside of the patriotic adoption of simpler dress regimes meant the middle and upper classes needed fewer clothes for their daily lives, continuing a pre-war trend towards more flexible dressing, while those on more limited incomes and without pre-war stocks to fall back on endeavoured to retain sufficient clothing appropriate to their lifestyles and occupations. This had the appearance of narrowing the gap between classes but was rather, in reality, the outcome of the necessary retrenchments of war on the more affluent. As conventional approaches to dress adapted to wartime conditions in general, so those old boundaries between classes, established by the stricter pre-war clothing protocols of the more affluent, certainly became less visible. Men were encouraged to wear flannel trousers to work or come into town in country clothing, and by early 1943, Hugh Dalton was openly embracing the changing dress codes, expressing the view that to cling to the past was 'quite wrong and out of date'. For him, the 'right clothes are the clothes we already have'.[36]

The reality of rationing was, therefore, to make the most of existing wardrobes by renovating or remodelling as need directed and to buy new only very infrequently and carefully. Value for money was a prime factor. Styles continued to reflect simplicity and practicality with the whimsical and, at times, rather eccentric entering the fashion lexicon, so broadening the parameters of the wearable. The austerity regulations would continue the focus on simple, undecorated lines, taking away residual elements of surface decoration and trimming that had created variation on the slim, graceful line of much pre-war daywear across the fashion markets. As more Utility clothing began to enter the shops, as discussed in Chapter 14, non-Utility fabric became far less available and very expensive. During 1943, 245 million square yards of cotton Utility cloth was produced compared to 64 million non-Utility and 115 million square yards of Utility rayon compared to 31 million of non-Utility rayon.[37] Between August and December Utility represented 80 per cent of the home civilian market for cotton apparel cloth and 83 per cent for rayon apparel cloth. By 1943, these still accounted for 79 per cent and 78 per cent respectively. By 1944, 84 per cent and 81 per cent respectively.[38] The removal of purchase tax from Utility cloth and clothing in August 1942 rendered Utility even more cost effective.[39]

Designers like Norman Hartnell and Digby Morton were also taking on Utility work,[40] despite representing that end of the industry furthest from volume production, while their bespoke services were still in demand. In an interview for Mass Observation in March 1942, Morton suggested that his house had never been busier, notwithstanding rationing. He expressed the view that 'really people seem to manage all right on coupons' and that women were using their husband's coupons, 'their relations' aunts' and so forth. But then most of our customers come from the country, and in the country people don't need their coupons so much, village people on estates and so on, you know, they're just lying idle. . . . We don't care much where they come from . . . I think now they're saving coupons to get one thing that's going to be good and worth having, instead of going into one shop here and another shop there and frittering away coupons on nothing.'[41] This painted a much cosier picture of rationing for those with more than enough and without the drains on their resources experienced by so many others. By the time Morton gave this interview, the Utility scheme was well underway, but it was clear that a percentage of the outfits being created by his house were not Utility. He was producing garments made from an increasingly small supply of expensive non-Utility fabric and was employing a much-reduced work force. These factors would have made the finished outfits slower to arrive and ever more expensive. Morton commented on this: 'We can't afford to ask less. . . . It's about 23 guineas for a suit and then the purchase tax. . . . I shall have to cut down overheads, concentrate on the simple styles: of course now I have to economise on material, I'm making dresses out of less than 3 yards of material, whereas I used to use about 3 1/2 or 4 yards. Then trimmings come under purchase tax, so they will have to go. Things will be very simple. I'm making little frocks out of men's suiting, little check dresses that look good and are rather tailored and plain.'[42] These prices were at the highest end of the price scale and much in excess of the ready-to-wear Utility prices from department stores like D. H. Evans.[43] Whatever the price of a non-Utility designer suit, there were still patrons able to buy. As Morton remarked, 'people pay quite willingly, they know they have to pay about £19 for a readymade suit or something at a place like Harrods, and for about £25 they can have it made to fit them. What I expect will happen will be that when most of the cloth manufactured is Utility, there'll always be a little non-Utility cloth, and people will have to either buy Utility or come and have models made for £30 or so.'[44] High society still clearly placed a premium on not dressing quite like the rest. Not only could they afford the extra, as they were buying so much less, but they were also, arguably, keeping alive the most aesthetically valuable element of the fashion market wherein lay the conceptual edge and innovative skill of an inherently British fashion.

Coupons for clothing together with the price and cloth controls that constituted the Utility scheme delivered a sustainable range of garments to the nation at largely affordable prices for all. The desire for the distinctive in quality and style that only money could buy clearly never disappeared, but with improvements in quality and manufacture in general, more people experienced value for money when purchasing new clothes than ever before. Thus fashionable clothing continued, within limits, to be offered on the British High Street, underpinned be a comprehensive system of coupon control that brought suitable, fit-for-purpose clothing within reach of all.

# –13–

# Keep Smiling Through: Good Health and Natural Beauty

The editor of *Weldon's Ladies Journal* assured her readers in the autumn of 1939 that the *Journal* would 'help the women of this country . . . to keep a cheerful heart and to maintain a calm competence'.[1] Keeping to the theme of boosting morale, it was also imperative to 'look your best, not to let yourself go whatever the circumstances'.[2] Magazines reflected two separate yet related aspects of body culture: the underlying need for inner well-being and strength, and a well-maintained external appearance. The right attitude of mind would help inform the presentation of the outer self both in matters of grooming and dress. A well-balanced and steady woman would always be clean and fresh and attired in clothing that reflected her competency, reliability and femininity. Although women increasingly took on men's roles in the workplace, femininity need not be compromised if more traditional approaches to grooming and presentation were retained. J.B. Priestley, in one of his Sunday evening radio broadcasts entitled *Postscripts,* paid tribute to the working women who had kept going, and shown their 'high courage and resolution . . . [the] crowds of nurses, secretaries, clerks, telephone girls, shop assistants, waitresses, who morning after morning, have turned up for duty neat as ever—rather pink about the eyes, perhaps, and smiling rather tremulously, but still smiling'.[3] His tribute to women was early evidence of the emerging spirit of resilience and determination that had begun to construct a new dimension to femininity. The energetic body language, the 'neat' visual aesthetic, reflected an inner capability and reliability that, for Priestley, revealed an essential womanhood that was 'magnificent'.[4] The media promoted the clear message that physical and mental stamina could be managed and that there was an undeniable relationship between looking and feeling good and good morale. The health of the nation was seen as 'invaluable to our war effort'[5] and was to be secured, as a Ministry of Health booklet advocated, by a 'conscious effort from each one of us'.[6]

Achieving this level of well-being required acknowledging the importance of basic hygiene, personal grooming and proper diet, and much advice was given out on all three through varied channels ranging from official government media to the popular weekly and monthly magazines. This type of information and guidance has to be seen in the context of the changing social mix brought about by war and the recognition that different standards of hygiene were practiced by different elements of the population. The poorest families, who lived without convenient access to sanitation and running water, did not necessarily practice poor personal hygiene, but where they did, it was understandable, if not to be condoned.[7] The principles of hygiene featured prominently, therefore, because of the greater incidence of community living during war. Service life or the enforced togetherness of a night shelter brought strangers into a proximity only bearable if reasonable standards of personal cleanliness were maintained. Washing properly and regularly were essential. Magazines carried advertisements for antiseptic products like Dettol and Milton, both of which could be used in the bath, and the Vinolia soap company reminded service women that 'personal daintiness' should be maintained alongside of service duties. 'Freshness' was the 'secret of the attractive woman', and a 'daily bath with fragrant Vinolia' was considered both wise and economical.[8]

Soap was rationed in February 1942, leaving the average household with a rather modest amount for both personal washing and the laundering of clothes. A sixteen-ounce block[9] was given to a household for the month, and *Good Housekeeping* magazine gave advice on how to presoften water so that the soap ration would go further.[10] Regular bathing was further challenged by a fuel shortage that hit Britain at the same time, causing the appearance of '"Plimsoll lines"' round 'hotel and public baths' as the population was 'urged to take fewer baths, and to use no more than five inches of hot water. . . . Shared baths are also encouraged.'[11] By 1943, the Ministry of Health booklet *Keeping Well in Wartime* continued to remind the public that there was 'one simple remedy against lousiness', a particular problem evacuation had uncovered, and that was 'cleanliness. This means a bath and a thorough wash all over at least once a week. A child's head must be washed weekly, too, and thoroughly combed and brushed every night.'[12]

Personal hygiene required washing hair regularly and maintaining a cut or style commensurate with lifestyle. During the first year of war, the more elaborate hairstyles fashionable for women often required salon care. As women took on war work or joined up, they had less time for sophisticated curling or setting, and these styles gave way to a simpler look. By spring 1941, shampoo preparations in liquid or powder form, wave-setting lotions, hair dyes and tonics and brilliantine for men were all controlled by a Limitation of Supplies Order Perfumery and Toilet Preparations,[13] and shorter, easier-to-wash styles emerged. Emphasis was also placed on choosing hairstyles appropriate for war work after the much-publicized horror stories of women munitions workers who had caught their hair in machinery.[14] By June 1941, *Vogue* had commissioned the designer Meyerhoff to come up with both a turban and a cap to protect hair during this type of work. These provided a neat and stylish solution to the problem, promoting the idea that a woman dressed up smartly will 'be smart on the job'.[15] *Vogue*'s 'Fashions for Factories'[16] also featured a range of clothing, including an overall and boiler suit with shoulder or rear fastenings to maximize safety, that established that wearing the right type of clothing was the only way to look really smart at work. The magazine also commissioned a suitable hairstyle to go with the clothing and turban, which took all hair off the face and set it with more discreet front and side waves. Longer hair was teased into tight ringlets at the back and drawn together at the nape of the neck. The style was easily covered by the new headpieces, and the completely dressed factory worker devoid of 'strings, loops or laces'[17] gave off an air of almost surgical precision.

By January 1942, *Woman's Own* was describing 'a steady trend towards the neater, more patriotic hairstyle . . . and mannish? No, not a bit of it.'[18] While longer hair did not go out of fashion, the 'Liberty Cut' and its derivatives proved popular. With a range of curls waved across the head in a way to suit the individual, the overall length of the hair was much shorter and looked neater for the wearing of uniform. Shoulder-length hair was considered 'untidy under a service cap' and unhygienic.[19] Grooming etiquette was very strict on the subject of hair length, and all hairstyles had to 'obey the fashion dictum, that hair is invariably dressed well above the collar-line when simple tailored clothes—uniform or civilian—are worn'.[20] Why shoulder-length hair was unhygienic was not clear. Perhaps shorter hair was simply quicker to wash and dry more often. Ursula Bloom writing for *Woman's Own* in May declared shorter hair meant 'cleaner and healthier scalps',[21] which may have been referring indirectly to controlling lice. By May 1943, Helen Temple's Beauty Parlour in *Woman* magazine gave the following advice about keeping hair looking good: 'Use a shampoo or soapy liquid made by pouring boiling water onto shredded bland soap. Make two lathers with a good rinse in between . . . rub with clean towels and whenever possible finish the drying in sunshine or fresh air.' Hair was also to be given 'one hundred strokes each night and morning'.[22] A healthy, well-kept hairstyle reflected appropriate attention to personal grooming and that all-important desire to maintain standards.

Skincare was another important element of maintaining a good appearance. Advice here fell into two discrete areas. The first was how skin should be cared for to achieve the clear complexion commensurate with generally good health. The second concerned the appropriate use of cosmetics. For good skin, women were advised to review their diet. Foods containing vitamin C, for example, were good for 'clear skin' and a 'fresh complexion' along with 'buoyant vitality'.[23] *Vogue*, in a piece entitled 'Eat for Beauty',[24] considered 'The Malady [of] Night blindness; dry, scaly, irritating skin and gooseflesh; dull

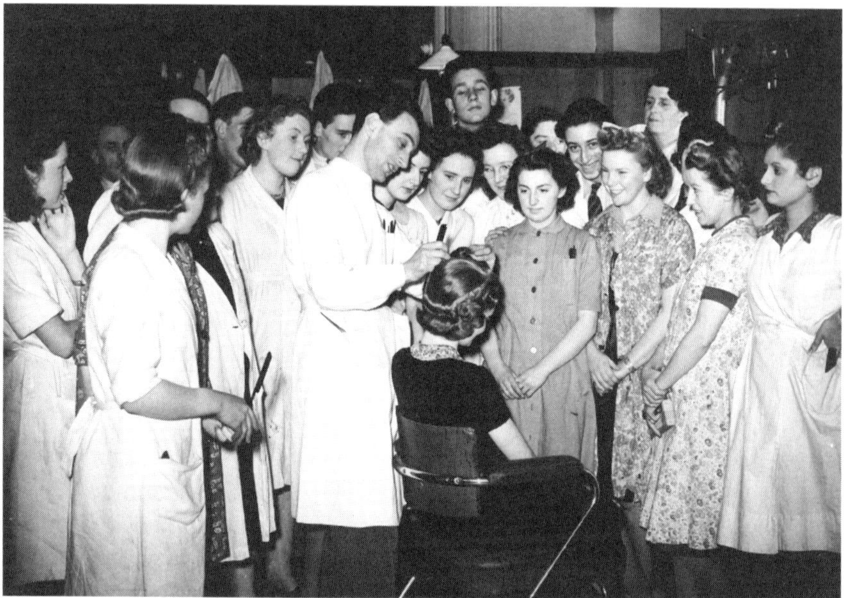

**Figure 23** The new 'service girl' hairstyle devised to be worn under uniform caps, 31 December 1943. Popperfoto/Getty Images (79655731).

and greying hair; dry and brittle nails'. All these were capable of remedy by a combination of vitamin A, vitamin D and calcium depending on the particular ailment, and advice was given on which foods contained these vitamins. *Vogue* stated that 'the right food is beauty's first aid'.[25] The Ministry of Health booklet on *How to Keep Well in Wartime* referred to the 'sunshine vitamins' A and D. Vitamin D was 'not found in many foods, though there is some in fat fish (like herring and salmon), so unless fish-liver oils are taken we have to depend for Vitamin D largely on the action of sunlight on the skin'. Dr Clegg urged mothers-to-be and children under five to 'therefore [take] full advantage' of the cod liver oil supplements available at Welfare Centres, and to eat fish, 'especially fat fish', whenever possible.[26] Dr Clegg also suggested that 'the play of sun and air on the bare skin is stimulating and generally tones you up, especially if you have a sluggish circulation'. Stringent precautions with regard to the dangers of sunbathing were also included.[27] Reminiscent of interwar European interest in the benefits of air and light and connected to modernist thinking on health and hygiene,[28] this advice was part of the much-wider theory of healthy living that had included the development of 'the sun-cure (heliotherapy)' used as a part of the treatment of tuberculosis—'the greatest and most omnipresent threat to public health'[29]—and also helped in cases of malnutrition.[30] The danger of overexposure to the sun was of course to be avoided.[31] Amidst the blackout and shelter life common sense advice on the importance of well-ventilated rooms and avoiding stuffy, confined areas[32] illustrated a related aspect of modernist concern for clean, bright, airy space where light could filter and a more hygienic environment could be maintained. Thus Ministry of Health recommendations had their roots in the medical developments and practice of the interwar years which had highlighted the specific interrelationship between human health and the natural and built environment.[33]

One step on from skincare was the application of cosmetics to enhance the appearance. The most elegant faces of the later 1930s had been achieved through the faultless applications of expensive foundation creams, face powders and lipsticks to obtain a highly groomed look considered the apex of beauty culture at the time. Eyebrows were shaped to achieve a clean arch and eyes carefully enhanced by mascara. Mulvagh suggests that 'artifice replaced nature', and 'page after page of beauty tips adapted from film and stage make-up appeared in *Vogue*. A plague of beauty spots and tattoos, false eyelashes, plucked and pencilled eyebrows, and garish lipstick streaked across the Western world.'[34] For the really soigné, skincare, including expensive salon beauty treatments and make-up routines, could be somewhat self-indulgent and time consuming. War changed this in two simple ways. Products became increasingly unavailable, and many women had other things to do. The woman whose appearance was too considered in terms of her make-up soon became unfashionable. She was clearly not spending her time usefully. Simple cleansing and moisturizing followed by face creams or powders that took only minutes to apply produced a natural refreshed look that became much more desirable.

In November 1940 during the blitz, Ursula Bloom, beauty correspondent for *Woman's Own*, was providing practical beauty tips for women entering air-raid shelters for the night: 'Invest in a warm dressing gown with large pockets to keep your air raid beauty make-up in. Some little refreshers for cleansing of any surplus grease (they'll cost 6d), a tube of powder cream, which, in an instant takes off all the shine and leaves you matt and composed (6d again), a handkerchief-puff well-filled with powder, and a tiny mirror. If you're fussy, have a lipstick, but it isn't necessary. In the second pocket put a small comb, a bottle of smelling salts, a flask with something in it to keep cold out and your favourite tablets to quieten the nerves. You may need them.'[35] Bloom revealed that being 'matt and composed' was what counted as well as being prepared to maintain standards whatever the situation. Who knows how many women organized themselves for an air raid in this way—perhaps what was more important was that it might appear that they did. The limitations on cosmetic production gave rise to home-made beauty aids which included 'cooked beetroot for lipstick' and 'gravy browning "paint" . . . substituting for silk stockings, with pencilled-in seams'.[36]

The British cosmetics firm Yardley rallied women to 'put your best face forward' and promoted a 'truly natural' look[37] suitable for war work. They reminded women how important it was to maintain their good looks as a duty and to 'honour the subtle bond between good looks and good morale'.[38] Icilma encouraged 'beauty in a few minutes' through their range of beauty basics that were 'making it possible for thousands of women to do their essential duty of being beautiful'.[39] Traditional femininity was preserved by familiar if attenuated grooming protocols, and looking healthy and smart now equated with a form of patriotism. For most women, taking care of appearance was also fun, and dressing up to go out was as important as it had ever been.

Lipstick remained an important beauty aid. Hartley quotes the advice given to ambulance drivers in France to 'remember to wear lipstick because it cheers the wounded'.[40] Little is said of mascara, although *Vogue* mentions its use briefly in an article about make-up routines in 1941. Here it is included in a 'before breakfast' make-up—that is, 'easy-to-apply, light but lasting'—and which featured 'powder foundation—cream or lotion; cream rouge; touch of oil on lids and lips; mascara, if you must; powder and lipstick, need we add?'[41] The slightly dismissive tone for the mascara indicated it was deemed unnecessary, possibly because of the practical difficulties in keeping it looking good in an otherwise low-maintenance make-up programme. *Vogue* followed up this advice with a 'before dinner' routine, in readiness for the evening ahead, where the make-up was to be the 'most flattering you can achieve in the time'.[42] Foundation, rouge and face powder were finished off by a this-time acceptable brush of mascara and lipstick.

The only other factor that had an impact on cosmetics was the dwindling supply of good-quality stockings both before as well as after clothes rationing. In their absence, or to save really good pairs, women turned to leg make-up purchased by the bottle. *Mother and Home* informed women that they could 'pour out about 8 pairs of stockings from the 1/3d size bottle' and that the cream should be applied with 'a large pad of cotton wool, stroking it on rapidly, then draw[ing] in the seam with a brown eye-brow pencil'.[43] This advice came as early as July 1940, by which time the lack of sheer stockings must have been already noticeable. After June 1941, obtaining sheers proved both difficult and uneconomic. Cyclax of London produced a 'stockingless cream' that was advertised as 'Non-greasy. Non tacky. Will not mark either skirt or shoes. Definitely non-staining to the skin. Quickly removed with soap and water. The extreme of elegance, comfort and economy.'[44] Here was leg make-up for the 'style-minded', promising 'all the slim beauty of the sheerest ankle clinging hose'.[45]

In addition to practicing good hygiene and careful grooming, women were encouraged to pursue physical and mental fitness through the correct balance of diet and exercise. Against a background of growing athletic participation

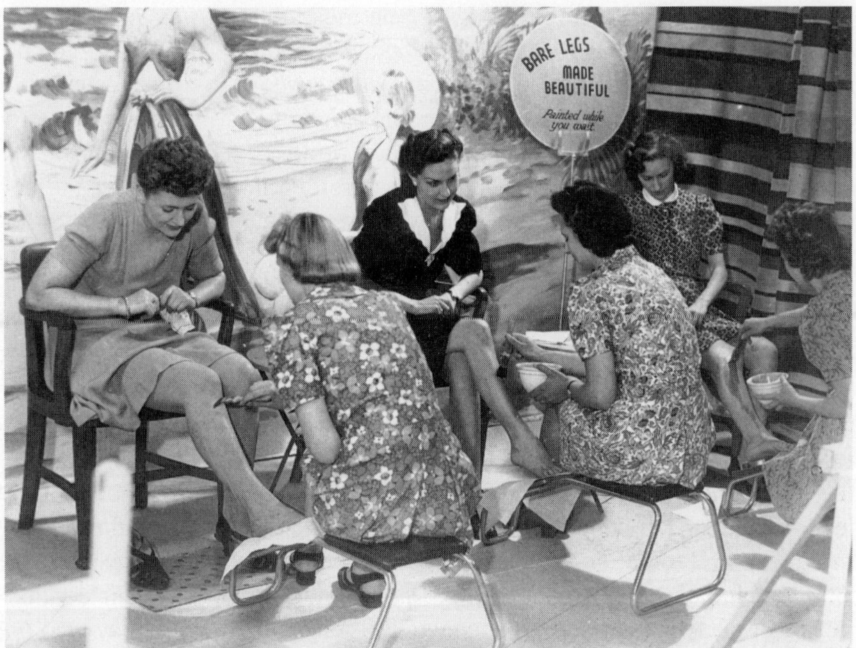


**Figure 24** Leg make-up, here being applied in Croydon, South London, England, was one method of overcoming the need for stockings, 19 July 1941. Keystone/Getty Images (3435288).

by women, and in the context of organizations like the Women's League of Health and Beauty, it is easy to lose sight of the fact that a great many women were still very unfit.[46] While this was generally seen as connected to economic disadvantage, another important perspective surfaced in an article that appeared in *Picture Post* in April 1939. Here, fragile health was seen as emerging from a post-lapsarian history of female suffering that stretched back to mistakes in the Garden of Eden. The fact that this could have had any serious bearing on women's health issues may strike us as extraordinary today. The article raised some disquieting, mythic issues about the nature of gender difference at the time which, with hindsight, helps in understanding ingrained prejudices against women especially in the context of health and well-being.

Under the section 'Science To-day', an article entitled 'A Square Deal for Women's Health' by John Langdon-Davies attempted to discover why women's health care had been neglected.[47] While the main focus was on better maternity care, certain preconceptions about the nature of women emerged. Langdon wrote that 'we are only just beginning to break down the idea that woman is a sort of natural invalid, and many people are still confused as to how far it is a good thing to get rid of this idea altogether'.[48] He cited as evidence of this the declining practice of men giving up their seats to women in the Underground during the rush hour. That some did and many did not was seen as a move, in modern manners, away from treating women as the weaker sex. In other areas there had been similar confusion as to how to break down old taboos. In the case of childbearing, Langdon wrote: 'The neglect of women's health by medical science can only be understood if we remember the social background of the problem. For example, society was for hundreds of years dominated by a belief that childbirth should be painful in order to punish women for Eve's part in the fall of man. Every advance in obstetrics has been held up by this attitude.'[49] When the restricted and repressed lifestyle of women in the Victorian era is recalled, it should not perhaps be surprising that residual elements of a philosophy that positioned women as weaker mentally and physically should still be in existence. Continuing ambivalence towards women in the arena of physical strength and stamina was rooted in the mythic perception that fragility and delicacy were defining elements of femininity. Langdon ended up by neatly diverting criticism away from human society and on to nature. Referring to the inherent physical inequalities that differentiate between men and women, he asked his readers to consider that 'although society has been an enemy to women's health, there may also be a certain amount of truth in the assertion that nature has not after all been too kind to it either'.[50]

If nature had laid down a type of genetic blueprint that appeared to underpin physical inequality, then how strong were women? What was their optimum physical capacity? There was also mental as much as physical strength to consider. These were questions which at this time could not be easily answered. All that could be done was to gear work or training to the standard believed commensurate with women's more limited strength and to monitor the way in which women performed as the war progressed. Much of the rhetoric of praise recording delight in women's war work achievements came from a recognition of new levels of endurance and stamina that had simply been untried until this time. In the propaganda booklet *Eve in Overalls*, women's roles in both military and civilian life were celebrated, and the author was keen to emphasize how well women were taking on a huge range of tasks, previously done by men, that often required physical and psychological strength. The writer featured women working in '"pick and shovel" gang[s] trench-digging and laying a power cable at a Southern Railway depot',[51] painting the underside of bridges and tethering a barrage balloon, which had to be hoisted and then positioned by pulling on mooring ropes 'regulated in accordance with the velocity of the wind, the visibility and the hygrometric condition of the air. All this requires a considerable amount of dexterity, method, co-ordination and physical strength.'[52] The Balloon Barrage defence girls from the WAAF were described as 'all radiantly healthy'[53] and perfect examples of fit, intelligent women. Similarly, the Women's Land Army was taking on a variety of jobs on farms that required enormous amounts of physical stamina. Wauters described how they 'work the cutting, binding and threshing machines. They drive the tractors. . . . They carry heavy trusses of fodder in great armfuls. They saw up the trees and steep them in sulphate.' He reflected on the 'joy of living, suppleness of gait, vivacity and moral balance' they demonstrated[54] and suggested that the Land Army girls had 'made it possible to win the battle of supplies in the British Isles',[55] overcoming the initial 'scepticism' and fear of farm owners.[56] J.B. Priestley described the 'vitality, drive and enthusiasm' of a woman air-raid warden working in London and representative of many such women active during raids, helping the injured and applying first aid.[57] He also was deeply complimentary about the Women's Land Army, with its 'hard and sometimes unrewarding work', and recognized the predictable prejudice that Land Girls had had to endure: 'At first many farmers could not believe that they would have any real help from these trim young women who descended upon them.'[58] His remarks are indicative of the whole process of overcoming misconceptions about the nature of women and how new attitudes had begun to form accepting women as stronger and more capable than their lives had yet been able to reveal. The built-in prejudices of a patriarchal society were now being fundamentally undermined by the emergence of this new image of woman, in large enough numbers to be representative of real change.

In line with this, and a part of the break with older ideas, was the less traditional attitude now revealed towards monthly periods. Feminine hygiene products such as Tampax, and pain remedies like Anti-Kamnia analgesic tablets, began to undermine representations of the female hormonal cycle as somehow disabling, a weakness or the commonly used label 'Women's Troubles'.[59] The advertising rhetoric for such products emphasized the user's ability to carry on through these times and that there was no need to suffer any more. Even the subject of menopause was raised in magazines including *Good Housekeeping* and *Woman and Home*, with both giving space to Menopax, a product advertised as helping alleviate the symptoms experienced by middle-aged women.[60] This rhetoric and ethos that encouraged women to carry on arguably helped to undermine entrenched attitudes about female weakness and suffering that were still entertained by some men and women.

While the population at large were encouraged to become ever fitter, the question of mental health was certainly not overlooked. The fear that the nation's mental health would be seriously endangered with the advent of saturation bombing has already been explored. Although air attack on the scale envisaged never happened, nor the mass hysteria predicted as possible, residual fear over the mental strain and anxiety caused by war remained. Advertising offered simple dietary salves for worry and distress which included drinks and foods with restorative vitamins. Bournvita's mix of milk, eggs, cocoa and malt provided energy as well as apparently fostering a 'cool, calm state of mind',[61] while Ovaltine supposedly helped strengthen nerves and assisted with restful sleep, a commodity much prized given the disturbance to normal sleep patterns that could be caused by the war.[62] Allenbury's Diet, a 'pre-digested nightcap', offered itself as helping to beat the 'Black-out Blues' while Wincarnis Tonic Wine apparently helped to ward of 'Blitz Dreams'.[63] In January 1942, *Woman and Home* carried an advertisement for Dr Niblett's Vital Renewer Nerve Sedative. The caption stated that Dr Niblett had a 'seventy years reputation in the treatment of nerve shock, neuritis, headaches, brain fag, sleeplessness, brain storms, irritability and other nervous disorders',[64] while Koray advocated their 'amazing pink tablet' for 'nerve trouble of all kinds' as well as all types of pain.[65] These, and other products available across the counter in high street chemists, offered a self-diagnosable line of defence against the very real worries and anxieties of war.[66] From September 1940, there was little let-up from air assault, or the anticipation of it, and in this context there was a continuing and unremitting need to maintain good health and combat nervous strain in order to keep civil defence strong and domestic life functioning as soundly as possible. Wauters commended women for their 'remarkable courage and professional conscientiousness' as members of 'the fire services, the police and the organisations created to take care of air-raid victims'.[67] During an air raid on London, he had seen women dealing with casualties, the majority of which 'were not a pleasing sight. It must have taken a great deal of strength of character to approach these mutilated limbs, these gaping heads and torn bodies. The women who were looking after them did so quietly and methodically without any sound or agitation or flurry, and above all without any fuss. . . . The following day I found them all back at their normal tasks. . . . This tranquil heroism is to be found wherever the women of Britain are calmly and quietly carrying out their civic duties.'[68] This strength was further endorsed by Douie, writing about the experiences of women in both the armed forces and civil defence. She confirmed their ability to stay calm under pressure, no matter how distressing that pressure might be. In particular, she cited the work of army nurses stationed in India in 1945 for a service period of five years. The work was hard, no leave was possible and they could not even 'go sick'. She believed it 'remarkable that more did not break down under the strain'.[69] The story seemed the same everywhere. Herbert Morrison speaking as early as December 1940 during the blitz stated that 'the women of this country have shown that when air raids come they have just as high courage and just as steady nerves as men'.[70] From the Women's Voluntary Service members who constructed emergency mortuaries, to the women who went into Belsen shortly after it had been liberated, to the teachers who stayed with children in air-raid shelters, the steadfastness and courage was the same.[71]

Women were beginning to be recognized as essentially different from older stereotypes that had dominated the past and limited their capacity to take a more active role in society. Priestley believed that those who thought all women would be happy to return to their restricted pre-war lives had clearly not fully appreciated the changes war had brought. His 'guess' was that women would be 'dissatisfied with any social and economic conditions approximating to those they knew before the war, conditions that pressed harder upon women and children than they did even upon men. . . . Their courage and endurance, their enterprise and growing initiative, will not utterly disappear just because the guns have ceased firing.'[72] Rose endorses this view, recognizing that as women took on what had been perceived as men's work, it became clear that women lacked the 'civil and social rights equal to men's'.[73] Women were able to rise to many of the physical and mental challenges of war with the same capacity as men. They negotiated their way around traditional preconceptions about themselves while adapting to new circumstances and opportunities. Traditional imageries that embedded women in purely leisured or maternal roles became disingenuous.

The active, reliable woman, who took care of herself and took responsibility for and beyond her home, responded to the exigencies of war in ways that had not been entirely predictable. The combination of energy and resilience with a less studied form of personal appearance resulted in a subtly different type of imagery surrounding the feminine, fine-tuned to the experience of war and indicative of a strength and capability that had, arguably, been significantly underestimated in the past.

# –14–

# Utility and Austerity

By early 1942, Utility garments were making a noticeable contribution to spring fashions. Garments made from the Utility fabrics were shown alongside of non-Utility ranges, with which they were still in competition, offering similarly styled products but at lower prices. The time required to specify particular qualities of cloth and then put them into production had meant a lapse between the inauguration of the scheme the previous year and the appearance of these clothes six to seven months later.[1] During summer 1942, closer specifications were drawn up for cotton and rayon so that by August there were more and better cloths entering the scheme.[2] While the process of cloth manufacture was being improved, the Board of Trade also introduced the series of austerity measures that would significantly affect the way clothing was constructed and finished.[3] To keep producing interesting and distinctive fashions in the face of so many limitations was the creative challenge of the second half of the war. Limited cloth allocations, restrictions on the making-up and finishing of garments, together with the new sizing requirements, all provided strict new parameters within which industry had to operate and represented a level of government intervention in the textile and clothing trades never before experienced. By autumn 1942, therefore, the Board of Trade had in place a comprehensive framework for the manufacture and finishing of all commercially sold clothing. The story of Utility and austerity becomes the story of fashion and dress for the remainder of the war.

The Board of Trade had introduced female journalists to the concept of Utility in November 1941. The Parliamentary Secretary to the Board, Captain Charles Waterhouse, had stressed that the civilian population was not going to be 'dragoon[ed] into wearing some sort of State uniform'.[4] There was to be no standardizing of dress, and new lines would be free of any curbs on design. At this stage only the cloth and price were affected by the Utility regulations, and the Board hoped that the new year stock would merge in appearance with other garments whilst holding down prices. By January 1942, the *Drapers' Record* was reporting no great interest from retailers in the variable amounts of Utility clothing now beginning to appear.[5] This was largely due to plentiful supplies of existing stock and a desire to handle the known product first. This attitude was still prevailing by mid-February when a new report from the *Drapers' Record* suggested that there was 'public prejudice against Utility',[6] leading the paper to ask retailers how they were going to combat this. The small sample of women questioned about Utility was largely negative in their responses to it, having formed the impression that such clothing would tend towards '"drabness", "heaviness", "standardization"'.[7]

That such a view could be held so early on implied poor forward promotion of the new products and an ostrich approach by retailers. They were warned that 'in six months or so', Utility would be 'the greater part of *your* trade' and that a dismissive attitude was counterproductive to everyone engaged in the making and selling of Utility, as well as the public who would have to buy it.[8] Criticism ranged from the name of the scheme—*utility* implying 'a uniform, government stuff, sackcloth'—through poor quality and lack of warmth to dark, drab, uninteresting colours.[9] Thus while some comments were based on a level of informed opinion—early Utility was not particularly good quality—the concerns over standardization and lack of colour were both clearly not, the latter especially so, as there were no restrictions on colour or pattern either at the outset of the scheme or at any future stage of it. Customers needed to be educated into a more positive approach towards Utility if a sales slump was to be avoided, and the shop floor had a specific role to play in this process. By March, Jean Guest for the *Drapers' Record* was providing shop assistants with a ready-made answer to customers enquiring about Utility: 'The garments are styled and made from cloths constructed on specified lines or price-stipulated by the Board of Trade. The margin of profit is controlled at every stage. Utility represents reliable value; but of course, there's no control on style.'[10] The first part referred to the difference between the cloth-specified rayon and cotton and the price-specified wool. While Guest did not expect shop assistants to bore their customers with too much detail on the CC41 clothing, she did expect them to be fully informed as to the value and quality of it. The following week, Guest was summarizing the difference between the Utility and non-Utility garment for the shop floor: 'You may expect a little more detail in the ordinary one [non-Utility]. The maker hasn't to work to such strict prices; he can calculate his own price for the ordinary coat. And, of course, he's completely free in his choice of fabric. He probably doesn't make so many to one style.' Guest was keen to point out that, while you might pay more for the style and fabric variations, the cut, however, would 'not necessarily' be better than for Utility.[11] This would be increasingly true as sizing methods became more accurate after April.

Mass Observation was also investigating both retail and public response to the new Utility lines. In February 1942, their reporter was in London's West End looking at shop window displays and gauging shoppers' reactions. D.H. Evans in Oxford Street had a collection of Utility dresses and coats in the main front window in a range of prices from the cheapest afternoon dress at fifteen shillings to coats at between eight to nine pounds. There was evidence of variety in style and colour, and the observer was told that Utility frocks were selling well. However, a member of staff suggested that while the current Utility clothes were 'lovely', those to come would not be: 'You see they have still got some of their old nice materials, but after this they won't be anything like so nice.'[12] This confirmed the misinformation that the *Drapers' Record* had encountered. The prejudice that continued to surround Utility, based to some extent on its government-controlled status, was increasingly born out of ignorance of the true product.

Another Mass Observation report carried out in March confirmed that ranges of Utility goods were now coming into stores at the cheaper and medium end of the market.[13] Only Marshall and Snelgrove continued to have no Utility garments, implying that they had plenty of non-Utility yet to sell. This could have been because of the higher prices of the goods there, which had slowed sales down, or that good stocks had allowed business to continue without Utility. Mass Observation noticed that the price differential between Utility and non-Utility was becoming very marked in certain shops. In Peter Robinson and D. H. Evans, windows were 'often adjacent showing the same type of clothes, some controlled, and others uncontrolled at double, treble or even several times the price. Thus wool dresses are £3–£4 in controlled prices, but are double this on an average in ordinary lines and even in Bourne and Hollingsworth some woollen dresses or two-pieces are 12.1/2 gns, or even 15 gns.' The differences appeared to lie in the quality of material, with higher prices also revealing 'better cut and originality of design'. While this was true, the observer noted that 'the general trend of design and line however is similar'.[14] In this transitional period, as old and new were side by side, it was even more necessary that retailers understood why their products were changing and how best to market them to the public. Garments were not like for like at this stage, and Utility wear could lose in the comparison. As more Utility garments began to reflect higher investment in better-quality fabrics, so the controlled margins came to offer ever-better value for money, and the tiered production of Utility was able to provide a range of garments at qualities and prices to suit most buyers. At the cheapest end, Utility delivered the value fabrics in cotton and rayon that had been available before the war but were now closely specified in order to maintain quality and, where appropriate, a level of finish commensurate with wear such as crease resistant or waterproofed.[15] Wool, which had remained unspecified with regard to construction, was the most unpredictable fabric in terms of quality, but the manufacture of Utility shoddy was monitored so that it sustained a quality arguably better than before the war.[16] The poorest fabrics and garments, of whatever fabric, were all but eradicated while at the other end of production the unnecessarily expensive, prestige ranges were increasingly relegated to the realms of the severely curtailed non-Utility market, subject to purchase tax. The *Working Party Reports: Light Clothing* published in 1947 as a review of the industry at that time confirmed, 'Undoubtedly the general standard of clothing now being produced is better than it was before rationing, due to the almost complete elimination of the cheapest cut-price production.'[17]

While the shops began the process of integrating Utility with existing lines, other work was going on behind the scenes to make the Utility concept more acceptable to the public. As early as February 1942, the *Drapers' Record* had reported rumours that a group of leading designers were going to create sample Utility garments 'to show the trade how good they can look'.[18] Each of the Mayfair houses approached had 'agreed to make a dress, a coat and a suit which will be modelled at shows sponsored by BoT [Board of Trade] for makers-up'.[19] The designers taking part were all members of the Incorporated Society of London Fashion Designers (IncSoc), a relatively new body that had been formed in June 1941 to combine and showcase the talents of the British couture industry both at home and, importantly, abroad.[20] Hartnell described how the 'leading London houses' had already combined together to dress a group of mannequins for a South America export drive.[21] Having proved that it was possible for the various designers to work alongside one another in a joint venture, Hartnell believed that further liaison was both manageable and desirable: 'Although we were rivals, there seemed no good reason why we should not achieve a unity which might help us with the authorities. We might even gain world-wide recognition for clothes based on a native style and dignity.'[22] In his autobiography, Hartnell recalled that he decided 'with some misgiving' to sound out his colleagues over such a joint venture and with a view to presenting a 'common front' to the Board of Trade.[23]

Hardy Amies, however, recalled the society coming into being 'at the Board's request'[24] and brought together by Harry Yoxall, managing editor of *Vogue* London. Yoxall also saw it this way. Aware that after the fall of France a number of well-known designers had made England their home,[25] Yoxall held a cocktail party for all the leading designers to see 'if they could be persuaded to work together, and I planned to introduce them to the few American buyers who were still venturing to stay in London'.[26] In a letter to Edna Chase, then editor of American *Vogue* and a great supporter of British fashion, Yoxall saw himself as a 'kind of midhusband at the birth' of a body where 'all the limbs . . . are kicking in different directions. . . . But I feel that the couture boys and girls here will never get anywhere unless they form some kind of professional association and maintain as a permanent policy the temporary unity which was rather precariously achieved for the South American collection.'[27] Thus, while Hartnell's actual role in the formation of IncSoc remains unclear, he shared Yoxall's perception that the export collection to Latin America had been a catalyst to band couture designers closer together in hard times. The first members included Norman Hartnell, Victor Stiebel, Bianca Mosca, Peter

Russell, Digby Morton, Hardy Amies and the House of Worth led by Elspeth Champcommunal.[28] A constitution was drawn up by Harry Yoxall and Margaret Havinden from Crawford's Advertising Agency, and with society leading lady Mrs. Reginald Fellowes as first president, IncSoc came into being.[29]

To get the best designers to lead from the top on Utility was an imaginative answer to scepticism over the product. It was hoped that these designers, used to working with the highest-quality fabrics and on the most distinctive and intricate use of cut and make, would not only inspire manufacturers, but would also convince the public of Utility's positive contribution to fashion. Digby Morton had already begun working on Utility clothing for commercial production, choosing fabrics and designing models which could then be 'distributed straight to the buyers and retailers'.[30] Ann Seymour confirmed that Morton had become involved in designing for the scheme: 'As far as I know Digby Morton is the only one [of all the London designers] who has actually done any yet, he's been working on them right from the start. His go to Bourne and Hollingsworths.'[31] Morton thought the scheme 'a very good idea' and believed it was the role of designers like himself to 'advise the Board of Trade on style and material and so on, I suppose, make up the models'.[32] Seymour suggested that other couturiers were also now ready to become involved with Utility.[33]

IncSoc's brief to design for a Utility prototype collection was their first joint action, although each house designed their contribution separately. Hargreaves and Gowing related that the Board of Trade saw the exercise as a demonstration of what could be achieved within the cloth specification restrictions and new austerity regulations which would begin affecting the industry from May 1942.[34] The clothes would not be revealed until the following August, by which time the cut and make restrictions had all been implemented, adding further prohibitions to the design process alongside of the fabric restrictions and price margins already operating. While the austerity measures did not formally restrict creative freedom, they limited the number of design options available, either because of the undue labour they caused or the production inefficiencies they introduced. The designers therefore took on a task in March that they could not fully appreciate in all its diversity until mid-June, when the last of the austerity regulations had been introduced. From then until August, they set about constructing their own solutions to the design conundrums now surrounding their craft.

In the meantime, Mass Observation reported that by the end of March, a greater supply of Utility wear had now reached the high street. With a wider variety of products now visible, the reporter believed the tide was turning and that 'people have become gradually more interested and favourable in their attitude'.[35] The 'large popular stores, such as D.H. Evans, Peter Robinson and Selfridges', were reported as having generous stocks of Utility wear, with the 'simple, well-designed styles' attracting the most praise.[36] Although the lower profit margins for retailers were hitting the independent traders harder, the chain stores were working well with Utility.[37] These popular high street shops with a secure customer base purchased Utility in relatively large quantities, confident in being able to sell enough to maintain profits. In April, and to follow up burgeoning interest in Utility, the first trade show of Utility garments took place. Seventeen fashion firms presented collections of coats, suits and dresses to press and other trade representatives to demonstrate the industry's early achievements with Utility cloths.[38] Norman Hartnell also contributed his collection of Utility wear for Berker Sportscraft, Ltd., known as Berkertex. The show revealed Utility as varied, stylish and good quality, and the collections subsequently toured provincial department stores to publicize the new ranges. One element of the show that further raised the profile of Utility was the 'Twins' collection. Here, 'one firm showed almost identical models', Utility and non-Utility, and asked the audience to guess which. Jean Guest reported that the differences 'appeared almost negligible'.[39] The ranges displayed revealed a continuation of the wartime emphasis on suits, in 'solid tweeds, herringbones and checks' with 'waisted, commendably long, jackets, and [a] most popular skirt [with] . . . three inverted pleats at front and one at back'. Coats 'followed the season's formula with important sleeve-heads, deep armholes and skirts generously pleated in back under a tie belt'.[40] Photographs of the show revealed pre-austerity generosity in terms of wide lapels on suiting and varied use of pleating on suits and dresses while the silhouette remained smartly tailored and slim fitting.

On 18 April, the *Drapers' Record* published the first of the new austerity restrictions.[41] The industry was asked to simplify their output. Rather than imposing a style or 'standardizing' a product, the Board laid down all the ways in which they had calculated that time and money could be saved in the manufacture of clothing. As long as these simplifications were followed, designers could do as they pleased. It was of course a moot point as to how much freedom this actually left designers. Their hands became increasingly tied but always in the direction of the less-is-more chic Settle had been advocating in 1937. Not just Settle. Hardy Amies recalled Molyneux telling him before the war: 'I remove everything that is not necessary. . . . Plainness is all.'[42] But as Amies went on to say, Molyneux 'paid great attention to cut, finish and above all, proportion'. This was the way ahead now for those employed in making clothes at whatever level. Attention to, and care with, the finer detail of seaming, of openings, closures, the setting of a sleeve, collar or cuff, would allow room for inventiveness and finesse at the higher end of the market and an unadorned gracefulness—at its best—lower down. Plain need not mean homespun, nor simple, austere. Amies remembered that when he and Molyneux heard that the new regulations for Utility had been introduced, 'we both laughed. "We have been making utility clothes for years," we said.'[43]

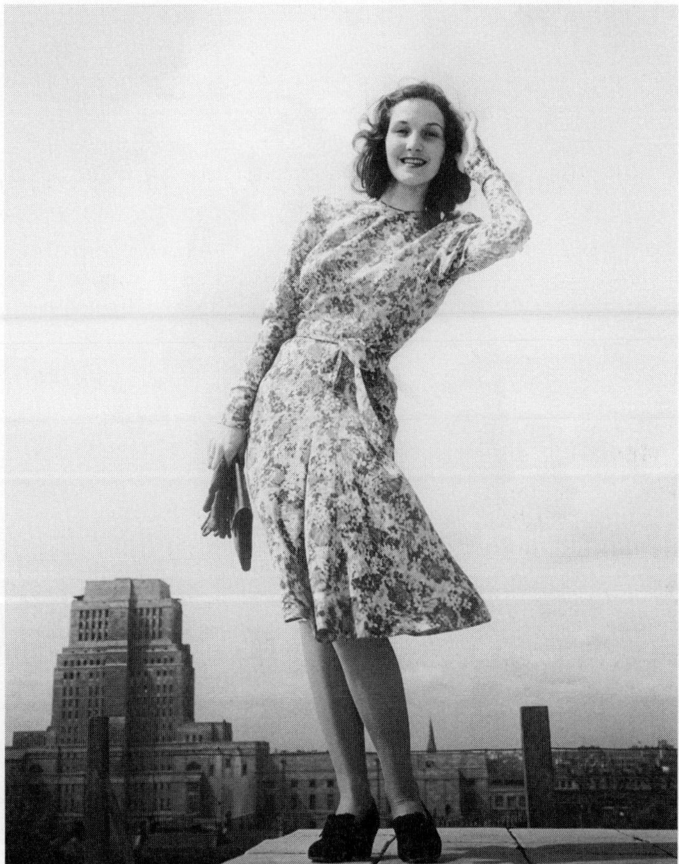

**Figure 25** Norman Hartnell austerity dress in purple, green and mauve with self-tie fabric belt at the waist, 1943. Ministry of Information Second World War Official Collection. © Imperial War Museum (D14820).

The new sizing regulations that had appeared in the *Drapers' Record* on 25 April[44] gave details of the much more accurately sized garments the public would now be able to enjoy. These, together with the supplementary making-up specifications published in June[45] regarding type and quality of seaming and finishing and constraints on production and finishing of various garments including domestic overalls and aprons, completed the reorientation of the clothing industry. After this there would be no further stringencies other than those imposed on the buying public by lowering the ration.[46]

In August, the *Drapers' Record* reported that eight London fashion designers were currently involved in designing for the Utility scheme and that their templates and technical instructions would be ready by the end of September. This was a little late for the approaching autumn/winter season,

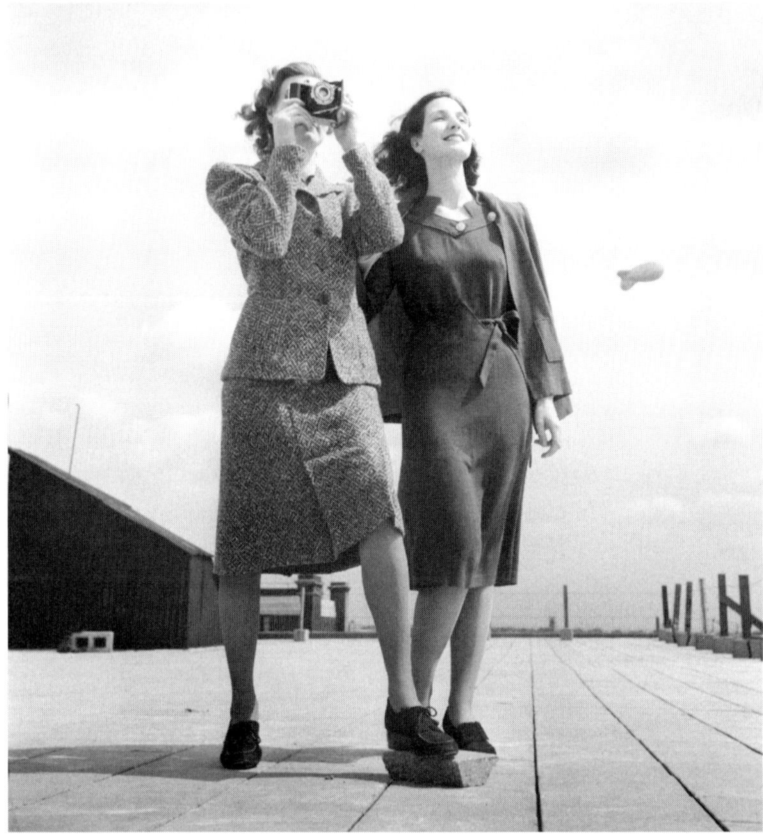

**Figure 26** Austerity fashions, 1943. The blue-flecked tweed Utility suit to the left is by Dereta while the emerald green woollen dress with matching jacket is by Norman Hartnell. Ministry of Information Second World War Official Collection. © Imperial War Museum (D14818).

but the collection that later appeared covered all climate possibilities with garments ranging from heavy top coats in thick tweeds to lighter suit ensembles with blouses and summer-weight dresses. Fabrics and colours were also chosen that could do duty throughout the year. The reporter believed that although there were a lot of similar pieces being produced, this was no bad thing as the more 'officially commissioned models are featured the greater should be the scope for makers-up to provide alternative designs'.[47] When the clothes were shown in the week of 26 September, the *Drapers' Record* recorded that the press had been 'somewhat critical'.[48] The models had featured side by side with mass-production copies, with the changes 'entirely of a simplifying nature to facilitate making and save time'.[49] By 12 October, the nature of the criticism was becoming clearer. The *Drapers' Record* ran

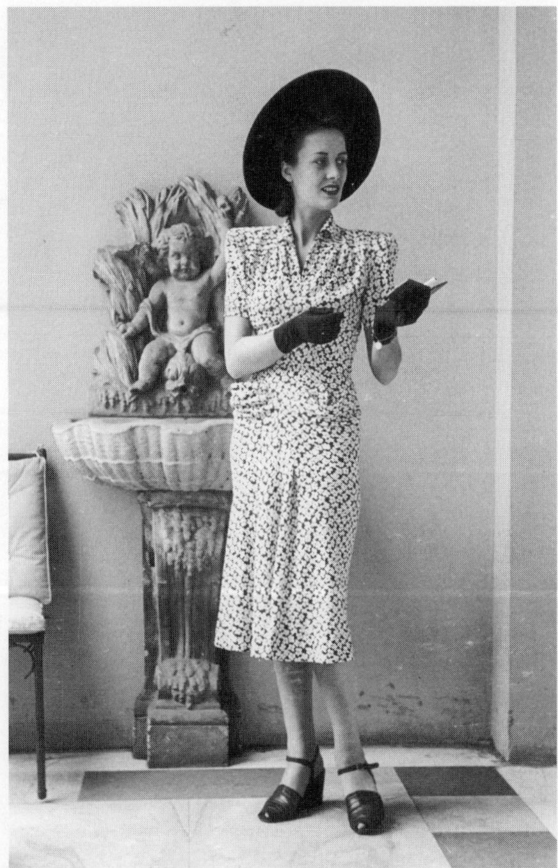

**Figure 27** 'Austerity Clothes for the Fourth Year of the War', 29 August 1942. In this fashion feature, *Picture Post* compared wartime austerity clothing such as this print frock by Rhavis with those more generous pre-war styles they replaced. Felix Man/Getty Images (2696616).

the headline 'Trade Cold-Shoulders "Mayfair Utility"', informing their industry readers that there had been 'very little interest and practically no enthusiasm' from the West End making-up trade contacted by them about the collection. The reason for this was that the trade felt 'resentment that Mayfair designers were brought in to show a long-established industry its job'. There was 'disappointment (tinged with a certain amount of satisfaction) that designers have not produced anything startlingly saleable, and a lofty determination to have nothing to do with the patterns'.[50] Several model houses had already produced Utility designs that complied with the new restrictions much more quickly as an article in *Picture Post* from 29 August 1942 makes

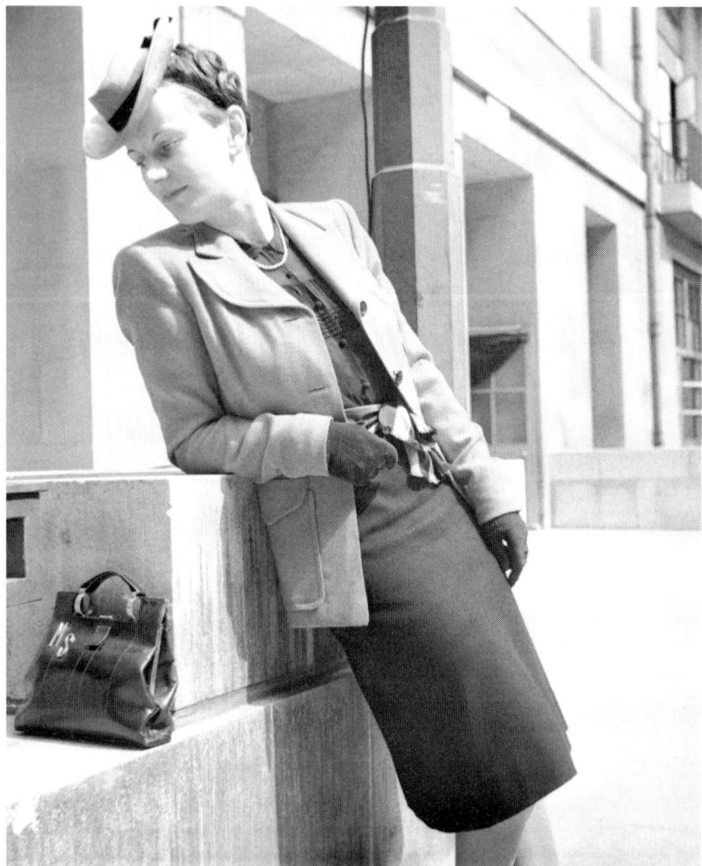

**Figure 28** Utility jacket and skirt, 1943. The cyclamen Utility jacket was from a suit bought at Dickins and Jones costing 82s 2d and requiring 18 coupons. The black skirt is from another suit and promotes the concept of co-ordinating existing clothing for variety. Ministry of Information Second World War Official Collection. © Imperial War Museum (D14790).

clear. It carried photographs of stylish and well-cut austerity fashions from manufacturers such as Rhavis, Rose and Blairman and Spectator Sports, alongside the more lavish pre-war garments they replaced.[51] With the benefit of hindsight, it might have appeared patronizing to manufacturers and model houses that the couture sector should be approached to represent fashion as a whole. Arguably it was a small, if highly regarded, element of fashion but one much less familiar with the constraints of the mass market, and it was for this sector that Utility *had* to work. On the other hand, those members of the Board of Trade who had commissioned the work would in all likelihood have assumed, not incorrectly, that the couture sector always gave the

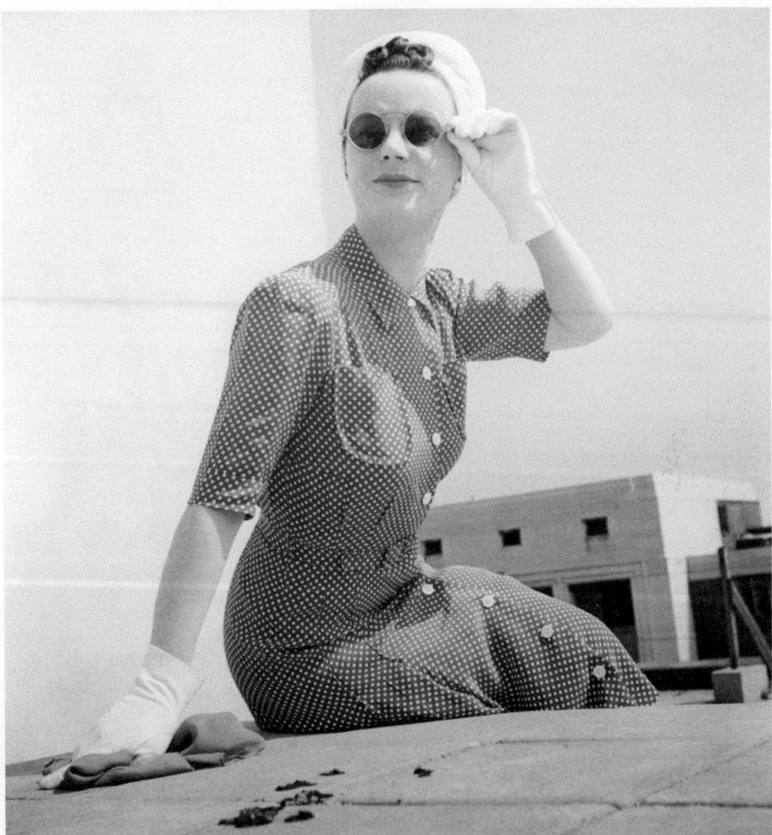

**Figure 29** Scarlet and white spot-printed Utility rayon shirt dress, accessorised with white turban, gloves and sunglasses. The dress required seven coupons and cost 53s. Ministry of Information Second World War Official Collection. © Imperial War Museum (D14784).

lead in fashion terms and sought its cooperation in promoting Utility on that basis. While wires had been crossed to some degree, not all manufacturers felt aggrieved. Hargreaves and Gowing reported that after the first trade show, 'over 100 manufacturers' asked for the patterns.[52]

The Utility prototype garments are not necessarily the best produced at the time, but they are the most intact collection to survive. They provided ideas for the industry as a whole and remain an interesting study of austerity couture. The collection complied with the regulations with an often-imaginative and unpredictable use of elements such as seaming, button placement and top stitching, producing stylish pieces for both couture and high street buyer alike. There are seven suits, six coats, three dresses and two blouses. Most can be linked to a designer although provenance is not

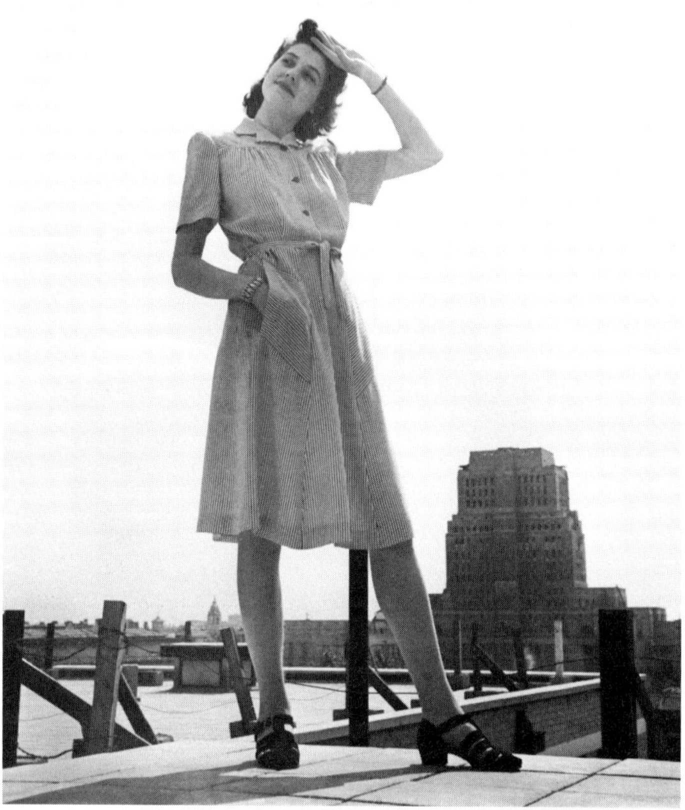

**Figure 30** White and brown striped Atrima Utility dress in rayon, 1943. Ministry of Information Second World War Official Collection. © Imperial War Museum (D14836).

always positive. All the prototype designs were originally shown anonymously on the basis that it was not who had designed a garment but rather what had been designed that counted, and while some garments bear clear signature design features, others remain a puzzle. The designers represented are Digby Morton, Charles Creed, Victor Steibel, Bianca Mosca, Elspeth Champcommunal for Worth, Peter Russell, Edward Molyneux and Hardy Amies—who did not have a house but was part of IncSoc as an invited private member.[53]

A Victor Stiebel dress in brilliant tomato red rayon took the template of an apparently simple button-through dress but added new interest by emphasizing the front yoke seaming, collar and cuffs with top stitching in a toning shade of deep pink. The collar and front yoke were also shaped into a gently scalloped design that softened and feminized the narrow, tubular line. While the number of buttons was limited to the strictly necessary, and no more than five, there were no rules as to button type or shape, so matching fabric-covered buttons were used for a little extra style in the finish. Using the allowance for stitching specified within the regulations added an eye-catching element at very little extra time and cost. Similarly, Creed created a heavy black rayon crepe dress in a simple, front-buttoning design with an asymmetrical pocket hanging to the left of the garment at the hip line. This gave an illusion of additional width to an otherwise narrow skirt and took advantage of the fact that, while only two pockets were allowed by the regulations, there were no stipulations as to how they might be added to a garment. A rayon crepe day dress in brick red, attributed to Molyneux, combined a softly pleated skirt and button-through bodice with three-quarter-length tapering sleeves to create a simple waisted style, starkly plain and relieved only by a softly falling pointed collar. This had been cut all in one with the yoke seam to save on fabric and labour and relied on the gently draping quality of rayon crepe to achieve its affect. Two pockets with flaps were the only detail.[54] This type of dress was highly representative of wartime style.

An example of a similarly simple button-through Utility dress, this time produced for the high street, reveals commercial production also adhering strictly to the austerity rules.[55] The buttons, for example, were placed not less than four inches apart, the simple fabric tie belt was made to be no more than two inches wide with no metal components and the collar and front bodice were cut in the economy style. On the inside of the collar, the CC41 logo on a cotton label was clearly visible, with the four-figure fabric specification number, and next to it, also printed on a cotton label, the registered trade name of the manufacturer and the size as specified by the new British standard regulations. In this case, the dress had been made to conform to a size C, which indicated a bust measurement of thirty-six inches and hips of thirty-eight inches. The length was forty-five inches.[56]

Clever cutting could lead to distinctive elements on garments, such as the shaped panels on the front of an otherwise standard wartime winter coat for the Utility prototype collection by Victor Stiebel. This navy-blue wool felt coat had gently curved front panels in a loosely hourglass shape, narrowing at the waist. Three tomato-red buttons (this coat was part of an ensemble with the tomato-red dress described earlier) were carefully placed to bring attention to the moulded cutting, as well as a line of topstitching which subtly defined the shape. One button was placed at the centre waist, the other two above on the upper bodice. A fourth allowed button was hidden under the turned-down collar and used to close the collar to the neck in stormier weather. The red-and-blue ensemble was anything but drab.[57]

Digby Morton's three-piece herringbone suit for the collection, in grey with red fleck, used pattern as detail. The herringbone travels vertically on the arms and horizontally across the bodice. The six seams in the skirt conformed to the allowance, and there were no pockets or general lining. The petersham lining the waistband and slight boning in the rear waistband reveal traditional tailoring methods that kept the skirt in place without the need of a belt.[58] The blouse revealed a raw selvedge edge used without a hem at the base of the garment and petersham as a front tie. The fully lined jacket, featuring revers which conformed to the limited width restrictions, was finished with decorative top sewing to enhance the line. A beautiful finishing detail of this ensemble, also seen in a claret-coloured coat by Morton, was a set of CC41 buttons. These were made—unusually—out of metal for the suit and Bakelite for the coat. Morton's buttons would remind his clients they were wearing rationed fashion, just as Bianca Mosca's buttons inscribed with 'Austerity Bianca Mosca' from her summer collection would identify austerity design.[59]

In the two and three quarter years left of war, the story of fashion and dress had three themes. The first was the fine-tuning of a wartime look which integrated pared-back design with a fitter and healthier body image, if necessary without the need for a foundation garment. With Utility corsets being in short supply and also rarely reaching to pre-war standards, it was now up to women to make slack muscles work and correct a sloppy posture without artificial aids.[60] The new emphasis on maintaining a disciplined approach to diet and fitness played a central role in providing both the physique ideal for the fashions and the get-up-and-go attitude that went with them. The second theme was the consistent desire to maintain a sense of fashion in clothing despite the lack of seasonal changes. The industry now had to create excitement, or at the very least interest, in other less remarkable ways. This required designers and manufacturers to devise smaller yet still distinctive style signatures that would continue to keep fashion alive and desirable. The third theme was not to become apparent until autumn 1944. After the success of the D-Day invasion had made winning the war likely to be only a matter of time,[61] a more philosophical line of debate opened up about the future of fashion. This discussion was made more pertinent as unsettling images from the first Paris couture shows for four years reached Britain.

In July 1942 in a feature called 'Fighting Trim', *Vogue* expressed the view that fashion was undergoing 'a compulsory course of slimming and simplification; and is emerging from those reducing rollers, the new dress restrictions, in fine shape'.[62] Couched in the language of the beauty parlour, the association between fashion and fitness was clearly established. Fashion had become leaner in response to the requirements of war but more fit-for-purpose in the process. *Vogue* remarked that 'modern eyes, apt to approve slimness, rest appreciatively on the spare elegance that results from this decree'.[63] In August, *Vogue* promoted 'The Look-Alive Look' as 'today's new beauty standard'.[64] This was the 'kind of beauty we hunger for today' and was to be found in '*feeling* healthily alive. And it is *looking* glowingly healthy.' To achieve this look readers needed to embrace 'four fundamental cosmetics . . . which don't come out of jars and bottles':[65] sleep, a proper diet, exercise and relaxation. Appropriate clothes were pictured as informal and ingénue, represented by the bike-riding model photographed in knee-length socks, practical knee-length skirt and open-necked shirt with rolled-up sleeves. By spring 1944, this theme was still important. In an article called 'Beauty follows Fashion', *Vogue* saw beauty as an 'alchemy part fashion, part health, part person, plus a new magic—the fitness of things'.[66] In a clever play on words, this fitness was now applied to the snug fit of simple clothing lines around the honed and athletic fashion figure. The stylish woman now looked to 'the way a head fits a hat; a hand fits a glove; a fashion fits a time. . . . Smooth fit is beauty at work in 1944.' To achieve this look, women were counselled to 'Take exercise. Make time. Fit fashion to you.'[67] The slim, toned figure remained fashionable into 1945, but some subtle changes were now developing. In an article entitled 'New Clothes Need a Figure', *Vogue* suggested women look again at honing theirs in readiness for the fashions coming. 'At best' the figure now was 'long. The legs are springy, the hips flat, the neck straight, the shoulders wide', and a main point of emphasis in this upright, spare image was the waist. With new attention being paid in clothing to accentuating the waist, exercises were suggested to lose extra inches, and a Susan Small advertisement for February 1945 revealed the way fashion appeared to be headed.[68] The cinched-in waist and flared peplum, later emblematic of Dior's New Look, had already begun to evolve.[69]

Fashion during the remaining war years consolidated along the lines of the softly tailored suit in durable wool fabrics, the button-through shirt dress or variations on this theme and interchangeable two-piece outfits where skirt suits, jackets and blouses became part of mix-and-match wardrobes offering variety with economy. Changes came through use of detail, not silhouette, and in June 1943, *Picture Post* warned its readers not to 'ache to find something "different"'[70] and confirmed that the slower pace of fashion had allowed time for improvement in general standards of dress with style residing in the successful combination of simplicity with thoughtful accessorizing. The 'really good lines and fabrics' had 'time to crystallize' and 'classic clothes fit the mood of today'.[71] Once bought, a garment had to give service for an indefinite period of time and for a variety of different occasions. By November 1943, *Vogue* was reaffirming the necessity for the 'Good Coat and the Good Suit' with 'value being paramount at every income level'.[72] Key themes for the wardrobe remained classic, interchangeable pieces and accessories, in practical yet varied colours and weaves. Fashion had 'few surprises, few thrills', and small developments, such as the collarless suits of late 1943 or the larger decorative stitching on coats for spring 1944, worked within the strictly limited design parameters of Utility and austerity.[73] Cutaway jackets and bright contrast binding were further apparently new details for spring 1944 grafted onto the lean and tailored look.

Fashion continued to reflect the conservative, cylindrical and interchangeable. Capsule wardrobes were intrinsic to coupon value, but a mild note of dissatisfaction had begun to creep into *Vogue* editorial. Might not more variety be achieved within the rules?[74] Hartnell's recently exhibited collection of wire mannequin dolls dressed in the traditional costumes of the countries of Latin America had provided a colourful and opulent spectacle that *Picture Post* reported as a 'mental feast for luxury-starved women's eyes' that had inspired 'a number of vivid ideas for not-so-Utility fashion touches'.[75] When the first Paris collections appeared after the liberation of August 1944,[76] the British public again witnessed a splendour much out of kilter with domestic austerity restrictions.[77] British fashion now began to look ahead to its own future, both with regard to its place in the world of fashion and the type of fashions peace would bring.

In September 1944, *Vogue* asked, 'Where is fashion going?'[78] Comparing the classic simplicity of contemporary British and American clothing with the highly sculpted, curvaceous lines revealed by Paris, the question arose of how women would want to dress in the future and why. *Vogue* believed that fashion changes were not 'imposed by the experts. They arise from a deeply felt, shared impulse among women.'[79] Opinion varied but revolved substantially around the contending merits of the current active, neat chic or the sensual opulence suggested by Hartnell's miniature South American collection that had proved popular for its exuberance and colour. *Vogue*'s desire for greater variety in all likelihood reflected a broader view that, while it was unpatriotic to complain, and British clothing was undoubtedly better in quality than pre-war, it had become predictable and prosaic. In November, *Vogue* was hoping that the austerity regulations could be dispensed with as soon as practicable so that designers could regain their freedom, the unspoken likely agenda here being that Britain could then become competitive in less restricted markets elsewhere.[80]

The year ended, however, with few variations on the familiar themes of tailored outerwear, slender-waisted daywear and coordinated knits. There were no firm indications of fashion change. While the rhetoric might grumble slightly, the party line supporting wartime chic did not waiver. By the early months of 1945, some changes, consistent with the regulations, were evident. These followed the more rounded feminine lines that had been suggested by Paris, both in the first images to appear immediately after the liberation and in the somewhat more restrained shows held in the autumn of 1944.[81] There was a gentle softening of the familiar box shape, achieved in a number of small ways, all of which seemed to indicate a less angular line for the future and a move away from the stricter symmetries that had underpinned civilian clothing. In March 1945, *Vogue* believed 'fashion is going feminine' and described how there were 'tricks' to create a more natural rounded shoulder. Revers were becoming more rounded, as well as jacket edgings, and the waist, the key design feature of this look, was contrived to look very fitted by careful seaming and/or a belt.[82] *Vogue* also confirmed that the optical illusion of the narrower waist was being achieved by some gathering of front and back bodice pieces and hip pleating. Even padding was being used in certain belted coats. Skirts were to have a 'distinct suppleness' with 'slight flares, small gathers . . . fullness mainly at the front . . . though some swing it to the back'.[83] Here were early indications of an evolving aesthetic much at odds with wartime simplicity. War lines had relied on no artificial aids to silhouette other than shoulder pads and, for those still requiring support, a decent corset when one could be had. Now elements of an arguably retrogressive repertoire of design subterfuges were beginning to creep back. If *Vogue* was right, Parisian designers working with more curvaceous lines were anticipating what women really wanted. In the same way, British designers were sensing the need for some level of change after three and a half years of rationing and over two and a half years of austerity regulations. British and French designers worked in parallel and within the means at their disposal to reorientate clothing away from the severity of wartime style in the context of approaching peace. The smart, efficient, poised silhouettes of wartime civilian clothing had represented a nation facing up to war. Now, 'throughout fashion, there is a reaction against anything that looks hard, sharp, cold, bold. Every couturier emphasises femininity. We hear of much print: of soft-detailed satin blouses to counteract the sternness of tweeds: of smoother, more dressy materials.'[84] The rhetoric alone expressed the sense of change coming, not only in the visual appearance of clothing, but in what that clothing stood for.

# Conclusion

This work has endeavoured to provide a comprehensive account of dress and dress practice for women during the Second World War. A range of social, economic, political and aesthetic factors created the infrastructure for the making and wearing of clothing in the years immediately before and during the war, and only by exploring these all together can a truly critical understanding of the visual narratives of dress be reached. At the same time, the bringing together of different types of history around the central focus of dress has endorsed the proposition that such a history offers its own specific and distinct cultural discourse.

Contemporary understanding of, and attitudes towards, dress and style, both before and during the war, have been revealing of the way society was structured by class and how the changing social and political priorities of war had an impact on the types of clothing worn and the methods of purchasing clothing on the high street. Having begun to experience a growing consumer culture in the years before the war, Britain was forced to make stringent consumer retrenchments in order to maintain adequate standards of civilian dress alongside war demands for textiles and garments. As the availability of raw materials became less certain and the goods they produced more rigorously restricted, the capacity for shopping on the high street was significantly reduced and pre-war patterns of spending effectively reversed. What people could now buy and the mechanisms adopted to constitute fair shares for the whole population brought about revised practices in domestic economy and a reevaluation of what type of clothing it was either necessary or appropriate to own and wear in wartime conditions. Attitudes towards buying new changed considerably, and as civilian life continued to place different demands on women, gradual but distinctive shifts in dress style resulted reflective of the changing social circumstances.

There were no sudden breaks from the ideas of good taste and dressing well that had underpinned the clothing priorities of the past. Alice Settle's belief that taste resided in simple, chic style gained even greater currency for wartime when the elaborate or overly elegant became out of kilter with busy and unpredictable wartime lives. This clearly affected the dress practice of the more affluent classes rather than those on limited incomes for whom the restricted opportunities to buy and the need to make-do and mend were all-too-familiar aspects of daily life. Practicality and flexibility became key wardrobe elements, and the familiar tailored and smart dresses, suits and coats evocative of a distinctive British fashion during the pre-war years now submitted to the subtle revisions appropriate to wartime use. The need for economy, however, from fabric construction to finished garment on the high street, was the most influential factor operating on fashion's advance during the wartime years. Limitation of supplies severely curtailed the amount of material available for the civilian clothing and domestic textiles market, undermining and in due course eliminating much of the choice that had existed in fabrics and clothing ranges before the war. The occasion clothing and dress diversity that had defined pre-war days and seasons for the better-off were also much reduced, and the designs that continued to be produced reflected a war-ready aesthetic that arguably offered better quality for more people, if in more limited ranges and styles. Women were encouraged to approach fashion with greater resourcefulness and ingenuity to make the most out of what they already had and of what the high street could now offer. Fashion became more democratic by default as limitations and rationing created the new dress priorities associated with patriotic thrift.

The methods of production that had sustained commercial buoyancy in women's fashions on the high street prior to war now offered models for wartime volume production with the result that the sound marketing methodologies and merchandising practices already established by chains such as Marks and Spencer created continuities between pre-war and wartime manufacturing. These were progressed in the context of developing technologies in garment make and finish. Where products were found wanting in value for money, where quality was not commensurate with wear, government found ways, in conjunction with the clothing industries, of ameliorating bad practice and encouraging better production and an ever more fit-for-purpose standard of clothing. Thus from pre-war to wartime, the buying and wearing of clothing went from greater to less choice but from less predictable to more predictable quality and value.

New perspectives on social need, opened up by the process of evacuation, revealed shocking levels of social deprivation in British society. This was particularly reflected in the inadequate amount and substandard quality clothing worn by a deeply disadvantaged sector of the population. Confrontation with such highly visual poverty, in tandem with an escalating cost-of-living index, were crucial factors that induced government to exert strenuous quality controls on both textile construction and clothing manufacture and direct and regulate prices. Costs had to be controlled and the specific needs of the disadvantaged addressed if unanimity of purpose across society as a whole was to be maintained. Rationing, Utility and the austerity restrictions together created the complex economic and social solution to the problem of clothing the civilian nation at war.

As women assumed more responsibilities beyond the home, particularly where this involved taking over men's jobs, there was growing public recognition that women were now revealing skills and qualities that extended more traditional notions of femininity. The adoption by women of work clothes and overalls usually worn by men, while entirely practical, emphasized this shift in function. Alongside of an often-cautious acceptance of the developing range of clothing women could now wear, the fresh-faced soap-and-water beauty associated with a more practical, relaxed style introduced another perspective on the nature of femininity in contrast to the often-poised and artificial charm of pre-war years.

Renewed emphasis on home crafts and patriotic thrift created diversity of design within a culture of austerity. As everyday dressing began to include the products of making-do and recycling, an alternative type of fashion arose that would became a significant component of wartime style. As a result, less rigid and inflexible dress practices emerged accepting of a broader and potentially challenging range of clothing most noticeable in practical and informal wear. Maintaining a sufficient wardrobe of wearable clothes in the face of commercial limitations and lack of choice united women across classes in principle, if not always in practice, and provided firm foundations for a make-do culture that underpinned and strengthened new priorities for national economy and greater self-sufficiency. It also opened up more distant continuities with a past before ready-made clothing solutions had presented themselves when hand-made had been fundamental in providing clothes, accessories and the distinctive refinements of personal dress. The strong presence of a female culture supporting home-craft initiatives within the home and community clearly acted as a corollary to the greater visibility of women in home front defence roles and helped consolidate a view of woman as capable, imaginative and lateral thinking. This was especially born out through the application of home-crafting skills to shortfalls in essential supplies of domestic, community and national clothing.

Altering social and economic perspectives that emerged in the face of failing infrastructures of public assistance and domestic welfare created a new desire for fairness and political inclusion that broke with a less democratic past. The clothes rationing system and its corollaries in terms of Utility and the austerity programmes were all founded on the principal of fair shares and the prospect of a better quality of life that came with sound commodities at affordable prices. The tiered approach to Utility production provided various, if limited, cloth ranges across a now much-circumscribed price spectrum, all of reasonable quality so that there would be clothes in price bands that virtually all could afford. The scheme was not intended to erode class difference, nor did it. Rather, it ensured all classes had adequate clothing at appropriate prices. In this way, it made its own contribution towards a type of democratization of fashion. This was neither complete nor lasting but revealed a conscious desire to neutralize an inappropriate level of social privilege on the one hand and relieve real distress and hardship on the other. Full employment was the economic fulcrum upon which a reorientating war economy turned, which largely eradicated residual elements of long-term unemployment and dependence on the dole and enabled the newly employed to now have access to value goods, however limited in choice, with a durability and fitness for purpose some had never known. This reflected a signal and a significant break with the past as it halted the cycle of deprivation and brought about new prosperity and hope for the future.

Clothing control in all its complexity provided an economic infrastructure that facilitated the design, production and distribution of appropriate and sufficient clothing for a nation at war. Unfit merchandise and exploitative selling mechanisms were rendered largely unnecessary by the combined results of controlled manufacture and extended employment opportunities so that there is little doubt that the standard of clothing of the poorest communities was improved. The desire to implement rationing can be seen as a testament to the Board of Trade's perception of the broader cultural significance of having access to adequate and affordable clothing by right.

Finally, in design terms, women's clothing in general continued to reflect the classic slim lines of the 1930s. Skirts and dresses did not become redundant in the face of the various forms of practical and work-related clothing, and off-duty women still enjoyed dressing up in much the same way as before the war. Standards of good taste became less rigid in accepting the new functionality of certain garments but in other ways remained relatively untouched by the war years. Designers continued to advocate a less-is-more style whether in terms of the tailored classic or simple soft separates for casual wear, consolidating a British fashion that came to represent the lasting design signature of the war years.

# Notes

## INTRODUCTION

1. Comforts referred to the home-made garments that supplemented the official supply of wartime clothing for serving personnel.

## CHAPTER 1 BUYING INTO FASHION

1. The term *ready-made* has a specific meaning in the history of fashion, with origins in the eighteenth-century seaport 'slop shops'. The garment manufacturers that supplied such enterprises were 'well-established' by the early nineteenth century. See E. Wilson and L. Taylor, *Through the Looking Glass* (BBC Books, 1989), p. 33.
2. P. Brendon, *The Dark Valley: A Panorama of the 1930s* (Jonathan Cape, 2000), p. 367.
3. A. De Courcy, *1939: The Last Season* (Thames and Hudson, 1989), p. 14.
4. Ibid., p. 32. De Courcy explains that 'marriage—to the right sort of man, needless to say—was both goal and expected destination. And to achieve the best, in terms of both love and money, a wide acquaintance and careful preparation were necessary. These, fortunately, could be achieved through that established ritual known as the Season'.
5. For a full description of some of the gowns and outfits worn during these occasions see Ibid., pp. 36–42.
6. Ibid., p. 15.
7. N. Hartnell, *Silver and Gold* (Evans Brothers, 1955), p. 62.
8. J. Mulvagh, *Vogue History of Twentieth Century Fashion* (Bloomsbury Books, 1992), p. 132.
9. Ibid., p. 125.
10. G. O'Hara, *The Encyclopaedia of Fashion from 1840 to the 1980s* (Thames and Hudson, 1989), p. 213. Schiaparelli also used rhodophane—a 'mixture of cellophane and other synthetics developed in the 1920s by the French fabric company Colcombet'. Ibid. Mulvagh described this fabric as creating 'glass-like tunics' in line with the popular silhouette of the day. See Mulvagh, *Vogue History*, p. 125.
11. Paillettes are flat metallic spangles sometimes called sequins that can come in a variety of sheens and colours, as opposed to rounded, elongated and hollow bugle beads. Both are decorative finishes adding

lustre and opulence. The description is as cited by Mulvagh, *Vogue History,* pp. 141–2.

12. O'Hara, *The Encyclopaedia of Fashion,* p. 183.
13. J. Struther, *Mrs Miniver* (Chatto and Windus, 1939).
14. The name *miniver* derives from a white fur, the ermine in winter coat. Whether the name was used deliberately by Struther is unknown.
15. Struther, *Mrs Miniver*, p. x. Struther was invited to write her column by Peter Fleming, the brother of Ian, who thought her background suited her to this topic. For a fuller account of Struther's life see Struther, *Mrs Miniver*, pp. vii–xiv.
16. H.M. Glancy, *When Hollywood Loved Britain: The Hollywood 'British' Film 1939–1945* (Manchester University Press, 1999), p. 142, quoting E.M. Forster, 'The Top Drawer But One', *New Statesman and Nation* (4 November 1939), p. 648.
17. J. Stevenson, *The Pelican Social History of Britain: British Society 1914–1945* (Penguin Books Ltd., 1984), pp. 340–1.
18. Ibid., p. 344.
19. P. Oliver, I. Davis, and I. Bentley, *Dunroamin: The Suburban Semi and Its Enemies* (Barrie and Jenkins, 1981), p. 71.
20. Wilson and Taylor, *Through the Looking Glass*, p. 78. See also Oliver, Davis and Bentley, *Dunroamin,* and R. Samuel, 'Suburbs under siege: The middle class between the wars', Part 111, *New Socialist* 11 (May/June 1983).
21. A clearer delineation of the shopping experiences of these class divisions will be addressed in Chapter 2, "Shopping for Fashion in the Pre-War Years."
22. J. Hilton, *Rich Man, Poor Man* (Allen and Unwin Ltd., 1944), p. 25.
23. Ibid., pp. 78–9.
24. Ibid., p. 92.
25. PRO, BT64/871. Rationing of Clothing and Footwear; Notice to the Public June 1st 1941.
26. To review working-class clothing costs within the cost of living index across the war years see E.L. Hargreaves and M.M. Gowing, *Civil Industry and Trade* (HMSO, 1952), p. 648. Clothing costs rose more than any other commodity in the index. See also this work, Chapter 9.

## CHAPTER 2 SHOPPING FOR FASHION IN THE PRE-WAR YEARS

1. E. Wilson and L. Taylor, *Through the Looking Glass* (BBC Books, 1989), p. 91.
2. R. Opie, *The 1930s Scrapbook* (New Cavendish Books, 1997), p. 4.

3. A. De Courcy, *1939: The Last Season* (Phoenix, 1989), p. 89. De Courcy suggests '"a good tweed suit will take you *anywhere*", mothers would tell their daughters in satisfied tones (no doubt caused in part by a subliminal recognition of its an-aphrodisiac qualities). It was worn with Aertex jerseys, shirts or blouses, wool or silk stockings according to the occasion, and highly polished brogues or, for racing, Newmarket boots'. Ibid., p. 89.
4. See this work, Chapter 14.
5. Wilson and Taylor, *Through the Looking Glass*, pp. 90–1.
6. Board of Trade, *The Working Party Report on Light Clothing* (HMSO, 1947), p. 8. See also M. Wray, *The Women's Outerwear Industry* (Duckworth and Co Ltd, 1957), p. 18. Wray goes on to discuss the development of ready-to-wear from these early beginnings through 'pioneer manufacturers [who] began in the 1890s and early 1900s, to produce aprons, mobcaps, sun bonnets, frillings, blouses, overalls and cloaks'. These included the Co-Operative Wholesale Society. After 1900, blouses and skirts were produced in response to new fashions, and Wray points out that, before 1914, these garments were created by manufacturers for sale to wholesalers, who would then distribute them amongst their retail clientele. A different model of production was established, however, by Dean and Thompson, who manufactured dresses and sold them directly to retail drapers through the system of using travellers to advertise their wares. Thus, at this early stage of pre-First World War supply, there were already two tiers of production for the light clothing industry, one where small manufacturers produced ranges for sale to wholesalers, who would then store and sell on, and the other where individual manufacturing concerns dealt directly with distributors. A further variant of this second method of practice saw the retailer initiating contact with the manufacturer for a specific product. See also footnote 60.
7. Board of Trade, *The Working Party Report*, p. 8.
8. Advertisements for women's clothing, particularly undergarments and corsetry, that appeared in magazines and newspapers during the later nineteenth and early twentieth century do, however, refer to apparel produced in small manufacturing (or sometimes wholesale) units. Outworkers, operating from small workshops, or home workers were also much used, and it was this form of production that became associated with sweated labour owing to the very low rates of pay and often poor environmental conditions in which the largely female operatives worked.
9. Board of Trade, *The Working Party Report*, p. 10.
10. Ibid., p. 10.
11. This work is not concerned with the development of industrial production in men's wear. However, it is an important trigger in the development of both the factory manufacture of clothing and, in due course,

the concept of mass production, and it is thus outlined briefly here. For further information on both the prerequisite mechanization and the early developers of the mass men's wear market see Board of Trade, *The Working Party Report*, pp. 8–9; J. Thomas, *A History of the Leeds Clothing Industry* (Universities of Hull, Leeds and Sheffield, 1955), Chapter 1, 'The Introduction of the Clothing Industry to Leeds', pp. 8–16; Wray, *The Women's Outerwear Industry*, pp. 16–17; K. Honeyman, Montague Burton Ltd: The Creators of Well-Dressed Men', in *Leeds City Business 1893–1993* (Leeds University Press, 1993), pp. 186–93; and A. Godley, *The Emergence of Mass Production in the UK Clothing Industry* (University of Reading, 1994–95).

12. The rise of John Barran in Leeds from 1852, Moses and Sons in London and other similar factory producers, as well as the men's multiple trading and wholesale bespoke market represented by Montague Burton from 1900 and Henry Price, both also in Leeds, are well covered in Thomas, *A History of the Leeds Clothing Industry*, pp. 8–14 and pp. 47–50; Honeyman 'Montague Burton Ltd', pp. 186–93; and G. Waddell, *How Fashion Works: Couture, Ready-to-Wear and Mass Production* (Blackwell Science Ltd, 2004), pp. 78–81.
13. S. Chapman, 'The Decline and Rise of Textile Merchanting 1880–1990', *Business History* 32/4 (1990), pp. 175–6.
14. See notes 6 and 60.
15. Wray cites 'a considerable production' after 1900 of 'ready-made blouses and skirts and also of coat frocks, in response to new fashion demands'. She footnotes that 'pre-1914 production was mainly for sale to wholesalers' and cross references the Board of Trade's *Working Party Reports Light Clothing*, pp. 10–11, Wray, *The Women's Outerwear Industry*, pp. 18–19. From 1907, as this report pointed out, the light clothing industry 'consisted chiefly of manufacturers of the following merchandise which was sold mainly to the wholesaler: dress skirts, underskirts, blouses, underclothing, aprons and overalls and infants' pinafores. . . . The apron trade flourished and the overall was beginning to take the place of the apron'. Board of Trade, *The Working Party Report*, pp. 10–11.
16. Wray, *The Women's Outerwear Industry*, p. 19.
17. Minimum wages and working hours were brought in for women's wear in 1919, and the demise of cheap labour sources was largely caused by a ban on immigration in 1918 that affected the continued employment of cheap Jewish labour. Ibid., p. 19.
18. Ibid., p. 19.
19. Godley, *The Emergence of Mass Production*, p. 21. Godley states that 'already before 1914, [men's wear] was being reduced to a series of standardized products, susceptible to mass- production and mass marketing

techniques, thus allowing a few firms to grow and dominate the market, with Montague Burton being the most obvious example'. Ibid., p. 21.

20. Ibid., p. 23.
21. Honeyman provides an aerial view of Burton's vast Hudson Road Mill site, which was purchased in 1920 (Honeyman, 'Montague Burton Ltd', p. 193), while Thomas states that in addition to Burton's five Leeds factories already working to full capacity, he bought the Hudson Road Estate and 'made plans for the building of the largest clothing factory in the world. In 1921 when the firm celebrated its coming-of-age, it was already the largest clothing manufacturing company in Europe, with shops in the West End of London and most provincial towns'. Thomas, *A History of the Leeds Clothing Industry*, p. 52.
22. Wray, *The Women's Outerwear Industry*, p. 20. Wray describes a number of different improvements enhancing factory output of women's wear including better quality lockstitch, felling and buttonholing facilities, as well as the adaptation of lockstitch machinery for hemming and facing so that these processes no longer needed to be done by hand. See also Board of Trade, *The Working Party Report*, p. 14, which comments on the variety of decorative surface work and stitching available to the industry that can be achieved 'not only by hand, but by the use of numerous types of machines and accessories. . . . These include hemstitching, cornelly, faggotting, tucking, gauging, scalloping and pinking machines.' These machines also helped the industry create a diverse range of products out of the relatively simple dress shapes of the later 1920s and the 1930s through variations in the details of the making-up and by the addition of various forms of surface decoration.
23. Wray, *The Women's Outerwear Industry*, p. 39.
24. Ibid., pp. 40–1.
25. Ibid., p. 41, and see also chapters 9 and 14.
26. Ibid., p. 34.
27. Ibid., p. 28. Wray points out that there are no separate figures for women's wear, p. 27.
28. I am dependent on Wray again as she provides the most comprehensive and accurate account of the development of factory production. Ibid., p. 30.
29. Ibid., p. 21, 25.
30. These examples were not the first to establish named brands from manufacturing businesses. Chapman cites various manufacturers before the end of the nineteenth century who, in order to break away from a dependency on wholesalers and wholesalers' charges, created their 'own brands with consumers, which gave . . . opportunity to increase profit . . . and establish . . . marketing organisations'. These included

'Horrocks of Preston, Hollins (Vyella Shirts) and Wolsey (underwear)', amongst others. Chapman, 'The Decline and Rise of Textile Merchanting', pp. 176–7.

31. Chapman is clear that branded goods, from their inception, did not entirely sidestep the wholesaler even though they had often been created to do just that. Small amounts of branded merchandise continued to be sold by wholesalers, and he suggests that 'in press advertisements the branded goods manufacturers were at pains to stress that they only sold through particular warehouses'. Ibid., p. 177.
32. See Godley, *The Emergence of Mass Production*, pp. 21–2.
33. Board of Trade, *The Working Party Report*, p. 11. See also Wray, *The Women's Outerwear Industry*, pp. 20–1.
34. Board of Trade, *The Working Party Report*, p. 9.
35. Wray, *The Women's Outerwear Industry*, p. 22.
36. E. Ostick, *What You Should Know about Cloth* (The Tailor and Cutter Ltd, [1936?–1939?], p. 15, 41.
37. Ibid., p. 41, 46.
38. Ibid., p. 41.
39. Ibid., p. 46.
40. Wray, *The Women's Outerwear Industry*, p. 23. The report gives the figures of £5,473,000 and £3,168,999 for rayon and cotton respectively. For the broader economic history of British production of rayon see Wray pp. 22–3.
41. Wilson and Taylor, *Through the Looking Glass*, p. 98.
42. E.L. Hargreaves and M.M. Gowing, *Civil Industry and Trade* (HMSO, 1952), p. 12.
43. The only other new fabric of note was nylon. First produced in 1938 for the Du Pont company in Delaware, USA, it had no impact on the home market in Britain. It is worth footnoting, however, as it was made into stockings in the United States by 1940, and some of these arrived in Britain from 1942 onwards as unofficial imports via US services personnel. Nylon was also the 'only approved silk substitute for man-carrying parachutes', and its production rose during the war from 'nothing to one million lbs a year'. Ibid., p. 373.
44. M. Spring Rice, *Working Class Wives: Their Health and Conditions* (Virago, 1981, first published Penguin, 1939).
45. Ibid., p. 212.
46. Ibid., pp. 170–2.
47. I. Sieff, *Memoirs* (Weidenfeld and Nicolson, 1970), pp. 56–8.
48. A. Briggs, *Marks & Spencer Limited 1884–1984* (Octopus Books, 1984), p. 17. Briggs suggests Marks may have traded in the towns of Castleford and Wakefield.

49. The exact date at which Marks began the penny trading is not known. See Briggs, *Marks & Spencer*, p. 18. Helen Chislett gives a slightly different version of this story in *Marks in Time: 125 Years of Marks & Spencer* (Weidenfeld and Nicolson, 2009), p. 9, suggesting that Marks's poor English had already caused him to coin the slogan 'Don't Ask the Price, It's a Penny' to append to his pedlar's tray.
50. Briggs cites dealing in 'ironmongery, turnery, household fittings and utensils, ornaments, pictures, works of art, stationery and fancy goods . . . hardware, safes, clocks and watches, jewellery, plated goods, glass, leather goods, photo-components, musical instruments', as well as the role of Marks and Spencer as 'drapers, upholsterers, decorators, furniture removers, depositories and manufacturers as well as dealers'. See Briggs, *Marks & Spencer Limited 1884–198,* p. 26.
51. Ibid., p. 74.
52. This rate was subsequently reduced in 1922–1923 because of an economic slump and was not raised again until 1937. By 1946, the rate was 1s 3d per hour or 1s 4½d for piece or conveyor workers. See Board of Trade, *The Working Party Report*, p. 10. Interestingly, Walter Greenwood's young apprentice engineer living at home, in his fictionalized account of the poverty in Salford in the early 1930s, had 1s a week to spend in 1933. This, together with the half crown's worth of tips earned from his works, made him feel well off. See W. Greenwood, *Love on the Dole* (Jonathan Cape, 1933), pp. 56–8. This again puts the pricing policy of Marks and Spencer into perspective.
53. Briggs, *Marks & Spencer Limited 1884–1984*, p. 22.
54. Sieff, *Memoirs*, p. 141.
55. Chislett, *Marks in Time* (Weidenfeld and Nicolson, 2009), pp. 18–19.
56. R. Worth, *Fashion for the People: A History of Clothing at Marks & Spencer* (Berg, 2007), quoting Sieff, *Memoirs*, p. 21.
57. Wray, *The Women's Outerwear Industry* p. 36.
58. Sieff, *Memoirs*, pp. 144–5.
59. Wray, *The Women's Outerwear Industry*, p. 37, quoting L. E. Neal, *Retailing and the Public* (Aberdeen University Press Ltd, 1932), p. 51.
60. Chapman, 'The Decline and Rise of Textile Merchanting', p. 178. Chapman interestingly writes, 'The pressure of the WTA is evident in the advertisements of branded goods manufacturers, in which they insisted that they sold only through the wholesalers; in reality many of them were simultaneously involved in subterfuges to sell direct to chain stores'. Chapman goes on to say that 'as late as 1953, the WTA was advertising in the *Drapers' Record* that the "Wholesaler ensures that only the cream of the world's production is presented to the retail trade. He enables the Shopkeeper to examine the products of hundreds of manufacturers

under one roof . . . " By such pressures, the old merchant houses were able to resist the tide of change for a couple of generations', leading to their eventual 'incorporation into vertical combines' in the 1960s. Thus the wholesaler offered choice, which arguably was the advantage over something more specific between retailer and manufacturer.

61. Sieff, *Memoirs*, p. 150. The customers referred to were likely to be wholesalers, possibly with more upmarket business.
62. Ibid., pp. 150–1. Sieff also confirmed that establishing this type of business had been 'hard going for several years. We did not have the same good fortune with all the manufacturers. Several of them used to come in at the back door of our offices in London for several years: if they had been . . . spotted by somebody in the Wholesalers' Association . . . they would have been . . . expelled from that, then, august body.' Ibid., p. 153.
63. Ibid., p. 153.
64. Ibid., p. 154.
65. Ibid.
66. Wray, *The Women's Outerwear Industry*, p. 37.
67. J.B. Jefferys, *Retail Trading in Britain 1850–1950* (Cambridge University Press, 1954), pp. 341–2.
68. Hargreaves and Gowing, *Civil Industry and Trade*, p. 373. It is interesting to note that by the outbreak of war, the chain stores had become 'a more important outlet, measured by value of sales, for underwear and hosiery than the specialist women's wear multiple shop organizations'. See Jefferys, *Retail Trading in Britain*, p. 342.
69. Jefferys, *Retail Trading in Britain*, p. 340.
70. Wray, *The Women's Outerwear Industry*, pp. 37–8. Wilson and Taylor also place the level of true mass production in context when they cite figures from a Board of Trade survey of 1942 reporting that of '842 firms in the women's tailoring trades 1 per cent were using the conveyor belt system (complete mechanisation), 40 per cent the sectional system (whereby individual workers concentrated on one part or section of a garment, making sleeves or collars all day) and 50 per cent the complete garment (one skilled worker making up a whole garment); for 807 dress, blouse and overall manufacturers the figures were 2 per cent, 18 per cent and 72 per cent'. See Wilson and Taylor, *Through the Looking Glass*, p. 101. This report was also carried out after a substantial amount of concentration within the cotton and wool industries, which reduced the number of small firms and tended to favour businesses with higher production capacity. See Hargreaves and Gowing, *Civil Industry and Trade*, p. 354, 390.
71. Jefferys, *Retail Trading in Britain*, pp. 333–4. Jefferys comments that some 'four fifths of hosiery goods were branded at the end of the inter-war years', citing H. A. Silverman, *Studies in Industrial Organization* (Methuen & Co., 1946), p. 9.

72. See BBC TV series *Through the Looking Glass,* first broadcast BBC2 November 1989, produced by S. Davis and R. Albury, Part 2, 'Health and Beauty off the Peg', for further information on the 'madam' shop; see also Wilson and Taylor, *Through the Looking Glass*, pp. 93–4.
73. The practice of wholesalers selling small amounts of goods had been made necessary by the turn of the century. Chapman quoting the *Statist* journal for 1897 stated that the 'little shopkeepers' who by this time were beginning to be in direct competition with the larger department stores wanted 'more and more concessions from the warehouses in the way of making up small parcels, such as quarter dozens, one-sixth dozens, and perhaps now and then one-twelfth dozens, until it is hard to distinguish so-called wholesale from retail trade'. See Chapman, 'The Decline and Rise of Textile Merchanting', p. 176.
74. All wholesaling material from the Hodson Shop Dress Collection. I am indebted to the staff of Walsall Museum for making available clothes from both the Hodson Shop Collection and the Museum's complementary garment collection as well as information on wholesalers used by the Hodson sisters, complete with invoices. The buying of very small amounts of wholesale clothing is evident here. Sheila Shreave, Curator, Hodson Shop Collection, states the shop's profit margin was 'only 20q'. Shop prices can be estimated from this (unpublished notes sent to author).
75. *Vogue* (25 January 25 1939), p. 48.
76. Ibid., p. 42.
77. Briggs, *Marks & Spencer*, p. 59.
78. M. Tebbutt, *Making Ends Meet: Pawnbroking and Working Class Credit* (Leicester University Press, 1983), p. 157.
79. Briggs, *Marks & Spencer*, p. 119.
80. Wray, *The Women's Outerwear Industry*, p. 30.
81. Worth, *Fashion for the People*, p. 41.
82. Briggs, *Marks & Spencer*, pp. 53–4.
83. The work of the laboratory and the merchandise development unit will be returned to in Chapter 9, 'The Utility Clothing Scheme'. See also Sieff, *Memoirs*, pp. 156–7; Worth, *Fashion for the People*, pp. 42–44; Chislett, *Marks in Time*, p. 32, for information on these two departments.
84. J. Hilton, *Rich Man, Poor Man* (Allen and Unwin Ltd, 1944), p. 115.
85. P. Oliver, I. Davis and I. Bentley, *Dunroamin: The Suburban Semi and Its Enemies* (Barrie and Jenkins, 1981), p. 71.
86. Since 1914, department stores had become more varied in terms of target customer, providing for both the 'high-medium' and 'medium-low' income brackets. Medium-priced stores included Lewis's of Manchester and Liverpool and Blacketts of Sunderland. See Jefferys, *Retail Trading in Britain*, p. 345.

87. Wilson and Taylor, *Through the Looking Glass*, pp. 91-2; J. Clark and A. de la Haye, *Jaeger 125* (Jaeger, 2009), p.42; see also J. Mulvagh, *Vogue History of Twentieth Century Fashion* (Bloomsbury Books, 1992), p. 124.
88. Jefferys, *Retail Trading in Britain*, pp. 339–41.

## CHAPTER 3 BEING CHIC AND BEING BRITISH

1. A. Settle, *Clothes Line* (Methuen and Co, 1937). Settle became editor of British *Vogue* in 1926.
2. Ibid., p. 140. It is useful to remember that the general housekeeping budget for some of the very poorest and/or unemployed families interviewed by Margery Spring Rice for her 1939 study, *Working Class Wives: Their Health and Conditions*, was as low as four shillings or under, per head per week, or about sixteen shillings a month, with better-off families having ten shillings or over, per head per week, or about forty shillings per month. This money had to stretch to cover all housekeeping needs; see Chapter 4 for more on Spring Rice and M. Spring Rice, *Working Class Wives: Their Health and Conditions* (Virago, 1981), p. 212. In this context, a dress allowance in the region of one hundred pounds a year purely for clothing and similar personal needs was very generous. As a couture dress, however, could cost forty-five pounds, as suggested in the previous chapter, and a commissioned suit twenty-five guineas or more during wartime (see Chapter 14), one hundred pounds was also not representative of a really wealthy woman's resources. See this work, chapters 4 and 10, for other budget examples.
3. Ibid., p. 88.
4. Ibid., pp. 137–8.
5. Ibid., p. 138.
6. Ibid., pp. 123–4.
7. Ibid., p. 139.
8. Ibid.
9. Ibid., pp. 184–5.
10. Ibid., p. 137.
11. Ibid.
12. J. Mulvagh, *Vogue History of Twentieth Century Fashion* (Bloomsbury Books, 1992), p. 150.
13. Ibid., p. 151.
14. Ibid.
15. The specific reasons for this will be discussed in detail in Chapter 6.
16. 'The Case for Slacks', *Vogue* (May 1939), p. 57.

17. Ibid., p. 58.
18. A. De Courcy, *1939: The Last Season* (Phoenix, 1989), p. 94.
19. 'The Cases for Slacks', *Vogue*, pp. 57–8.
20. *Vogue Pattern Book* (June–July 1939), p. 8.
21. Settle, *Clothes Line*, p. 164.
22. Ibid., p. 164.
23. Ibid., p. 168.
24. Ibid., pp. 168–9.
25. Ibid., pp. 82–6.
26. Ibid., p. 82.
27. Ibid.
28. Ibid., pp. 82–3.
29. Ibid., p. 84.

## CHAPTER 4 THE HEALTHY BODY AND THE POLITICS OF FITNESS

1. *Vogue Beauty Book* (23 August 1939), p. 7.
2. Ibid., p. 57.
3. J. Stevenson, *The Pelican Social History of Britain: British Society 1914–1945* (Penguin Books, 1984), p. 388.
4. Ibid., p. 389.
5. G. Horseman, *Growing Up in the Thirties* (Cottage Publishing, 1994), p. 237.
6. Stevenson, *The Pelican Social History of Britain*, p. 392.
7. Horseman, *Growing Up in the Thirties*, p. 218.
8. Ibid., p. 216.
9. Stevenson, *The Pelican Social History of Britain*, p. 392.
10. Ibid.
11. C. Wilk, 'The Healthy Body Culture', in *Modernism: Designing a New World 1914–1939* (Victoria and Albert Publications, 2006), pp. 256–7. This article is excellent in putting the idea of the fit and healthy body into its broader European context.
12. Ibid., p. 258.
13. E. Wilson and L. Taylor, *Through the Looking Glass: A History of Dress from 1860 to the Present Day* (BBC Books, 1989), p. 76.
14. For a fuller picture of the *Volksgemeinschaft* and the reorientation of the family in the Third Reich see L. Pine, *Nazi Family Policy 1933–1945* (Berg, 1999), chapters 1 and 2.
15. P. Bagot Stack, *Zest for Life: Mollie Bagot Stack and the League of Health and Beauty* (Peter Owen, 1988), p. 101.

16. Ibid.
17. Ibid., p. 104.
18. Ibid.
19. Ibid., p. 110.
20. Ibid., p. 117.
21. Ibid., p. 125.
22. Ibid., p. 114.
23. Ibid., p. 126.
24. Ibid., p. 136.
25. Ibid.
26. Ibid., p. 137.
27. M. Spring Rice, *Working Class Wives: Their Health and Conditions* (Virago, 1981).
28. Ibid., p. 212
29. D. Beddoe, *Back to Home and Duty: Women between the Wars 1918–1939* (Pandora, 1989), p. 112.
30. Spring Rice, *Working Class Wives*, p. xv.
31. B. Cartland, in J. Hartley, *Hearts Undefeated: Women's Writings of the Second World War* (Virago, 1994), p. 115.
32. Spring Rice, *Working Class Wives*, p. xv.
33. Ibid., p. 207.
34. Ibid., p. 69, and see also Beddoe, *Back to Home and Duty*, p. 111.
35. Beddoe, *Back to Home and Duty*, p. 20.
36. Ibid. Beddoe also mentions in this context the work of Dr. Truby King, who emerged as the 'chief authority' on child care at this time. See also Evelyn Pantin, SCN, *Preparing for Motherhood and Training in Infancy and Childhood* (Thorsons Publishers Ltd, 1932), and republished seven times between this date and 1943.
37. Ibid.
38. Ibid., p. 104. (See also this work, Chapter 1, alluding to the new housing estates.)
39. Ibid., p. 104.
40. R.M. Titmus, *Problems of Social Policy* (HMSO, 1950), p. 21.
41. Ibid.
42. Ibid., p. 18.
43. Ibid., p. 19.
44. Ibid., p. 18.
45. Ibid., p. 17.
46. Ibid. Titmus writes that when a 'special committee was established in 1937 to review the air raid precautions, hospital and fire brigade schemes, the maintenance of the morale of the people was stated to be the first aim of these services', p. 21. See also Ibid., Chapter 3, 'Preparations: Evacuation', pp. 23–44.

47. Ibid., p. 17. It is interesting to see the prescience in H.G. Well's 1898 fictional account of the mass exodus from London in Chapter 16 of *War of the Worlds*, where panic and frenzy to escape is described as the 'liquefaction of the social body'. See H.G. Wells, *The War of the Worlds* (Pan, 1975), p. 99. See also Alexander Korda's 1936 film, *Things to Come*, directed by William Cameron Menzies and with a screenplay by H.G. Wells, picturing London and then Britain reduced to wreckage during a world war in 1940.
48. Ibid., p. 20.
49. Ibid.

## CHAPTER 5 EVACUATION

1. See S. Rose, *Which People's War?: National Identity and Citizenship in Wartime Britain 1939–1945* (Oxford University Press, 2003), p. 30.
2. Stevenson clarifies that the Jarrow action was, in fact, 'one of the smallest' hunger marches and that it sidestepped politics and 'disassociated itself' from other action over unemployment organized by the NUWM with which it coincided. J. Stephenson, *The Pelican Social History of Britain: British Society 1914–1945* (Penguin, 1986), p. 291.
3. Ibid.
4. Rose, *Which People's War?* p. 31.
5. Ibid., quoting R. Graves and A. Hodge, *The Long Week-End: A Social History of Great Britain, 1918–1939* (W. W. Norton, 1994; originally published 1940), pp. 391–3.
6. R.M. Titmus, *Problems of Social Policy* (HMSO, 1950), p. 116.
7. Ibid.
8. Ibid. See also Ministry of Information, *Home Front Handbook* (first issued 15 September 1943, reprinted Imperial War Museum 2005), Chapter 14, 'Social Services', pp. 52–6, for a comprehensive account of the provision for national health insurance, unemployment insurance, unemployment assistance, public assistance and pensions. Winifred Holtby gives a moving fictional account of a Public Assistance Committee in session in *South Riding* (BBC Books, 2011, originally published 1935), pp. 297–309.
9. D. Ibberson, *Our Towns* (Oxford University Press, 1943). This publication was compiled by the Hygiene Committee for the Women's Group for Public Welfare and written up by Dora Ibberson. It was a specialist study of 'the conditions of town life [as disclosed by evacuation] in England which might be held responsible for those features in the physical condition, habits and conduct of the evacuees which were the subject of complaint by their hostesses' (p. X1). The study was conducted between 1939

and 1942 and was initially undertaken because of the deep concern expressed at the conditions of evacuees by the National Federation of Women's Institutes. The Women's Institutes were largely associated with the countryside (as opposed to the towns' Women's Guilds) and were thus on hand to witness the problems arising out of the social mismatch of the evacuation scheme.

10. Ibid., p. 55.
11. Ibid., p. 54.
12. Titmus, *Problems of Social Policy*, p. 117.
13. Ibid., p. 118.
14. Ibid., p. 92. The money was not made available until 23 August 1939, just days before the evacuation scheme began.
15. R. Samways, ed., *We Think You Ought to Go. An Account of the Evacuation of Children from London during the Second World War . . .'* (Corporation of London, 1945), p. 10.
16. All figures taken from R. M. Titmus's official war history, *Problems of Social Policy*, pp. 102–3.
17. R. Samways summarized movements out of the London area in *We Think You Ought to Go,* pp. 9–12. Plan II began evacuation on 1 September 1939. This was followed by plan IV in June 1940 as the military situation in Britain worsened. Plan V was called the 'trickle' evacuation which succeeded plan IV in July 1940 and continued until November 1942, during which time 64,200 people left the broader metropolitan area of London.
18. Mass Observation was an 'independent, scientific, fact-finding body' set up in 1937 to 'study real life' using trained investigators and 'voluntary informants'. Its findings charted aspects of everyday life across classes and the nature and process of social change. Taken from H. Spender, *Worktown People: Photographs from Northern England 1937–1938* (Falling Wall Press, 1982), p. 6.
19. T. Harrison and C. Madge, *War Begins at Home* (Chatto and Windus,1940), p. 297.
20. Ibid.
21. *Times* (1 September 1939), p. 7.
22. Harrison and Madge, *War Begins at Home*, p. 297.
23. *Times* (1 September 1939), p. 7.
24. Harrison and Madge, *War Begins at Home*, p. 327.
25. Ibid., pp. 301–2. The report was published by Liverpool University Press. Dr. Wagner had previously been a full-time member of the Mass Observation staff reporting from Worktown (Bolton).
26. Ibid., p. 328.
27. Ibid.

28. Titmus, *Problems of Social Policy*, p. 115.
29. A. Calder, *The People's War* (Pimlico, 1992), p. 38.
30. Harrison and Madge, *War Begins at Home*, p. 299.
31. Ibid., p. 300.
32. See Calder, *The People's War*, p. 40. Calder points out that official evacuees 'came disproportionately from the poorest strata of urban society for several reasons. Firstly, the well-to-do were more likely to have made their own arrangements. Secondly, the evacuation areas were mostly areas of high population density, where overcrowding was at its worst, while thc wealthier suburbs were often classed as "neutral" areas. Thirdly, the poorest classes had maintained a higher birth rate than their social superiors, . . . Large families . . . were a contributory cause of much poverty. (p. 40).
33. Ibberson, *Our Towns*, p. 54.
34. Ibid., p. 57.
35. Central Council for Health Education, 'War on Disease', undated, reprinted by the Imperial War Museum.
36. Ibid.
37. Ibid.
38. Calder, *The People's War*, quoting from Lord Chandos, *The Memoirs of Lord Chandos* (Bodley Head, 1962), p. 41.
39. Ibberson, *Our Towns,* p. 55.
40. Rose, *Which People's War?* p. 59.
41. Ibberson, *Our Towns*, p. 57.
42. W. Greenwood, *Love on the Dole* (Jonathan Cape, 1966, first published 1933).
43. Ibid., pp. 34–5.
44. Ibid., p. 45.
45. See this work, Chapter 2.
46. For a full account of the financial dealings of club operators see Ibberson, *Our Towns*, pp. 57–9.
47. Ibid., p. 59.
48. Ibid., p. 57.
49. G. Horseman, *Growing Up in the Thirties* (Cottage Publishing, 1994), p. 55–6.
50. Titmus, *Problems of Social Policy*, p. 119.
51. For an extensive and detailed account of the workings of the clothing scheme see Titmus, *Problems of Social Policy*, pp. 119–20, 165–6, and for later changes to it pp. 374–5.
52. See this work, Chapter 7.
53. M-OA TC5 5/1/M, *Daily Worker* (4 November 1939), p. 6.
54. Ibberson, *Our Towns*, p. 55, 65, and this chapter, note 55.

55. The full list of clothing as cited by the Women's Group for Public Welfare (cf. Ibberson, *Our Towns*, p. 65), but drawn up by the LCC, was as follows:

    Girl: 2 vests. 2 pairs knickers. 2 nightgowns or pyjamas. 2 bodices. 3 pairs stockings or socks. 2 either a) warm frocks b) jumper and skirt c) tunic and jumper. 1 coat and 1 mackintosh or 1 lined mackintosh. Either 2 pairs strong shoes or 1 pair shoes and 1 pair Wellingtons. 1 pair slippers or plimsolls.

    Boys: 2 vests. 2 pants. 3 shirts. 2 pairs pyjamas. 3 pairs socks. 1 jacket. 2 pairs knickers or trousers. 1 jersey or pullover. 1 coat and 1 mackintosh or 1 lined mackintosh. Either 2 pairs heavy boots or shoes or 1 pair of boots and 1 pair of Wellingtons. 1 pair of slippers or plimsolls.

56. Titmus, *Problems of Social Policy*, p. 166.
57. MO-A TC 5 5/1/L, 'Notes and Suggestions on Clothing' (26 January 1940).
58. London County Council Education Officer's Department, 'The Government's Evacuation Scheme Plan 1V' (19 March 1940), reprinted Imperial War Museum (undated), pp. 1–8.
59. Titmus, *Problems of Social Policy*, pp. 374–5.
60. Ibid., pp. 375–6.
61. Samways, *We Think You Ought to Go,* p. 15. When rationing was implemented, the LCC were issued with additional secret coupons to supplement want. See also Chapter 12 of this work for the role of the WVS in receiving and distributing clothing across the country.
62. Ibid., p. 16.
63. Parents contributed just over a third of the £178,000 the LCC had received from the Exchequer by 1943; see Titmus, *Problems of Social Policy*, p. 376.
64. M. Smith, *Britain and 1940: History, Myth and Popular Memory* (Routledge, 2000), p. 27.

## CHAPTER 6 FASHIONS FOR A PHONEY WAR

The phoney war lasted from Britain's declaration of war on Germany on 3 September 1939 to the Allied violation of Scandinavian neutrality on 8 April 1940. Calder explains that the term 'phoney' was 'an American usage later adopted by the British'. A. Calder, *The People's War* (Pimlico, 1994), p. 57.

1. J. Struther, *Mrs Miniver* (Virago, 1989; first published by Chatto and Windus, 1939), p. 139.

2. J. Hartley, *Hearts Undefeated: Women's Writing of the Second World War* (Virago, 1994), p. 104.
3. See C. Harris, *Women at War in Uniform 1939–1945* (Sutton Publishing Ltd, 2003), p. 31.
4. M-OA., TC 18/2/A, 18 December 1939. It is interesting that Mr. Scott also disapproved of recently appointed officers being able to 'go about in guardee uniform and all the rest of it, it's a very bad form of snobbishness'. Leslie Hore-Belisha was Minister for War until January 1940.
5. By early 1940, in response to complaints about having to wear uniform off duty, the rules were modified, and mufti—civilian clothing—was allowed for home leave. Harris, *Women at War in Uniform*, p. 31.
6. Harris suggests that rank was attained 'on the basis of little more than social or family connections. This was in part a reflection of the way things were done generally . . . [and] . . . typical of the frantic way in which preparations for the war were being made.' Harris, *Women at War in Uniform*, p. 11.
7. Figure obtained from individual numbers cited by M. Brayley and R. Ingram, *World War Two British Women's Uniforms* (Windrow and Greene, 1995), p. 4, 22, 68.
8. G. Braybon and P. Summerfield, *Out of the Cage: Women's Experiences in Two World Wars* (Pandora, 1987), p. 168, citing J. Hooks, *British Policies and Methods of Employing Women in Wartime* (U.S. Government, 1944), p. 16.
9. V. Douie, *Daughters of Britain: An Account of the Work of British Women during the Second World War* (Vincent Baxter Press, 1949), pp. 60–1.
10. For a full account of WVS uniform see M. McMurray (WRVS archivist),'WVS Uniform 1939–1945: The Introduction and Development of the Uniform of the Women's Voluntary Services for Civil Defence' (WRVS, 2009), <http://www.wrvs.org.uk/archiveandheritagecollection> accessed 12 January 2012. Uniform wearing was not compulsory unless specific roles demanded it (p. 6). An assisted purchase scheme ran from June 1942 as necessary (p. 9), and, after June 1941, coupon discounts for uniform were available (p. 14).
11. Douie, *Daughters of Britain*, p. 47.
12. Ministry of Information, *Home Front Handbook* (Ministry of Information, 1945; reprinted by Dept. of Printed Books, Imperial War Museum, 2005).
13. A. Wauters, *Eve in Overalls*, Historical Pamphlet Series No. 2 (Imperial War Museum, 1995).
14. The combining of unpaid domestic work with paid or voluntary work beyond the home altered women's perspective on life, however temporarily. For some, this type of work was seen as short-term, but for others, the war opened up new avenues of thought about the role of housewife and

a woman's capacity to work, particularly after marriage. Many authors deal with this complex issue and the debate over the extent to which women's lives changed because of their war work. See J.B. Priestley's *British Women Go to War* (Collins, 1943), for a contemporary view; also Braybon and Summerfield, *Out of the Cage*; H.L. Smith, ed., 'The Effect of the War on the Status of Women', in *War and Social Change: British Society in the Second World War* (Manchester University Press, 1986); and D. Sheridan, 'Ambivalent Memories: Women and the 1939–45 War in Britain', *Oral History* 18/1 (Spring 1990).

15. M-OA TC18/2/A, interview with James Laver, 20 March 1940.
16. *Vogue Pattern Book* (January 1940), p. 3.
17. The London Fashion Group had formed in 1936 to promote not just fashion but the arts as a whole. It had wanted to establish London as a fashion centre and to encourage American business. With a lack of funds, the group closed down at the outbreak of war. See also Margaret Havinden from Crawfords Advertising in M-OA TC 18/2/A, 27 February 1940, p. 1.
18. M-OA TC18/2/A, interview with Jean Smith, secretary of Fashion Group, 29 November 1939, p. 1.
19. M-OA TC 18/2/A, interview with H. Scott, Mercia and Co., 85 Wells St., 18 December 1939, p. 1.
20. Ibid.
21. 'Treasury's Strange War Cry', *Drapers' Record* (2 December 1939), p. 1.
22. *Tailor and Cutter* (15 September 1939), p. 879.
23. *Drapers' Record* (16 December 1939), p. 7.
24. M-OA TC18/2/A, interview with Jean Smith, secretary of Fashion Group, 29 November 1939, p. 2.
25. 'Here and Now', *Vogue* (20 September 1939), p. 44.
26. T. Harrison and C. Madge, *War Begins at Home* (Chatto and Windus, 1940), pp. 358–9.
27. 'Put Them Back into Evening Gowns! Fashion Trade Must Face-Up to War-Time Problems', *Drapers' Record* (2 December 1939), p. 10.
28. Ibid.
29. M-OA TC 18/2/A, interview with Mary Joyce, editor of *Woman's Wear News*, 7 December 1939, p. 1.
30. 'You Can't Ration Fashion', *Drapers' Record* (16 December 1939), p. 11.
31. M-OA TC 18/2/A, interview with Mary Joyce, p. 1.
32. All quotations from *Vogue* (November 1939), p. 20.
33. Harrison and Madge, *War Begins at Home*, p. 194.
34. Ibid., p. 221.
35. Ibid., p. 216. Harrison and Madge reported that three quarters of all road deaths took place in the blackout, and, of all deaths recorded, 'no less than 85% were [people] over 50 years of age, and of these

a third were over 70.' For further information on blackout detail see E. S. Turner, *The Phoney War* (Michael Joseph, 1961), Chapter 6, 'Carry a White Pekinese'.

36. After a blanket closure of all places of entertainment on the outbreak of war, the Home Office allowed the 're-opening, until ten p.m., of all theatres and cinemas in neutral and reception areas. . . . In the third week of war permission was given for places of entertainment to re-open in vulnerable areas . . . shut[ting] at ten p.m. except in the West End of London where curfew would operate at six.' It was not until December that these London venues were able to change the Home Office regulations, on condition that theatres and cinemas 'staggered their closing between ten and eleven'. See Turner, *The Phoney War*, p. 100.
37. As of 16 September 1939. *Daily Mirror* (4 September 1939), p. 1.
38. *Vogue* (November 1939), p. 20.
39. *Drapers' Record* (23 September 1939), p. 19.
40. *Vogue* (November 1939), pp. 22–3.
41. Turner, *The Phoney War*, pp. 70–1.
42. *Vogue* (November 1939).
43. Mass Observation, *Change: Home Propaganda*, Bulletin of The Advertising Service Guild, No. 2 (Advertising Service Guild, 1941), pp. 10–11.
44. Ibid., and Calder, *The People's War*, pp. 25–6.
45. *Drapers' Record* (9 September 1939), p. 10.
46. Harrison and Madge, *War Begins at Home*, p. 117.
47. *Vogue* (November 1939), p. 15.
48. J. Struther, 'Letters from Mrs Miniver to The Times Autumn 1939', in *Mrs Miniver*, (Virago, 1989). See letter entitled 'Peace-in-War', London, 5 October 1939, p. 141.
49. Harrison and Madge, *War Begins at Home*, p. 116.
50. *Drapers' Record* (23 September 23 1939), p. 19.
51. *Drapers' Record* (2 December 1939), p. 10.
52. *Drapers' Record* (23 September 1939), p. 18.
53. *Drapers' Record* (21 October 1939), p. 15.
54. M-OA TC18/1/G, 'Observations of shop windows 1939–40', concerning D. H. Evans, Oxford Street, London, 8 November 1939.
55. M-OA TC/18/1/G, 11 November 1939.
56. *Vogue* (November 1939), frontispiece advertisement for Fortnum and Mason Ltd.
57. *Vogue Pattern Book* (December 1939), frontispiece 'Siren into Suit' advertisement for 'Viyella Thirty-six Fashion Fabrics'.
58. *Vogue* (November 1939), p. 19.
59. M-OA TC 18/2/A, interview with Victor Stiebel, 1 December 1939, p. 1.

60. M-OA TC 18/2/A, interview with Jean Smith, secretary of Fashion Group, 29 November 1939, p. 1.
61. M-OA TC 18/2/A, interview with Victor Stiebel, 1 December 1939, p. 1.
62. *Vogue Pattern Book* (January 1940), p. 4.
63. M-OA TC 18/2/A, interview with Anne Seymour, editor of *Women and Beauty*, 5 December 1939, p. 2.
64. M-OA TC 18/2/A, interview with Madge Garland, editor of *Vogue*, 15 December 1939. See also the *Drapers' Record* (18 November 1939), p. 24. In an article entitled 'Ginger-Up Woman's Appetite for Fashion and Combat War Stagnation', regular writer Jean Guest suggests 'many women are becoming slack under present conditions. For example, two months ago, wearing a plain-Jane coat and heavy country shoes for a West-end lunch "date" would never have been considered. Similarly though the pre-war woman might have preferred to go hatless in the local High-street, she wouldn't have visited town looking like a gypsy or peasant girl. Now, one notices far too many passers-by "up West" who appear to have bundled on garments solely for warmth.'
65. *Vogue Pattern Book* (January 1940), p. 4.
66. *Drapers' Record* (9 March 1940), pp. 34–5.
67. *Drapers' Record* (6 April 1940), p. 18.
68. Ibid.
69. M-OA TC 18/2/A, 6 December 1939, p. 2.
70. M-OA TC 18/2/A, 5 December 1939, p. 2.
71. Brayley and Ingram, *World War Two British Women's Uniforms*, p. 6.
72. M-OA TC/18/2/B, interview with Digby Morton, 24 April 1940.
73. M-OA TC/18/1/H, Reports on Sales and Sales and Publicity 1939–1940, 6 January 1940.
74. M-OA TC/18/2/F, Priscilla Feare, 6 March 1940, p. 1.
75. D. Mercer, *Chronicle of the Twentieth Century* (JL International Publications, 1993), p. 524.
76. M-OA TC/18/2/F, Priscilla Feare, 6 March 1940, p. 1. Finland's engagement in the Russo-Finnish war resulted in Finland ceding territory to Russia. See M. Gilbert, *Second World War* (Phoenix Giant, 1995), chapter entitled 'Finland Defiant', pp. 31–43; P. Calvocoressi, G. Wint and J. Pritchard, *Total War: The Western Hemisphere*, vol. 1, *The Causes and Courses of the Second World War* (Penguin, 1989), pp. 115–18.
77. M-OA TC/18/2/F, Priscilla Feare, 6 March 1940, p. 1.
78. Mass Observation were reporting this duality as early as November 1939 as the contrast between high-fashion hats and the military look. See M-OA TC 18/2/F, 20 November 1939.
79. 'Birth of an Easter Bonnet', *Picture Post* (23 March 1940), pp. 44–5.
80. Ibid., p. 44.

## CHAPTER 7 CALLS FOR RATIONED FASHION

1. W.K. Hancock and M.M. Gowing, *The British War Economy* (HMSO, 1949), p. 20.
2. E.L. Hargreaves and M.M. Gowing, *Civil Industry and Trade* (HMSO, 1952), p. 4.
3. Hancock and Gowing, *The British War Economy*, pp. 20–1.
4. C. Sladen, *The Conscription of Fashion: Utility Cloth, Clothing and Footwear 1941–1952* (Scolar Press, 1995), p. 25.
5. Hancock and Gowing, *The British War Economy*, p. 43.
6. Ibid., pp. 46–7.
7. Ibid., p. 48.
8. Ibid., p. 50.
9. Ibid., p. 51.
10. Hargreaves and Gowing, *Civil Industry and Trade*, p. 13.
11. Reproduced here are all the figures that comprise the index: **Cost-of-Living Index 1 September 1939 = 100.**

| | *Food* | *Clothing* | *Fuel and light* | *Rent* | *All other items* |
|---|---|---|---|---|---|
| *Weightings* | 53% | 16% | 9% | 17% | 5% |
| *1939 Sept.* | 100 | 100 | 100 | 100 | 100 |
| *Oct.* | 109 | 107 | 101 | 100 | 106 |
| *Nov.* | 112 | 113 | 103 | 100 | 109 |
| *Dec.* | 114 | 118 | 107 | 100 | 112 |
| *1940 Jan.* | 114 | 120 | 110 | 100 | 112 |
| *Feb.* | 117 | 125 | 111 | 100 | 114 |
| *Mar.* | 117 | 128 | 113 | 100 | 115 |
| *Apr.* | 114 | 131 | 113 | 100 | 115 |
| *May* | 115 | 135 | 114 | 101 | 116 |
| *June* | 114 | 137 | 116 | 101 | 117 |

Source: W. K. Hancock and M.M. Gowing The British War Economy, p. 166.

See also J. Hurstfield, *The Control of Raw Materials* (HMSO, 1953), p. 366, for the increasing cost of importing raw cotton from America between 1938 and 1942, showing the price at source to have 'more than doubled' while the 'cost of ocean transport had increased fourfold, marine insurance had increased six fold and . . . a substantial sum had to be paid for war risks insurance'.

12. Order Prohibiting Importation without a Licence, S.R. & O. 1939 No. 1054. Hargreaves and Gowing, *Civil Industry and Trade*, p. 23.
13. H. Wadsworth, 'The Utility Cloth and Clothing Scheme', *Review of Economic Studies* 16(2), No. 40 (1948), p. 87.
14. 'Price Regulations from January 1st', *Tailor and Cutter* (22 December 1939). The act covered those goods 'of common use . . . which a man with a family earning £500 per year might be expected to buy'. Hargreaves and Gowing, *Civil Industry and Trade*, p. 82.
15. Hargreaves and Gowing, *Civil Industry and Trade*, p. 82.
16. Ibid.
17. Sladen, *The Conscription of Fashion*, p. 18.
18. Hargreaves and Gowing, *Civil Industry and Trade*, p. 83.
19. Hancock and Gowing, *The British War Economy*, p. 167.
20. The scheme was recommended by the Economic Policy Committee to the War Cabinet as cited in Hancock and Gowing, *The British War Economy*, p. 168.
21. Ibid., and Hargreaves and Gowing, *Civil Industry and Trade*, p. 88. Together these sources provide a comprehensive account of the criticism surrounding the scheme.
22. Hargreaves and Gowing, *Civil Industry and Trade*, p. 88.
23. Hancock and Gowing, *The British War Economy*, p. 168.
24. Ibid., and Hargreaves and Gowing, *Civil Industry and Trade*, pp. 88–9.
25. PRO, BT 96/46, letter from Alderman Bretherick, 29 April 1940.
26. One noticeable change was an unanticipated rise in demand for leather shoes as reduced unemployment allowed for the purchase of better quality footwear. This caused a further drain on footwear supplies. See Chapter 10.
27. PRO, BT 96/46, letter from Alderman Bretherick, 29 April 1940.
28. Hargreaves and Gowing, *Civil Industry and Trade,* p. 433.
29. G.L. Watkinson (as described in Sladden, *The Conscription of Fashion*, p. 123), was 'Principal Assistant Secretary (Industries and Manufacture) BoT, Under Secretary 1942–6, Deputy Secretary, Ministry Fuel and Power 1947–1955'.
30. PRO, BT 96/46, letter from G.L. Watkinson, 14 May 1940.
31. *Tailor and Cutter* (1 December 1939), p. 1059.
32. *Tailor and Cutter* (22 December 1939), p. 1110.
33. Ibid.
34. Ibid.
35. On 10 March 1943, orders were issued suspending new clothing in Germany completely except for mourning and maternity dress. Only uniform was still to be produced. See press handout from the president of the Board of Trade (Sir Hugh Dalton) on Thursday, 11 March 1943, PRO, BT 64/3025.

36. Hancock and Gowing, *The British War Economy*, p. 117.
37. Ibid. See also P. Ady, 'Utility Goods', *Bulletin* 4/15 (31 October 1942), p. 356.
38. Hargreaves and Gowing, *Civil Industry and Trade*, pp. 97–8.
39. Ibid., pp. 98–9.
40. Hancock and Gowing, *The British War Economy*, p. 117 (footnote). Traders preferred using their limited quota for retail and hoped the government would provide for essential use. See Hargreaves and Gowing, *Civil Industry and Trade*, pp. 104–5.
41. Ibid.
42. Hargreaves and Gowing, *Civil Industry and Trade*, p. 98.
43. Ibid. The call for export was superseded once the US Lend Lease proposal of 11 March 1941 was accepted. See Hancock and Gowing, *The British War Economy*, from p. 235.
44. Sladen, *The Conscription of Fashion*, p. 18.
45. Ibid.; Hurstfield, *The Control of Raw Materials*, p. 145. See also pp. 145–6 for special purchases of cotton and wool.
46. Hancock and Gowing, *The British War Economy*, p. 382.
47. Hargreaves and Gowing, *Civil Industry and Trade,* p. 102. See also the *Drapers' Record* (15 June 1940), pp. 4–5.
48. Hargreaves and Gowing, *Civil Industry and Trade*, p. 105.
49. Ibid., pp. 106–7.
50. Ibid., pp. 106–7 and see this chapter, note 40.
51. D. Mercer, *Chronicle of the 20th Century* (JL International Publications, 1993), p. 538.
52. Ibid., p. 539.
53. Hargreaves and Gowing, *Civil Industry and Trade*, p. 106.
54. Ibid., p. 107.
55. Ibid.
56. Ibid., p. 106.
57. Ibid., p. 303; Sladen, *The Conscription of Fashion*, p. 28; Hancock and Gowing, *The British War Economy*, p. 334.
58. Hargreaves and Gowing, *Civil Industry and Trade*, p. 303.
59. Ibid., p. 108, referring to SR & O 1940, No. 2031 Miscellaneous (No. 5) Order. There were some exceptions that got higher quotas such as corsets, which were restricted by 50 per cent, while furs and 'undoubted luxuries' were limited to only 25 per cent of the standard period. Ibid., p. 109.
60. Ibid., p. 108.
61. Ibid., p. 294. For a full account of the area officers see pp. 294–6.
62. Ibid., p. 202. Concentration was intended to be largely completed by May 1941. For the process and ramifications of concentration see Ibid., pp. 202–24.

63. *Manchester Guardian* (Saturday, 16 November 1940), and cited in Hargreaves and Gowing, *Civil Industry and Trade*, p. 304.
64. Ibid.
65. From an article on voluntary self-restraint, *Manchester Guardian* (Saturday, 16 November 1940), p. 6.
66. Ibid.
67. Ibid., p. 7.
68. Hancock and Gowing, *The British War Economy*, p. 304.
69. *Financial News* (11 November 1940), p. 2.
70. Raw cotton imports were 'exceptionally low in 1941', creating a fear 'that a shortage of raw material would limit cotton output'. There was no way of knowing at the time that this situation was only temporary and stocks would rise. Hargreaves and Gowing, *Civil Industry and Trade,* p. 351, and see also *Financial News* (11 November 1940), p. 2.
71. From an article entitled 'Consumption Control' in *Financial News* (11 November 1940), p. 2.
72. Ibid.
73. Ibid.
74. Hargreaves and Gowing, *Civil Industry and Trade*, p. 304.
75. For the debate on how to launch a rationing scheme see Ibid., pp. 304–7.
76. Ibid., pp. 202–24 for a full explanation of the concentration scheme as it affected the various clothing and textile industries.
77. Hancock and Gowing, *The British War Economy*, p. 334.
78. Sladen, *The Conscription of Fashion*, p. 28.
79. Hancock and Gowing, *The British War Economy*, p. 335.
80. PRO, BT 64/971.
81. Hargreaves and Gowing, *Civil Industry and Trade*, p. 312.
82. Sladen, *The Conscription of Fashion*, p. 20, quoting Oliver Lyttelton (Lord Chandos) from *The Memoirs of Lord Chandos* (Bodley Head, 1962), p. 205.
83. PRO, BT 64/971.
84. Ibid.
85. Ibid.
86. Ibid. *Don* is a term used for a fellow of a college, or a college authority, usually from Oxford or Cambridge.
87. Hargreaves and Gowing, *Civil Industry and Trade*, p. 313.
88. Ibid.

## CHAPTER 8 SETTING THE RATION

1. PRO, BT 64/871, public notice entitled 'Rationing of Clothing, Cloth and Footwear June 1st 1941'.

2. Ibid., and see this work, Chapter 7, for the inauguration of the German rationing scheme.
3. PRO, BT64/871, 'On the Rationing of Clothing and Footwear, Notice to the Public, 1st June 1941', Industries and Manufactures Department 2, Pine Court Hotel, Bournemouth.
4. Ibid.
5. PRO, BT 64/871, 'Rationing of Clothing, Cloth and Footwear'.
6. Ibid.
7. BoT papers, BS 41, *Cloth and Clothing, Coupons and Quotas. Clothes Rationing Manual for Manufacturers, Makers-Up, Wholesalers and Retail Traders*, from Board of Trade Miscellaneous Circulars, Memoranda etc., Nos 23–60, HMSO, p. 3.
8. Ibid.
9. Ibid., pp. 3–4.
10. See this chapter, note 28.
11. M. Spring Rice, *Working Class Wives: Their Health and Condition* (Virago, 1981, first published 1939), p. 106.
12. BT 64/3025, 'Cut the Clothing Ration? Comments on Mr. Lintott's Memorandum', hand dated to 23 July 1942, p. 1.
13. Spring Rice, *Working Class Wives*, p. 175, 115.
14. Spring Rice suggested that the three main causes of married women's difficulties were poverty, ill health and ignorance. She advocated higher wages, increased community responsibility for children and subsidies for better housing as the means to assuage poverty; better health services and health insurance, subsidies for essential foods and more recreational opportunities for resolving health issues; and greater education in home craft and family care for women to offset ignorance. Ibid., pp. 207–8.
15. D. Ibberson, *Our Towns: A Close-up* (Oxford University Press, 1943). For more information on *Our Towns,* see Chapter 5.
16. Ibberson, *Our Towns*, pp. 64–5. The Women's Group on Public Welfare Hygiene Committee suggested instalment purchase should be investigated, a new National Institute for Domestic Affairs be reviewed, a minimum standard of clothing for children be ascertained against which adequacy could be gauged, extended craft classes be set up both for adults and children and community laundering facilities be explored.
17. For Utility production and Utility clothing see chapters 9 and 14.
18. E. L. Hargreaves and M. M. Gowing, *Civil Industry and Trade* (HMSO 1952), p. 308.
19. Ibid.
20. Ibid., p. 307, 314.
21. PRO, BT 64/871.
22. Ibid.

23. Hargreaves and Gowing, *Civil Industry and Trade*, p. 314.
24. Ibid.
25. O. Lyttelton, *The Memoirs of Lord Chandos* (Bodley Head, 1962), p. 203.
26. A Mr. Leak. Ibid., p. 204.
27. Ibid.
28. Hargreaves and Gowing, *Civil Industry and Trade*, p. 307.
29. Ibid.
30. PRO, BT/64/3025, 17 July 1942.
31. Ibid.
32. Hargreaves and Gowing, *Civil Industry and Trade*, pp. 308–9.
33. Ibid., p. 308.
34. All the *Clothing Quiz* booklets are in the British Library, reference BS 41/151.
35. The information cited here with regard to the setting of the ration is an amalgamation of various sources as no one document/book creates the full picture. Most important have been the *Clothing Quiz* booklets which show facsimiles of the ration books giving all the types of coupon values and when they can be used. The official history *Civil Industry and Trade*, by E. L. Hargreaves and M. M. Gowing, gives a summary in context of the setting of the ration, pp. 314–31. Also useful has been the discussion of ration setting in the Board of Trade papers held at the PRO, specifically BT 64/3025. A calculator is helpful in showing how the ration breaks down over individual months and monthly periods.
36. Hargreaves and Gowing, *Civil Industry and Trade*, p. 329.
37. Ibid., p. 315; and PRO, BT64/4216, The 1944–45 Civilian Ration.
38. Hargreaves and Gowing, *Civil Industry and Trade*, p. 473. For a full account of the economics of the textile industry at this point see pp. 472–9.
39. PRO, BT64/421T(7), from a memo marked ‘Secret’ and dated 22 August 1945.
40. PRO, BT64/421T(7), press notice entitled ‘Red Clothing Coupons Valid on August 1st’, Ref:743, dated 24 July 1946.
41. PRO, unreferenced but catalogued under BT64/4218 (1946–7), from a confidential memo entitled ‘Consumer Goods Export, President’s Directive of January 1947’. Clothes rationing would continue throughout 1948. It was retained ‘until supplies were sufficient to permit a ration of something over 100 coupons per head’, see Hargreaves and Gowing, *Civil Industry and Trade*, p. 621. Clothes rationing was finally brought to an end on 15 March 1949 although the Utility scheme continued in production; see D. Mercer, *Chronicle of the Twentieth Century* (JL International Publications, 1993) p. 684. The Utility scheme was finally wound up in May 1952; see Sladen, *The Conscription of Fashion: Utility Cloth, Clothing and Footwear 1941–1952* (Scolar Press, 1995), p. 103, and

p. 115, footnote 9. It is not the remit of this work to investigate either rationing or Utility beyond the war years.

42. H. Channon, *Chips: Diaries of Sir Henry Channon* (Weidenfeld and Nicolson, 1967), p. 307.
43. Sladen, *The Conscription of Fashion*, p. 21.
44. Hargreaves and Gowing, *Civil Industry and Trade*, p. 329.

## CHAPTER 9 THE UTILITY CLOTHING SCHEME

1. *Clothing Quiz*, 1941–1942, second edition. A series of these were produced to accompany each new rationing year. They contained a complete listing of all pointings for garments as well as pointings for second-hand goods and fabrics of different kinds. Comparison between all the booklets reveals that, overall, pointings remained fairly constant for the main items of wear, with only minor fluctuations where particular items or fabrics became scarce. The full set can be seen at the British Library referenced BS 41/151.
2. Ibid. A new Utility mark was suggested in 1946, and Enid Marx 'prepared seven designs for S. C. Leslie, the first Director for the Council of Industrial Design, although none was adopted, the famous "CC41" mark being retained'. See Geffrye Museum, *CC41 Utility Furniture and Fashion 1941–1951* ( Inner London Education Authority, 1974), p. 30.
3. W.K. Hancock and M.M. Gowing, *British War Economy* (HMSO, 1949), p. 335.
4. Ibid., p. 336.
5. Ibid.
6. Ibid., pp. 335–6.
7. Ibid., p. 336.
8. E. L. Hargreaves and M. M. Gowing, *Civil Industry and Trade* (HMSO, 1952), p. 435.
9. Ibid.
10. P. Ady, 'Utility Goods', *Bulletin* 4/15 (31 October 1942), p. 358.
11. Ibid.
12. Ady gives a very good and succinct account of the methodology behind these first seven months of the Utility scheme. He describes the beginnings of cloth specification and the emphasis at this stage on durability (p. 359), with 'instructions to makers-up stressing points such as the re-enforcement of seams'. Price controls for each type of fabric through fixed spinners' and weavers' profit margins are described, as well as the importance of controlling profit margins at each stage of production from raw material through to finished product to create a fair price for the consumer.

13. Ady explains 'manufacturers' prices were fixed at the level of June 30th. Wholesalers' profit margins were fixed at 30% and retailers' at 37.5%'. Ibid., p. 361.
14. 'Designated firms agreed to devote not less than 75% of their production capacity either to Utility clothing, to other government contract work (for example, service uniforms) or to exports; they would in turn receive at least 65% of the available Utility yardage.' C. Sladen, *The Conscription of Fashion: Utility Cloth, Clothing and Footwear 1941–1952* (Scolar Press, 1995), p. 33.
15. The terms 'designated' for firms and 'key certificates' for orders of cloth and clothing are specific to the process whereby the Board of Trade established Utility production. See Ady, 'Utility Goods', p. 360 (designation and key certificates); Hargeaves and Gowing, *Civil Industry and Trade*, pp. 403–11 (designation) and p. 445 (key certificates); Sladen, *The Conscription of Fashion*, pp. 33–6 (designation).
16. Purchase Tax (Exemptions) (No. 4) Order, SR & O 1942 No. 1506; Sladen, *The Conscription of Fashion*, p. 36.
17. H. Wadsworth, 'Utility Cloth and Clothing Scheme', *Review of Economic Studies* 16(2), No. 40 (1948), p. 3. From a paper read before the Manchester Statistical Society, 10 November 1948. The author was on the staff of the Cotton Board.
18. H. Wadsworth, 'Utility Cloth and Clothing Scheme', p. 87. See also Hargreaves and Gowing, *Civil Industry and Trade*, pp. 440–1.
19. Wadsworth, *Utility Cloth and Clothing Scheme*, p. 99.
20. Hargreaves and Gowing, *Civil Industry and Trade*, pp. 453–4.
21. PRO, BT 64/78 SR & O 1941, No. 1387, Goods and Services (Price Control), pp. 2–4. While Wadsworth cites nineteen woollens, this cloth schedule (SR & O 1387) for 11 September 1941 quotes twenty-two.
22. Ibid., and Hargreaves and Gowing, *Civil Industry and Trade*, pp. 451–2.
23. Hargreaves and Gowing, *Civil Industry and Trade*, p. 451.
24. Ibid., p. 458.
25. Ibid.
26. Ibid.
27. Ibid., p. 457.
28. PRO, BT 64/78 SR & O 1941, No. 1387, pp. 4–5.
29. Ibid.
30. See Chapter 2.
31. PRO, BT 64/85, 'Draft Minute', July 1942.
32. Ibid.
33. Ibid.
34. Hargreaves and Gowing, *Civil Industry and Trade*, p. 441.
35. BL BS/BOT 23 and BS/BOT 24 for rayon and cotton respectively.

36. Hargreaves and Gowing, *Civil Industry and Trade*, p. 442. See also Wadsworth, *Utility Cloth and Clothing Scheme*, p. 84. The specifications were worked on by the Cotton Board, including members of the 'Cotton Control, Shirley Institute, the Manchester Chamber of Commerce Testing House and weavers and converters, with special knowledge of each group of cloths considered, drawn from panels appointed by the Cotton Spinners and Manufacturers Association and the Cotton and Rayon Merchants' Association respectively. Those for rayon were initially drafted by members of the Rayon Weaving Association and the Silk and Rayon Users' Association in consultation with other rayon interests under B.S.I. Auspices.'
37. BL BS/BOT 23 and BS/BOT 24 for rayon and cotton respectively, and for 'Shrink Resistance of Certain Woollen Garments', October 1942, see BS/BOT 30.
38. I. Sieff, *Memoirs* (Weidenfeld and Nicolson, 1970), p. 156.
39. A. Briggs, *Marks & Spencer Limited 1884–1984: A Centenary History* (Octopus Books Ltd, 1984), p. 67. Dr. Kann, 'a refugee from Nazi Germany', had originally worked for the German chain store Samuel Schocken.
40. Sieff, *Memoirs*, p. 156.
41. H. Worth, *Fashion for the People: A History of Clothing at Marks & Spencer* (Berg, 2007), p. 47, and also P. Bookbinder, *Marks & Spencer: The War Years* (Century Benham, 1989), p. 45. The details in Bookbinder are interesting but not referenced. The list of people and groups involved with setting up the BSI specifications are given in this chapter, note 36.
42. For the impact of austerity restriction on design see this work, Chapter 14.
43. Hargreaves and Gowing, *Civil Industry and Trade*, p. 437.
44. Ibid.
45. PRO, BT 64/3025, 11 March 1943.
46. Hargreaves and Gowing, *Civil Industry and Trade*, p. 439.
47. PRO, BT 64/3025, 11 March 1943.
48. Hargreaves and Gowing, *Civil Industry and Trade*, p. 437.
49. Ibid., p. 438. Neither boys' nor men's socks were to exceed a leg length of nine and a half inches—designed to save on worsted wool.
50. Ibid., p. 437, and see this work, Chapter 14.
51. See this work, Chapter 14 for a more detailed account.
52. Sladen, *The Conscription of Fashion*, p. 39.
53. *Drapers' Record* (18 April 1942), p. 14.
54. *Drapers' Record* (2 May 1942), p. 34.
55. *Drapers' Record* (9 May 1942), p. 28.
56. A.M. Miall, *Making Clothes for Children* (London, 1946, first published 1934), p. 1.

57. See this work, Chapter 11.
58. Hargreaves and Gowing, *Civil Industry and Trade*, p. 437.
59. J. Waller, *Knitting Fashions of the 1940s: Styles, Patterns and History* (Crowood Press Ltd, 2006), p. 74.
60. War Emergency British Standard Specification, BS/BOT1, Women's Dresses, April 1942, and BS/BOT2, Women's Underwear, April 1942. See also *Drapers' Record* (25 April 1942), p. 15, 24.
61. Hargreaves and Gowing, *Civil Industry and Trade*, p. 438.
62. Ibid.
63. Wadsworth, 'Utility Cloth and Clothing Scheme', p. 95.
64. It was decided not to make demobilization suiting with austerity restrictions; see Hargreaves and Gowing, *Civil Industry and Trade*, p. 439.
65. Ibid., p. 434. For information on Utility production of different cloths see Hargreaves and Gowing, *Civil Industry and Trade*, Chapter 17, 'Clothing Policy'. See also Wadsworth, 'Utility Cloth and Clothing Scheme'.

## CHAPTER 10 ASSESSING THE IMPACT OF CLOTHES RATIONING

1. O. Lyttelton, *The Memoirs of Lord Chandos* (Bodley Head, 1962), p. 163. This was a pun on the Nazi slogan 'Strength through Joy' (*Kraft durch Freude*) that referred to the Nazi policy of providing German workers with opportunities for active leisure pursuits.
2. Churchill's perception of clothes rationing. Ibid., p. 205.
3. An expert later to be 'Advisor on Consumer Needs to the Board'. See E. L. Hargreaves and M. M. Gowing, *Civil Industry and Trade* (HMSO, 1952), pp. 282–3.
4. For monitoring the buying populations of towns see Ibid., pp. 292–3.
5. Ibid., p. 297.
6. Ibid.
7. Wardrobe checks were carried out three times: in April and December 1942 and April 1944. Ibid., p. 298.
8. PRO, BT/41/01, 'An Investigation of Consumer Reaction to the Clothes Rationing Order'.
9. Ibid., p. 9.
10. Ibid.
11. Ibid., p. 18.
12. Ibid., p. 19.
13. Hargreaves and Gowing, *Civil Industry and Trade*, p. 23, referring to the early elimination of shoe imports for women. The worsening situation in the Atlantic during autumn 1940 and into 1941 also curtailed importation of leather from South America. As the situation deteriorated in the Mediterranean during 1940 with the Nazi conquest of Europe and Italy joining the

Axis in June, the Mediterranean was closed to Allied ships. A much-longer route would now be required to import Commonwealth goods from Australia and Asia. The invasion of Malaya three days after Pearl Harbor on 10 December 1941 meant rubber, amongst other commodities, would no longer be available even were shipping space allocated to it. In general, all importations of clothing and textiles were largely suspended after the first year of war, although during this time wool and cotton had been imported in large quantities so providing excellent buffer stock, as we have seen elsewhere. For a definitive account from the official war history, see J. Hurstfield, *The Control of Raw Materials* (HMSO, 1953), Chapter 11, 'Overseas Supplies: Sources', pp. 151–75; Hargreaves and Gowing, *Civil Industry and Trade*, p. 381. See also A. Calder, *A People's War* (Pimlico, 1992), p. 69, 114, 276.

14. See Chapter 14.
15. In the 1942–1943 coupon schedule for the new ration year, section 9, 'industrial overalls', made clear which *Utility* cloth overalls could now be bought at the lower rates of boiler suit (four), bib-and-brace overall (three), overall long coat (three), wrap-over coat overall (three), overall jacket or trousers (two) and apron (two), as opposed to the pointing for overalls in section 7, 'principle articles of adults and children's clothing'. Overalls were now a much-bigger category, here including the original domestic garment of 1941 at six and four and a new range of others. Aprons were the lowest at one, with group 2 (non-wool) overalls at seven and five and a group 1 (containing more than 15% wool by weight) overall and non-industrial boiler suit the highest at eleven and eight. As before, men and women's weightings were the same. See BS 41/151, 1942–1943 *Clothing Quiz*, August 1942, p. V1., p. 9, 6.
16. Hargreaves and Gowing, *Civil Industry and Trade*, p. 322.
17. Although taken together, the combined comments on boots and shoes for working adults and shoes for children far outweighed this category.
18. The full listing of second-hand item prices and how to work out whether coupons were necessary or not appeared in the supplemental *Clothing Quiz* for 1941 and in all subsequent *Quizzes*: 'Second-hand goods require coupons if sold above certain prices. These prices are fixed by multiplying the number of coupons that would be required for the article if new by the price given in the list below.

| | s | d |
|---|---|---|
| 1) Hand knitting yarn, cloth and stockings and woollen socks for men and boys | | 8 |
| 2) Undergarments, stockings and socks other than those in the preceding item | 1 | 0 |
| 3) Boots, bootees, shoes, overshoes, slippers and sandals | 1 | 6 |
| 4) Other rationed goods | 2 | 0 |

If sold above these prices rationed goods, even though genuinely second-hand, require the full number of coupons. See BS 41/151, 1942–1943 *Clothing Quiz*, August 1942, p. X11.

19. PRO, BT64/3025, 'The Clothing Ration', 3 July 1942.
20. Hargreaves and Gowing, *Civil Industry and Trade*, pp. 317–18. The new rationing year 1942–1943 would reduce the ration (see this work, Chapter 8), and children under eighteen would be immediately compensated by an additional ten coupons (Ibid., p. 318). On top of this, the board continued with a sliding scale of supplements. Seventeen- and eighteen-year-olds received a further ten, fourteen- to sixteen-year-olds received twenty. 'Outsize' children below thirteen years eight months who weighed over seven stone twelve pounds and/or were taller than five foot three inches on or before 31 October 1942 were now given twenty coupons. See BS 41/151, 1942–1943 *Clothing Quiz*, 'Questions Answered'. The rules were clear: 'The weights and measurements must be taken without boots or shoes, jackets or waistcoats, and 2 1/2 lbs deducted for the weight of other clothing.' See PRO, BT64/3025, 'Extra Coupons for Older Children'.
21. Hargreaves and Gowing, *Civil Industry and Trade*, p. 318.
22. PRO, BT64/3025, 'The Clothing Ration', 3 July 1942, p. 1.
23. Ibid. Miners had been given a very high supplement of sixty extra coupons in the first rationing year. This was not to be repeated. See Hargreaves and Gowing, *Civil Industry and Trade*, pp. 320–1.
24. PRO, BT64/3025, 'The Clothing Ration', 3 July 1942, p. 1.
25. Ibid., pp. 1–2.
26. Ibid., p. 2.
27. Ibid.
28. Ibid.
29. PRO, BT64/3025, 'Secret': 'The question of reducing the ration falls into three parts', 17 July 1942, p. 1.
30. Hargreaves and Gowing, *Civil Industry and Trade*, p. 319.
31. PRO BT64/ 3025, 'Secret': 'The question of reducing the ration falls into three parts', 17 July 1942, p. 2.
32. PRO, BT64/3025, 'Statement by the President of the Board of Trade: Clothes Rationing—General Occupational Supplement 1942–1943'. Prepared for a statement to be made on 18 September 1942. For a further industrial supplement called the 'iron ration' see Hargreaves and Gowing, *Civil Industry and Trade*, p. 321.
33. PRO BT64/3025, 'Secret': 'The question of reducing the ration falls into three parts', 17 July 1942, p. 2.
34. Hargreaves and Gowing, *Civil Industry and Trade*, p. 426.
35. Ibid.

36. Ibid., pp. 426–7.
37. PRO BT64/3025, a notice, 'Some Facts about Coupon Spending', 1 June 1943.
38. PRO BT64/3025, 'Anniversary of Clothes Rationing', p. 2.
39. Ibid.
40. For full details on rationing year by year see the annual *Clothing Quiz* booklets, BS 41/151.
41. Hargreaves and Gowing, *Civil Industry and Trade*, pp. 333–5. The buying permit system is explained in detail here as well as the priority docket, whereby certain specialized consumers became entitled to particular types of clothing and footwear. One example given as a docket purchase was clogs.
42. Hargreaves and Gowing, *Civil Industry and Trade*, pp. 635–6.
43. A.M. Curtis, *Consider the Lilies: The Warden's Address to the Community on the Clothes Rationing Order of June 1st 1941* (Christian Contemplatives Charity, 1941).
44. Mass Observation, *Change 1–5 No. 1 Bulletin of the Advertising Service Guild August 1941 Clothes Rationing Survey: An Interim Report* (Advertising Services Guild, 1941), p. 57.
45. The results were:

    33% of A- and B-class women
    13% of C- and D-class women
    36% of A- and B-class men
    16% of C- and D-class men

    Ibid., p. 11.
46. Ibid., pp. 14–15.
47. Ibid., p. 28, 63.
48. Ibid., pp. 31–2, 41.
49. The following figures were for those who had never worn trousers:

    82% of Worcester women
    80% of Bolton women
    57% of London women
    38% of younger women wore trousers 'sometimes' as opposed to 18% of those over 30. In classes A and B, 37% of women wore trousers; in C, 29%, and in D, only 14%. For full details of the MO findings see Ibid., pp. 52–3.

50. Ibid., p. 55.
51. Ibid., pp. 62–4.
52. Ibid., pp. 55–7.
53. Lyttelton, *The Memoirs of Lord Chandos*, pp. 206–7.

54. BS 41/151, *Clothing Quiz*, 'Forward from the President of the Board of Trade', 1944–1945.

## CHAPTER 11 HOME FRONT CLOTHING INITIATIVES

1. *Picture Post* (17 February 1940), pp. 29–30.
2. Ibid., p. 30.
3. Ephemera Box C, 'Fashion', Imperial War Museum. Officers were provided with battle dress but not service dress (with thanks to Ron Johnson for this information). Some patterns can be dated by serial numbers, as explained in an unpublished talk by Claire Dolman, chair, West Midlands Costume Society, England.
4. Ibid., citing Margaret Watts, Honourable Secretary, Merchant Navy Comforts Service.
5. R. Broad and S. Fleming (eds.), *Nella Last's War: The Second World War Diaries of Housewife, 49* (Profile Books Ltd, 2006), p. 80.
6. Ephemera Box C, 'Fashion', Imperial War Museum. The RAFCC had been appointed by the Air Council, October 1939.
7. Ibid. See also BT 64/871, Draft Press Notice, 26 August 1941, urging knitters to 'work for the common pool run by the Navy, Army and Air Force Authorities' so that 'comforts may be distributed fairly'.
8. Ibid.
9. Ibid.
10. Ibid.
11. Ibid.
12. Ibid.
13. *Stitchcraft* (September 1940), p. 24.
14. Ibid., p. 2.
15. *Picture Post* (24 February 1940), pp. 40–1.
16. All references Ibid., pp. 40–2.
17. *Britain Is a Woman: A Tribute to the War Effort of British Women* (British Movietone, 1940), DVD, IWM, 2006.
18. *WVS (Women's Voluntary Service)* (Verity Film, 1941), DVD, IWM, 2006.
19. Ibid.
20. *Willing Hands* (World Wide Pictures, 1944), DVD, IWM, 2006.
21. PRO, BT64/3023, 'Extension of the Life of Clothing: A Preliminary Investigation into Possibilities, by a Distribution Officer', 2 July 1941, p. 1.
22. Ibid., pp. 1–2.
23. PRO, BT64/3023, 'Extension of the Life of Clothing: The Need for a National Campaign to Stimulate the Public to Remake, Mend and Renovate', 2 July 1941.

24. Ibid.
25. PRO, BT64/871, twelfth meeting Publicity Committee, agenda item 5, 9 July 1941.
26. Ibid.
27. Ibid. See also PRO, BT64/3024, 'Joint Meeting of Standing Committee of Voluntary Organisation . . .', 25 September 1941.
28. PRO, BT64/3025, 'Background Clothing Campaign . . .', 11 July 1942.
29. *Clothing Quiz*, 1944–1945, see question 39.
30. *Clothing Quiz*, August 1941, p. X. See this work, Chapter 10.
31. Ibid., see question 47.
32. PRO, BT 64/871, twelfth meeting Publicity Committee, agenda item 5.
33. R.M. Titmuss, *Problems of Social Policy* (HMSO, 1950), p. 375.
34. PRO, BT64/871, twelfth meeting Publicity Committee, agenda item 5.
35. PRO, BT64/871, minutes of sixteenth meeting Publicity Committee, 10 September 1941, pp. 1–2.
36. PRO, BT64/3024. 'Joint Meeting of Standing Conference of Voluntary Organisations and Women's Group on Public Welfare to discuss the promotion of "Make-and-Mend" Classes', 25 September 1941, p. 2. The motion was signed off on 20 October 1941.
37. PRO, BT64/3023 '"Make and Mend" Campaign', 29 September 1941, p. 1.
38. PRO, BT64/3023, letter from L. Harford (WGPW), 9 April 1942, p. 1.
39. PRO, BT64/3023, 'Women's Group on Public Welfare, Make and Mend Campaign', undated but, given context, most likely April 1942.
40. Ibid., pp. 1–2.
41. Ibid., p. 3.
42. Ibid., p. 4. Dalton became President in February 1942.
43. PRO, BT64/3025, 'Background Clothing Campaign . . .', 11 July 1942.
44. PRO, BT64/3023, untitled paper dated 9 September 1942.
45. Letter from the Rt. Hon. Hugh Dalton, MP . . . , 16 September 1942.
46. *Pathe News Reels*, London, 1942.
47. In late 1942, Home Intelligence reported relatively negatively on the campaign. Respondents cited lack of time, lack of awareness and clothing too poor to work with. See I. Zweiniger-Bargielowska, *Austerity in Britain: Rationing, Controls and Consumption, 1939–1955* (Oxford University Press, 2000), p. 121. This must be offset by the numbers actively engaged in classes or groups.
48. *Make-Do and Mend*, (First published Ministry of Information, 1943, reprinted Imperial War Museum, 1997).
49. H. Reynolds reports, 'The Board of Trade was running 12,000 Make-Do and Mend dressmaking classes in their evening and technical schools. A similar number were also run by Women's Voluntary Organisations'. See

'Your Clothes are Materials of War: The British Government Promotion of Home Sewing during the Second World War', in B. Burman, ed., *The Culture of Sewing: Gender, Consumption and Home Dressmaking* (Berg, 1999), p. 331.

50. Ibid., p. 337.
51. For more on the debate surrounding altering perspectives on femininity during the Second World War see P. Summerfield, 'The Girl That Makes the Thing That Drills the Hole That Holds the Spring . . .'; Discourses of Women and Work in the Second World War', in C. Gledhill and G. Swanson, eds., *Nationalizing Femininity: Culture, Sexuality and British Cinema in the Second World War*, pp. 35–52 (Manchester University Press, 1996).
52. Ibid., pp. 39–40.

## CHAPTER 12 CLOTHES FOR COUPONS

1. PRO, BT 64/871, 'Rationing of Clothing, Cloth and Footwear', 1 June 1941.
2. M. Felton, *Civilian Supplies in Wartime Britain* (Originally published Ministry of Information, 1945, reprinted Imperial War Museum, 1997), p. 33.
3. *Times* (2 June 1941), p. 5.
4. *Woman* (28 June 1941), in an article on saving coupons, written by Anne Edwards, p. 7.
5. BS 41/151, *Clothing Quiz,* 1 June 1941, section 9, p. v.
6. All quotations *Woman* (28 June 1941), p. 7.
7. *Vogue Pattern Book* (June–July 1939), p. 45.
8. *Woman* (28 June 1941), p. 7.
9. E. L. Hargreaves and M. M. Gowing, *Civil Industry and Trade* (HMSO, 1952), p. 331. These bandings are different from those used by Mass Observation and are as follows: A and B = well-to-do, 5%; C = middle class, 15%; D and E as suggested. See Chapter 10.
10. Ibid., p. 648. Table X, 'Personal expenditure on consumers' goods and services revalued at 1938 prices', shows that in 1938, £446 million was spent on clothing. The figures for each year thereafter were as follows: 1939, £444 million; 1940, £372 million; 1941, £275 million; 1942, £273 million; 1943, £247 million. In 1944, the figure rose to £275 million and again in 1945 to £279 million.
11. Ibid. Table X1, 'Working-class cost-of-living index (prices at 1st September 1939 = 100) showed that on 31 May 1941 just before the introduction of rationing the figure stood at 177. This rose to 191 by 1 December 1941, 195 by 1 June 1942, 181 by 1 December 1942, 168 by 1 June 1943, 164 by 1 December 1943. This proved to be the lowest figure as

prices rose slightly in 1944 to 165 and 167 respectively for June and December, staying at 167 for June 1945 and then dropping to 166 by 1 December 1945. The biggest fall in the index for clothing—27%—clearly came over the year from June 1942 to June 1943, when the full impact of the Utility cloth and clothing scheme had had time to stabilize clothing and textile prices.

12. P. Bookbinder, *Marks & Spencer: The War Years 1939–1945* (Century Benham, 1989), p. 31.
13. Wilkinson and Riddell catalogue, May 1939, the Wholesale Catalogues Archive, Walsall Museum, Hodson Shop Collection, and notes kindly sent to me by Sheila Shreeve, curator, Hodson Shop Collection.
14. Wilkinson and Riddell catalogue, April 1939, the Wholesale Catalogue Archive, Walsall Museum, Hodson Shop Collection. See also Chapter 2, footnote 74.
15. *Vogue* (25 January 1939), p. 48.
16. As at May 1941, see Chapter 7. Purchase tax on clothing also had an effect. Hancock and Gowing quote the Cost of Living Index figure for clothing as 175p, May 1941 (W.K. Hancock and M.M. Gowing, The British War Economy (HMSO, 1949) p. 335). Hargreaves and Gowing quote the Working Class Cost of Living Index figure for clothing on May 31st as 177 (see footnote 11).
17. See H. Worth, *Fashion for the People: A History of Clothing at Marks & Spencer* (Berg, 2007), p. 46. Worth does not say exactly when. The inference from Bookbinder is mid-autumn 1939. He suggests 'manufacturers' demands for extra payments to cover rising costs due to war-risks insurance, shorter hours, higher wages and material costs forced considerable increases in the business' selling prices at the end of October 1939'. Bookbinder, *Marks & Spencer*, p. 37.
18. The Walsall Museum, Hodson Shop Collection, referring to an invoice from Wilkinson and Riddell to the Hodson sisters dated 28 April 1941. Two dresses invoiced for on 1 April 1941 were priced considerably higher at 59s 6d and 57s 6d wholesale prices. This could well reflect inflation, but also that there might be customers of the Hodson Shop with greater spending capacity.
19. The *Drapers' Record* (28 February 1942), p. 14. *Drapers'* (28 February 1942), p. 28, informed their readers that a full schedule showing clothing types and maximum selling prices fixed for makers-up or wholesalers and retailers had been compiled by the Wholesale Goods, Mantles and Millinery Association Ltd and was available to its members.
20. *Picture Post* (21 June 1941), pp. 28–9.
21. Ibid., p. 29.
22. M-OA TC 18/4/E.

23. *Picture Post* (5 July 1941), pp. 26–7.
24. *Vogue* (July 1941), p. 18.
25. Ibid.
26. Ibid.
27. Ibid.
28. Ibid.
29. *Gone with the Wind*, 1939, dr. Victor Fleming. It was the 'most expensive film ever produced up to that time' and the 'most-viewed cinema film of all time' [in 1939]. See A. Gronemeyer, *Film: A Concise History* (Lawrence King, 1999), p. 78.
30. M-OA TC 18/4/E, 27 February 1942.
31. M-OA TC 18/4/F, 3 March 1942.
32. Ibid.
33. *Vogue* (July 1941), p. 18.
34. *Draper's Record* (21 June 1941), p. 6.
35. PRO BT64/3025, press handout, 11 March 1943.
36. Ibid.
37. Hargreaves and Gowing, *Civil Industry and Trade*, p. 448. Table 29 provides figures for 'Deliveries of Cotton and Rayon Cloths to the Home Market for Civilian Consumption'.
38. All figures quoted from Hargreaves and Gowing, *Civil Industry and Trade*, p. 448, Table 30, 'Proportion of Cotton and Rayon Fabric Production for Home Civilian Market represented by Utility'.
39. Hargreaves and Gowing, *Civil Industry and Trade*, p. 606. Prices of Utility wear are discussed in this work, Chapter 14. D.H. Evans's cheapest dress according to Mass Observation was fifteen shillings (M-OA TC 18/4/E, 27 February 1942). Chain store prices would be lower again pro rata and thus nearer to preinflationary prices.
40. See this work, Chapter 14.
41. M-OA TC 18/4/E, 3 March 1942.
42. Ibid., pp. 1–2.
43. M-OA TC 18/4/E, 27 February 1942, and this work, Chapter 14.
44. M-OA TC 18/4/E, 3 March 1942.

## CHAPTER 13 KEEP SMILING THROUGH

1. J. Waller and M. Vaughan-Rees, *Women in Wartime: The Role of Women's Magazines 1939–1945* (Macdonald and Co. (Publishers) Ltd, 1990), p. 12.
2. Ibid., p. 13.
3. J.B. Priestley, *Postscripts* (Heinemann, 1940), transcript of broadcast aired on 22 September 1940, p. 78.

4. Ibid., p. 79.
5. Ministry of Health, 'Foreword', *How to Keep Well in Wartime* (Ministry of Information, 1943), booklet.
6. Ibid.
7. See the work of M. Spring Rice, *Working Class Wives* (Virago, 1981), and as discussed in this work, Chapter 2.
8. Waller and Vaughan-Rees, *Women in Wartime*, p. 99.
9. A. Calder, *The People's War* (Pimlico, 1992), p. 276.
10. B. Dixon (ed.), *Good Housekeeping Wartime Scrapbook* (Collins and Brown, 2005), p. 17.
11. D. Mercer (ed.), *Chronicle of the Twentieth Century* (JL International Publications, 1993), entry for 18 February 1942, p. 562.
12. Ministry of Health, *How to Keep Well in Wartime*, p. 19.
13. BoT BS41 'Limitation of Supplies of Perfumery and Toilet Preparations (No. 2) Order 1941 No. 1686'. See also 'I Take a Look at a Black Market', *Picture Post* (27 September 1941), pp. 22–3.
14. See Waller and Vaughan-Rees, *Women in Wartime*, p. 83.
15. *Vogue* (June 1941), p. 54.
16. Ibid.
17. Ibid.
18. Waller and Vaughan-Rees, *Women in Wartime*, p. 83.
19. Ibid., p. 82.
20. Ibid.
21. Ibid., p. 83.
22. 'As He Remembers You', *Woman* (1 May 1943), p. 6.
23. Dixon, *Good Housekeeping Wartime Scrapbook*, p. 33.
24. *Vogue* (August 1941), p. 40.
25. Ibid.
26. Ministry of Health, *How to Keep Well in Wartime*, p. 11. Vitamin D was 'the anti-rickets vitamin'. Ibid., p. 5.
27. Ibid., pp. 5–6.
28. C. Wilk, 'The Healthy Body Culture', in *Modernism: Designing a New World 1914–1939* (Victoria and Albert Publications, 2006), pp. 249–96. This chapter is an excellent summary of the major ideas positioning the body in a modernist context.
29. Ibid., p. 253; pp. 253–255; p. 255.
30. Ibid., p. 253.
31. Ibid., p. 253, 255.
32. Ministry of Health, *How to Keep Well in Wartime*, pp. 4–6.
33. Wilk, 'The Healthy Body Culture', pp. 250–258.
34. J. Mulvagh, *Vogue History of Twentieth Century Fashion* (Bloomsbury Books, 1992), p. 123.

35. Waller and Vaughan-Rees, *Women in Wartime*, p. 80.
36. Mercer, *Chronicle of the Twentieth Century*, p. 562.
37. Dixon, *Good Housekeeping Wartime Scrapbook*, p. 79.
38. Waller and Vaughan-Rees, *Women in Wartime*, p. 104.
39. Ibid., p. 100.
40. J. Hartley, *Hearts Undefeated: Women's Writings of the Second World War* (Virago, 1994), p. 105.
41. *Vogue* (August 1941), p. 44.
42. Ibid.
43. Waller and Vaughan-Rees, *Women in Wartime*, p. 88.
44. Ibid.
45. Ibid.
46. See this work, Chapter 4.
47. *Picture Post* (8 April 1939), p. 67.
48. Ibid., p. 69.
49. Ibid., p. 67.
50. Ibid., p. 69.
51. A. Wauters, *Eve in Overalls* (Reprinted Imperial War Museum, 1995). Undated and without provenance but probably Ministry of Information and in circulation from later 1942, as the text refers to having been at war for three years (p. 31). Imperial War Museum Historical Pamphlets Series (No. 11), 1995, p. 10.
52. Ibid., pp. 11, 13–14.
53. Ibid., p. 14.
54. Ibid., p. 31, 29.
55. Ibid., p. 27.
56. Ibid., p. 31, 27.
57. J. B. Priestley, *British Women Go to War* (Collins, 1943), p. 31
58. Ibid., p. 44.
59. Dixon, *Good Housekeeping Wartime Scrapbook*, p. 44–5.
60. Ibid.; see also *Woman and Home* (December 1939), p. 4.
61. *Woman and Home* (January 1940), p. 55.
62. *Woman and Home* (February 1940), p. 8; *Woman and Home* (March 1940), p. 10.
63. Waller and Vaughan-Rees, *Women in Wartime*, p. 25, 31.
64. *Woman and Home* (January 1942), p. 55.
65. Ibid., p. 43.
66. See also M. Brown, *Put That Light Out: Britain's Civil Defence Services at War 1939–1945* (Sutton Publishing, 1999), pp. 15–18. for continuing air attacks on Britain
67. Wauters, *Eve in Overalls*, p. 7.
68. Ibid., pp. 7–9.

69. V. Douie, *Daughters of Britain: An Account of the Work of British Women during the Second World War* (Vincent Baxter Press, 1949), p. 75.
70. Ibid., p. 65.
71. See for example: R. Garofalo and S. Joseph, *The Memoirs of Women Who Went to War* (Pegasus VCR, Imperial War Museum, undated); M. Nicholson, *What Did You Do in the War, Mummy?* (Pimlico, 1995); Ministry of Information, on behalf of the Board of Education, *The Schools in Wartime* (Originally published by the Ministry of Information, 1941, reprinted Imperial War Museum. Historical Pamphlet Series, (no. 1) 2001.
72. Priestley, *British Women Go to War*, p. 59.
73. S. Rose, *Which People's War?: National Identity and Citizenship in Wartime Britain 1939–1945* (Oxford University Press, 2003), p. 149.

## CHAPTER 14 UTILITY AND AUSTERITY

1. Initially the specification of cottons and rayons was fixed by three-figure numbers and regulated the cheaper end of the market. See Chapter 9. See also E.L. Hargreaves and M.M. Gowing, *Civil Industry and Trade* (HMSO,1952), pp. 432–4 and 441–64, for the official history account of Utility cloth production.
2. There were 102 cotton cloths and 69 rayon. See Hargreaves and Gowing, *Civil Industry and Trade*, p. 441.
3. The style regulations, reported in the *Drapers' Record*, were introduced over a period from April to June as follows: Restrictions for underwear and nightwear (SR & O 1942, No. 658), 18 April 1942, p. 14, to come into force after 31 May; coats, jackets, skirts and slacks (SR & O 1942, No. 701), p. 14, continued p. 33, to come into force 18 May; new dress sizings (BS/BoT 1), 25 April 1942, p. 15, and a detailed sizing chart, p. 25; restrictions for dresses, blouses, jumpers, cardigans and related suits (SR & O 1942, No. 784), 2 May 1942, p. 13, continued p. 34, to come into force 20 June; restrictions on infants' and girls' (SR & O 1942, No. 785), 9 May 1942, p. 28 and 30, to come into force 1 June; rules for simplified raincoats (SR & O 1942, No. 882), 16 May 1942, p. 12, to come into force 20 June; supplementary simplifications on garments covered in SR & O 1942, No. 784, 13 June 1942, pp. 28–9; rules on the correct use of the CC41 logo (SR & O 1942, No. 1012), 20 June 1942, p. 24. A full list of these and further garment regulation orders also appear in Hargreaves and Gowing, *Civil Industry and Trade*, pp. 436–8.
4. *Drapers' Record* (15 November 1941), p. 13.
5. *Drapers' Record* (31 January 1942), p. 20.
6. *Drapers' Record* (14 February 1942), p. 26.

7. Ibid., p. 27.
8. Ibid., p. 26.
9. Ibid., pp. 26–7.
10. *Drapers' Record* (14 March 1942), p. 37.
11. *Drapers' Record* (21 March 1942), pp. 18–19.
12. MO-A TC 18/4/E, 27 February 1942.
13. MO-A TC 18/4/E, 3 March 1942.
14. Ibid.
15. See Chapter 12.
16. See Chapter 9.
17. Board of Trade Working Party Reports, Light Clothing (HMSO, 1947), p. 21.
18. *Drapers' Record* (21 February 1942), p. 13.
19. Ibid.
20. *Vogue* recorded that the Incorporated Society had asked Mrs. Reginald Fellowes to be its first President in June 1941. *Vogue* (July 1941), p. 36.
21. N. Hartnell, *Silver and Gold* (Evans Brothers, 1955), p. 103.
22. Ibid., p. 106.
23. Ibid.
24. C. McDowell, *Forties Fashion and the New Look* (Bloomsbury Books, 1997), p. 8.
25. Yoxall refers to Molyneux, Charles Creed, Bianca Mosca and Angele Delanghe. See H. A. Yoxall, *A Fashion of Life* (Heinemann, 1966), p. 71.
26. Ibid. A different story again is told by Patrick Heron about his father, Tom, of Cresta Silks. Recounting that Tom Heron went to the Board of Trade as 'Advisor on Women's and Children's Clothing', he adds, 'One of the first things Heron did at the Board of Trade was to initiate the famous Utility Clothing scheme. The first of its kind, it began with Heron personally inviting all the leading couturiers—Digby Morton, Hardy Amies, Edward Molyneux and Bianca Mosca, among them—to design a "Utility" range of clothes for a wartime population.' See P. Heron, 'Tom Heron: A Biographical Note', *Journal of the Decorative Arts Society 1890–1940* 4 (1979), pp. 34–9.
27. Ibid.
28. *Drapers' Record* (21 February 1942), p. 13.
29. Yoxall, *Fashion of Life*, p. 72.
30. MO-A TC /18/4/E, 3 March 1942.
31. MO-A TC /18/4/E, 5 March 1942.
32. MO-A TC /18/4/E, 3 March 1942.
33. Ibid. Seymour mentions Peter Russell and House of Worth. Hartnell must also have been working on Utility for Berkertex as his collection for them is revealed as part of a Utility promotion covered by *Drapers' Record* on 4 April 1942.

34. See footnote 3; Hargreaves and Gowing, *Civil Industry and Trade*, pp. 433–4.
35. MO-A TC /18/4/E, 31 March 1942.
36. Ibid.
37. Ibid. and see also C. Sladen, *The Conscription of Fashion* (Scolar Press, 1995), p. 44.
38. *Drapers' Record* (4 April 1942), pp. 14–15.
39. Ibid.
40. Ibid., p. 14.
41. See this work, Chapter 9, and this chapter, note 3.
42. McDowell, *Forties Fashion and the New Look*, p. 11.
43. Ibid.
44. Under the orders BS/BoT 1 and 2. See Hargreaves and Gowing, *Civil Industry and Trade*, p. 438; *Drapers' Record* (25 April 1942), p. 15 and 24.
45. *Drapers' Record* (13 June 1942), pp. 28–9.
46. Austerity restrictions were not removed in bulk until January 1946 for men and March to April 1948 for women. See this work, Chapter 9.
47. *Drapers' Record* (22 August 1942), p. 9.
48. *Drapers' Record* (26 September 1942), p. 10.
49. Ibid.
50. *Drapers' Record* (3 October 1942), p. 10.
51. *Picture Post* (29 August 1942), pp. 22–3.
52. Hargreaves and Gowing, *Civil Industry and Trade*, p. 434.
53. McDowell, *Forties Fashion and the New Look*, p. 8. It is likely that one of the coats in the collection is by Molyneux, as well a day dress, which, given that Yoxall saw him as the first chairman of IncSoc, is most probable (See Yoxall, *A Fashion for Life*, p. 72). This would also provide a total of eight designers as mentioned by the *Drapers' Record* (22 August 1942, p. 9). Norman Hartnell, who had already produced Utility, but not austerity, clothing for Berketrex, was not represented.
54. All three dresses from Utility prototype collection, Victoria and Albert Museum, London.
55. The dress referred to is by the manufacturer Frazerton and bears a four-figure fabric specification. This dates the garment to 1943 or beyond, when the first four-figure numbers were introduced. The dress belongs to the writer.
56. The four-figure specification number of 1009 indicated a spun rayon dress fabric. See BS/BOT 23, 'Rayon Cloths'.
57. Utility prototype collection, Victoria and Albert Museum, London.
58. I am indebted to Hilary Tipping, professional pattern cutter and Senior Lecturer in Design Translation on the BA(Hons) Fashion Design course at

the University of Westminster, for advice on the cutting and making techniques of the Utility garments described.

59. 'Fighting Trim', *Vogue* (July 1942), p. 29.
60. Corsets were also controlled by the austerity regulations; see the *Drapers' Record* (9 May 1942), p. 19, under SR & O 1942, No. 833. Amongst a number of construction and trimming restrictions corsets were to have no more than one-quarter ounce of rubber or four ounces of metal, other than in suspenders. There was to be no double body cloth or reinforced linings. This produced a less robust article that quickly wore out. For the difficulties attendant on corset production and the reasons behind poor quality as a result of shortages of heavy-duty cotton, rubber and steel, see Hargreaves and Gowing, *Civil Industry and Trade*, pp. 466–7. Corsets for medical purposes were produced, strictly controlled by permit, and Hargreaves and Gowing mention a more expensive or super utility corset, designed to a higher specification, being introduced. These did not appear to solve the problem, however, as *Vogue*, as late as December 1944, was still making a plea for better-quality corsets to replace the 'trashy belts' that failed to 'give the support they should' and were a drain on coupons and cash. See 'The Case for the Corset', *Vogue* (December 1944), p. 57.
61. D-Day was the official start of Operation Overlord, the invasion of occupied Europe by the Allied forces from the south coast of Britain. It began on 6 June 1944. See S. Badsey, *D-Day: From the Normandy Beaches to the Liberation of France* (Tiger Books International, 1994); F. Flory, *Remember 44* (Editions Ouest-France, 1994); J. Gardiner, *D-Day: Those Who Were There* (Collins and Brown, 1994).
62. *Vogue* (July 1942), p. 27.
63. Ibid.
64. *Vogue* (August 1942), p. 25.
65. Ibid.
66. *Vogue* (February 1944), p. 29.
67. Ibid.
68. *Vogue* (February 1945), pp. 29–30, 11.
69. See this chapter, note 77.
70. *Picture Post* (June 1943), pp. 24, 24–5.
71. Ibid, p. 24.
72. 'Fashions around the Corner', *Vogue* (November 1943), p. 27.
73. 'Fashion Moves', *Vogue*, p. 28, and *Picture Post* (26 February 1944), p. 23.
74. 'Fashion Is Where You Find It', *Vogue* (January 1944), p. 43.
75. N. Hartnell, *Silver and Gold*. Hartnell places the exhibition as opening in October 1944 (p. 103–5), although *Picture Post* had already reviewed

it in November 1943 (*Picture Post*, 20 November 1943, pp. 19–20), and *Vogue* refers to it having happened in their January 1944 edition (p. 43).

76. Paris was liberated on 25 August 1944. D. Mercer, ed., *Chronicle of the Twentieth Century* (JL International Publications, 1993), p. 607.
77. *Picture Post* reported in 1943 on the opulent French couture fashions for wealthy German patrons and two thousand French collaborators who had 'cartes de haute couture' and could buy any clothes from the designer houses. The article had stressed the tremendous poverty that, in contrast, was being experienced by the majority of the occupied French; see *Picture Post* (1 May 1943), pp. 10–11. For a full account of the history of the French couture under Nazi occupation see D. Veillon, *Fashion under the Occupation* (Berg, 2002). For British reporting on Paris Fashions after the liberation, see *Picture Post*, 'Paris Fashions are Quick off the Mark', 7 October 1944, p. 19; *Picture Post*, 'What a Vogue Photographer sees in Paris', 25 November 1944, pp. 12–13; *Vogue*, 'Paris 1942–1944', October 1944, pp. 30–36; *Vogue*, report on 'Paris Fashions', November 1944, pp. 36–43. There are a variety of texts that together provide a more extensive picture of the French couture's justifications for continuing to provide opulent clothing under German occupation. See in particular H. R. Lottman, 'As War Ended', and N. Gasc, 'Haute Couture and Fashion 1939–1946', both in S. Train, ed., *Theatre de la Mode* (Rizzoli, 1991); D. Veillon, 'Haute Couture on German Time' and 'Conclusion', in *Fashion under the Occupation* (Berg 2002); L. Taylor, 'Paris Couture 1940–1944', in E. Wilson and J. Ash, eds., *Chic Thrills: A Dress History Reader* (Pandora, 1993); and L. Taylor, 'The Work and Function of the Paris Couture Industry during the German Occupation of 1940–1944', *Dress: The Annual Journal of the Costume Society of America* 22 (1995).
78. *Vogue* (September 1944), pp. 31–2.
79. Ibid., p. 31.
80. See 'Vogue's View on Austerity', *Vogue* (November 1944), p. 25.
81. See *Vogue* (November 1944), pp. 36–43, reporting that Paris was showing 'simpler clothes than those made under the occupation'.
82. *Vogue* (March 1945), p. 31.
83. Ibid.
84. Ibid.

# Bibliography


## PRIMARY SOURCES

### ARCHIVE COLLECTIONS

British Library, Board of Trade Archives; *Clothing Quizzes* 1941–1947; Orders; and Miscellaneous Circulars and Memoranda 1939–1945.

Imperial War Museum, Department of Documents, Ephemera 1941–1943; Photography, Fashion and Dress 1941–1945; Film and Video 1940–1945.

Mass Observation Archive, University of Sussex, Topic Collections (various) 1938–1945.

National Archives, Board of Trade Archives 1939–1945.

National Newspaper Library, magazines and journals 1939–1945.

University of Westminster, *Picture Post* 1938–1945.

Westminster Central Reference Library, *Vogue* 1938–1945.

### MUSEUM DRESS COLLECTIONS

Imperial War Museum

Victoria and Albert Museum, Department of Textiles and Dress, Utility Prototype Collection

Walsall Museum, Dress Collection and the Hodson Shop Collection

Worthing Museum and Art Gallery Costume Collection

### NEWSPAPERS AND JOURNALS OF THE PERIOD

*Drapers' Record*

*Film Fashionland*

*Financial News*

*Home Chats*

*Housewife*

*Journal of the Decorative Arts Society*

*Manchester Guardian*

*Picture Post*

*Tailor and Cutter*

*Times*

*Vogue* (British)

*Woman*

*Woman's Own*

## BOOKS, ARTICLES, PAMPHLETS

Barlow, Sir T. (1944), 'The Conception, Birth and Development of Utility Fabrics', *Journal of the Society of Dyers and Colourists*, 60 (March).

British Information Services (1943, September), *British Youth Answers the Call*, reprinted 2005 (New York), Historical Pamphlet Series No. 9, London: Imperial War Museum.

British Library papers from the Board of Trade (BS 41/151).

Board of Trade (annual 1941–1947), *Clothing Quiz*, London: HMSO.

Board of Trade (1941, August), 'Getting Ready for Baby', Leaflet No. 1, Ephemera Box C K74105, London: Imperial War Museum, HMSO.

Board of Trade Working Party Reports: Light Clothing, London: HMSO, 1947.

Committee of the Council for Fine Art and Industry (1945), 'Design and the Designer in the Dress Trade', London: HMSO.

Felton, M. (1945), *British Achievements of the War Years. Civilian Supplies in Wartime Britain*, reprinted 2007 (London: Ministry of Information), Historical Pamphlet Series No. 5, London: Imperial War Museum.

Hancock, J., and Gowing, M. M. (1949), *British War Economy*, London: HMSO.

Hargreaves, E. L., and Gowing, M. M. (1951), *Civil Industry and Trade*, London: HMSO.

Henderson, D. (1947), 'Post script: Concentration—Success or Failure?', in G.D.N. Worswick, *Studies in War Economics*, Oxford: Oxford University Institute of Statistics/Basil Blackwell.

Hurstfield, J. (1953), *The Control of Raw Materials*, London: HMSO.

Imperial War Museum Archives, Box C, 'Fashion Ephemera', includes: ration cards, examples of *Stitchcraft*, *Housewife*, *Weldons Ladies' Journal*; Weldon's *Win-the-War* and *Go-to-it* series, Board of Trade leaflet on 'Make-do and Mend'.

'Impresario' (1944, 31 March), *The Market Square. The Story of the Food Ration Book 1940–1944*, reprinted 1997 (London: Ministry of Information), Historical Pamphlet Series No. 6, London: Imperial War Museum.

Mass Observation Archive (M-OA), TC 18, Boxes 1–5, 'Personal Appearance and Clothes', University of Sussex.

Ministry of Information, for the Board of Education (1941), *The Schools in Wartime*, reprinted 2001 (London, HMSO), Historical Pamphlet Series No. 1, London: Imperial War Museum.

Ministry of Information, for the Board of Trade (1943), *Make Do and Mend*, reprinted 1997 (London, HMSO), Historical Pamphlet Series No. 4, London: Imperial War Museum.

Ministry of Information, for the Ministry of Food (1943), *Wise Eating in Wartime from the Ministry of Food's Kitchen Front Broadcasts*, reprinted 2002 (London, HMSO), Historical Pamphlet Series No. 7, London: Imperial War Museum.

Ministry of Information, for the Ministry of Health (1943), *How to Keep Well in Wartime*, reprinted 2005 (London: HMSO), Historical Pamphlet Series No. 11, London: Imperial War Museum.

Ministry of Information (September 1943, revised December 1943, April 1945), *Home Front Handbook*, reprinted 2005 (London: HMSO), Historical Pamphlet Series No. 11, London: Imperial War Museum.

Public Record Office Board of Trade, BT64, Industries and Manufacturers Department: Correspondence and Papers, Kew.

Titmuss, R.M. (1950), *Problems of Social Policy*, London: HMSO.

Wadsworth, H.E. (1948), 'The Utility Cloth and Clothing Scheme', *Review of Economic Studies*, 16/40.

Wauters, A. (late 1942, undated and without provenance), *Eve in Overalls*, reprinted 1995, Historical Pamphlet Series No. 2, London: Imperial War Museum.

## OTHER MEDIA

*Britannia Is a Woman: A Tribute to the War Effort of British Women* (1940), British Movietone News, Imperial War Museum Official Collection: Women and Children at War (2006), written by G. Sangerand and R. Landon.

*Diary for Timothy* (1945), Crown Film Unit, directed by H. Jennings.

*The Heart of Britain* (1941), Crown Film Unit, directed by H. Jennings.

*Hope and Glory* (1987), Columbia Pictures, directed by J. Boorman.

*I.T.M.A. It's That Man Again* (selected broadcasts 1939–1949), BBC Radio Collection, produced by F. Worsley.

Langley Moore, D. (recorded 1986), *The People's War*, Sound Archive, Imperial War Museum Vol. 44.

*Let the People Sing* (1942), British National, directed by J. Baxter.

*Listen to Britain* (1942), Crown Film Unit, directed by H. Jennings.

*Memoirs of Women Who Went to War* (undated), Classic Pictures Entertainment Ltd, produced by R. Garofalo.

*Millions Like Us* (1943), GFD/Gainsborough Pictures, directed by F. Launder and S. Gilliat.

*Mrs Miniver* (1942), MGM, directed by W. Wyler.

Pathe News (1939–1945), *A Year to Remember*, originally produced by British Pathe News, reproduced 1990 (London: Parkfield Publications).

*The Second World War in Colour* (1999), Carlton Television Ltd, series produced by S. Binns.

*Things to Come* (1936), London Films, directed by W.C. Menzies.

*This Happy Breed* (1944), GFD/Two Cities/Cinegold, directed by D. Lean.

*Through the Looking Glass* (1989), BBC TV, produced by S. Davies and R. Albury.

*Triumph of Will* (1935), N.S.D.A.P., directed by L. Riefenstahl.

*Willing Hands* (1944), World Wide Pictures for Ministry of Information, Imperial War Museum Official Collection: Women and Children at War, 2006, directed by Mary Francis.

*WVS Women's Voluntary Services* (1941), A Verity Film for the Ministry of Information, Imperial War Museum Official Collection: Women and Children at War, 2006, directed by L. Birt, commentary written by R. Howe.

## SECONDARY SOURCES

Ackroyd, P. (2002), *The Origins of the English Imagination*, London: Chatto and Windus.

Ady, P. (1942, 31 October), 'Utility Goods', *Bulletin*, 4/15.

Amies, H. (1984), *Still Here*, London: Weidenfeld and Nicolson.

Ardizzone, E., and Gorham, M. (2010), *The Local*, Dorset: Little Toller Books (first published 1939, Cassell and Co. Ltd).

Atkins, J. M. (ed.) (2005), *Wearing Propaganda: Textiles on the Home Front in Japan, Britain, and the United States, 1931–1945*, New Haven, CT, and London: Yale University Press.

Attfield, J. (ed.) (1999), *Utility Reassessed: The Role of Ethics in the Practice of Design,* Manchester: Manchester University Press.

Attfield, J., and Kirkham, P. (1989), 'Women and the Inter-War Handicrafts Revival' in *A View from the Interior: Feminism, Women and Design*, London: Women's Press.

Badsey, S. (1994), *D-Day: From the Normandy Beaches to the Liberation of France*, London: Tiger Books International.

Bates, H. E. (1994), *Flying Bombs over England*, Westerham: Froglet Publications Ltd.

Bayliss, M. (1997), 'My Wartime Clothes at St. Hilda's 1943–1947', unpublished manuscript given to author.

Beaton, C., and Hardy, W. (1954), *The Glass of Fashion*, London: Weidenfeld and Nicolson.

Beaven, B., and Griffiths, J. (1998), *Mass-Observation and Civilian Morale: Working Class Communities during the Blitz 1940–1941*, Falmer: University of Sussex.

Beddoe, D. (1989), *Back to Home and Duty: Women between the Wars 1918–1939*, London: Pandora.

Berry, S. (2000), *Screen Style Fashion and Femininity in 1930's Hollywood*, London: University of Minnesota Press.

Betjeman, J. (1986), *The Best of Betjeman*, London: Penguin Books.

Bevan, J. (2007), *The Rise and Fall of Marks & Spencer and How it Rose Again*, London: Profile Books.

Bookbinder, P. (1989), *Marks & Spencer: The War Years 1939–1945*, London: Century Banham.

Braybon, G., and Summerfield, P. (1987), *Out of the Cage: Women's Experiences in Two World Wars*, London: Pandora.

Brayley, M., and Ingram, R. (1995), *World War II British Women's Uniforms*, London: Windrow and Greene Ltd.

Brendon, P. (2000), *The Dark Valley: A Panorama of the 1930s*, London: Jonathan Cape.

Breward, C. (1995), *The Culture of Fashion*, Manchester: Manchester University Press.

Breward, C., Conekin, B., and Cox, C. (eds.) (2002), *The Englishness of English Dress*, Oxford: Berg.

Breward, C., Ehrman, E., and Evans, C. (2004), *The London Look: Fashion from Street to Catwalk*, London: Yale University Press in association with Museum of London.

Briggs, A. (2000), *Go To It! Working for Victory on the Home Front 1939–1945*, London: Mitchell Beazley in association with Imperial War Museum.

Briggs, A. (1984), *Marks & Spencer Limited 1884–1984: A Centenary History*, London: Octopus.

Briggs, S. (1975), *Keep Smiling Through: Home Front 1939–1945*, London: Weidenfeld and Nicolson.

British Universities Film and Video Council (2008), *Projecting Britain: The Guide to British Cinemagazines*, London: BUFVC Publication.

Brittain, V. (1988), *Testament of a Peace Lover: Letters from Vera Brittain*, London: Virago.

Brittain, V. (1979), *Testament of Experience*, London: Virago.

Brittain, V. (1989), *Vera Brittain's Diary 1939–1945*, London: Victor Gollancz Ltd.

Broad, R., and Fleming, S. (eds.) (2006), *Nella Last's War: The Second World War Diaries of Housewife, 49*, London: Profile Books Ltd.

Brown, M. (1999), *Put That Light Out! Britain's Civil Defence Services at War 1939–1945*, Stroud: Sutton Publishing.

Buckley, C., and Fawcett, H. (2002), *Fashioning the Feminine: Representation and Women's Fashion from the Fin de Siecle to the Present*, London: I.B. Taurus and Co. Ltd.

Burman, B. (ed.) (1999), *The Culture of Sewing: Gender, Consumption and Home Dressmaking*, Oxford: Berg.

Burman, B., and Leventon, M. (1987), 'The Men's Dress Reform Party 1929–1937', in *Costume: Journal of the Costume Society,* No. 21, pp. 75-87, London: Costume Society.

Calder, A. (1992), *The Myth of the Blitz*, London: Pimlico.

Calder, A. (1994), *The People's War: Britain 1939–1945*, London: Pimlico.

Calvocoressi, P., Wint, G., and Pritchard, J. (1989), *Total War: The Western Hemisphere*, vol. 1, *The Causes and Courses of the Second World War*, London: Penguin.

Cannadine, D. (ed.) (1989), *The Speeches of Winston Churchill*, London: Penguin.

Carroll, D. (1999), *The Home Guard*, Stroud: Sutton Publishing Ltd.

Carter, M. (2003), *Fashion Classics from Carlyle to Barthes*, Oxford: Berg.

Cartland, B. (1943), *The Isthmus Years*, London: Hutchinson and Co. Ltd.

Channon, H. (1967), *Chips: The Diaries of Sir Henry Channon*, London: Weidenfeld and Nicolson.

Chapman, S. (1990), 'The Decline and Rise of Textile Merchanting 1880–1990', *Business History*, 32/4.

Chinn, C. (1988), *They Worked All Their Lives*, Manchester: Manchester University Press.

Chislett, H. (2009), *Marks in Time: 125 Years of Marks & Spencer*, London: Weidenfeld and Nicolson

Clark, J., and de la Haye, A. (2009), *Jaeger 125,* London: Jaeger.

Cooke, D. (ed.) (1944), *Youth Organisations of Great Britain 1944–1945*, Bristol: Jordan and Sons Ltd.

Curtis, A.M., (1941),*Consider the Lillies of the Field: The Warden's Address to the Community on the Clothes Rationing Order of June 1st 1941*, Dorset: Christian Contemplatives Charity.

Dalton, H. (1957), *The Fateful Years: Memoirs 1931–1945*, London: Frederick Muller Ltd.

De Courcy, A. (1989), *1939: The Last Season*, London: Thames and Hudson

De la Haye, A. (1993), 'The Dissemination of Design from Haute Couture to Fashionable Ready-to-Wear during the 1920s, with Special Reference to the Hodson Dress Shop in Willenhall', *Textile History,* 24/1.

De la Haye, A. (2009), *Land Girls: Cinderellas of the Soil*, Brighton: Royal Pavilion and Museums.

de Marly, D. (1990), *Dior*, London: Batsford.

Dior, C. (1957), *Dior by Dior*, London: Weidenfeld and Nicolson.

Dixon, B. (ed.) (2005), *Good Housekeeping Wartime Scrapbook*, London: Collins and Brown.

Dobbs, S.P. (1928), *The Clothing Workers of Great Britain*, London: Routledge and Sons Ltd.

Douie, V. (1949), *Daughters of Britain: An Account of the Work of British Women during the Second World War*, Oxford: Vincent Baxter Press.

du Maurier, D. (1931), *The Loving Spirit*, London: Heinemann, reprinted 2004 (London: Virago).

du Maurier, D. (1938), *Rebecca*, London: Victor Gollancz, reprinted 2004 (London: Virago).

Evans, H. (1998), *The American Century: People, Power and Politics. An Illustrated History*, London: Jonathan Cape/Pimlico.

Ewing, E., revised by Mackrell, A. (2001), *History of Twentieth Century Fashion*, London: Batsford.

Flory, F. (1994), *Remember 44*, Rennes: Editions Ouest-France.

Fox, C. (1988), *Dame Laura Knight*, Oxford: Phaidon.

Franks, C. (undated c. 1930s), *The Pictorial Guide to Modern Home Dressmaking*, London: Odhams Press Ltd.

Fussell, P. (1980), *Abroad. British Literary Traveling between the Wars*, Oxford: Oxford University Press.

Gardiner, J. (1994), *D-Day: Those Who Were There*, London: Collins and Brown.

Garfield, S. (2006), *We Are at War: The Diaries of Five Ordinary People in Extraordinary Times*, London: Ebury Press.

Gilbert, M. (1995), *Second World War*, London: Phoenix Giant.

Glancy, H.M. (1999), *When Hollywood Loved Britain: The Hollywood 'British' Film 1939–1945*, Manchester: Manchester University Press.

Gledhill, C., and Swanson, G. (eds.) (1996), *Nationalizing Femininity: Culture, Sexuality and British Cinema in the Second World War*, Manchester: Manchester University Press.

Glover, E. (1940), *The Psychology of Fear and Courage*, Harmondsworth: Penguin.

Godley, A. (1994–1995), 'The Emergence of Mass Production in the UK Clothing Industry', *University of Reading, Department of Economics Series A*, 7/291.

Graves, R., and Hodge, A. (1940), *The Long Weekend: A Social History of Great Britain 1918–1939*, London: Faber and Faber, reprinted 1985 (London: Hutchinson).

Greenwood, W. (1933), *Love on the Dole*, London: Jonathan Cape, reprinted 1966.

Greenwood, W. (1967), *There Was a Time*, London: Jonathan Cape.

Gregg, J. (2001), *The Shelter of the Tubes: Tube Sheltering in Wartime London*, London: Capital Transport Publishing.

Gronemeyer, A. (1999), *Film: A Concise History*, London: Laurence King.

Gropius, W. (1968), *The New Architecture and the Bauhaus*, London: Faber and Faber Ltd., first published 1935.

Guenther, I. (2004), *Nazi Chic: Fashioning Women in the Third Reich*, Oxford: Berg.

Hackney, F. (2006), '"Use Your Hands for Happiness." Home Craft and Make-do-and-Mend in British Women's Magazines in the 1920s and 1930s', *Journal of Design History*, 19/1.

Hall, S., and Jefferson, T. (1993), *Resistance through Rituals: Youth Subcultures in Post-War Britain*, London: Routledge.

Harris, C. (2003), *Women at War in Uniform 1939–1945*, Stroud: Sutton Publishing Ltd.

Harrison, T., and Madge, C. (1940), *War Begins at Home*, London: Chatto and Windus.

Hartley, J. (1994), *Hearts Undefeated: Women's Writings of the Second World War*, London: Virago.

Hartnell, N. (1955), *Silver and Gold*, London: Evans Brothers.

Haste, C. (1992), *Rules of Desire: Sex in Britain World War I to the Present*, London: Chatto and Windus.

Hays, N., and Hill, J. (eds.) (1999), *Millions Like Us: British Culture in the Second World War*, Liverpool: Liverpool University Press.

Heron, P. (1979), 'Tom Heron: A Biographical Note', *Journal of the Decorative Arts Society 1890–1940*, 4.

Hillier, B. (1975), *Austerity Binge: The Decorative Arts of the Forties and Fifties*, London: Studio Vista.

Hilton, J. (1944), *Rich Man, Poor Man (The Sir Halley Stewart Lectures, 1938)*, London: Allen and Unwin Ltd.

Honeyman, K. (1993), 'Montague Burton Ltd: The Creators of Well-Dressed Men', in J. Chartres and K. Honeyman (eds), *Leeds City Businesses 1893–1993: Essays Marking the Centenary of the Incorporation*, Leeds: Leeds University Press.

Hopkins, H. (1963), *The New Look: A Social History of the Forties and Fifties in Britain*, London: Secker and Warburg.

Horseman, G. (1997), *Growing Up in the Forties*, London: Constable and Company Ltd.

Horseman, G. (1994), *Growing Up in the Thirties*, Bovey Tracey: Cottage Publishing.

Ibberson, D., for the Women's Group for Public Welfare (1943), *Our Towns*, Oxford: Oxford University Press.

Jefferys, J.B. (1954), *Retail Trading in Britain 1850–1950*, Cambridge: Cambridge University Press.

Jenkins, I. (1953), *The History of the Women's Institute Movement of England and Wales*, Oxford: Oxford University Press.

Jephcott, A.P. (1942), *Girls Growing Up: A Study of the Lives of Young Working Girls*, London: Faber and Faber Ltd.

Johnson, K.P., Torntore, S.J., and Eicher, J.B. (eds.) (2003), *Fashion Foundations: Early Writings on Fashion and Dress*, Oxford: Berg.

Kaes, A., Jay, M., and Dimendberg, E. (eds.) (1994), *The Weimar Republic Source Book*, London: University of California Press.

Kennet, S., Naden, D., and Stamp, R. (1989), *The Day War Broke Out*, London: Marshall Cavendish.

Kidwell, C.B., and Steele, V. (1989), *Men and Women: Dressing the Past*, Washington: Smithsonian Institute Press.

Lang, C. (1989), *Keep Smiling Through: Women in the Second World War*, Cambridge: Cambridge University Press.

Lovell, M.S. (2003), *The Mitford Girls: The Biography of an Extraordinary Family*, London: Abacus.

Lyttelton, O. (1962), *The Memoirs of Lord Chandos*, London: Bodley Head.

McDonough, F. (2002), *Hitler, Chamberlain and Appeasement*, Cambridge: Cambridge University Press.

McDonough, F. (1999), *Hitler and Nazi Germany*, Cambridge: Cambridge University Press.

McDowell, C. (1997), *Fashion Forties and the New Look*, London: Bloomsbury.

McLaine, I. (1979), *Ministry of Morale: Home Front Morale and the Ministry of Information in World War Two*, London: Allen and Unwin.

McNeil, P. (1993), '"Put Your Best Face Forward": The Impact of the Second World War on British Dress', *Journal of Design History*, 6/4.

Mens' Wear (1930), *Yearbook and Diary 1930*, London: Mens' Wear.

Mercer, D. (ed.) (1993), *Chronicle of the Twentieth Century*, Farnborough: JL Publications.

Miall, A.M. (1934), *Making Clothes for Children. Every Mother's Practical Guide to the Art of Making and Mending for the Children from Babyhood to Adolescence*, London: Pitman and Son, reprinted 1946.

Minns, R. (2001), *Bombers and Mash: The Domestic Front 1939–1945*, London: Virago.

Mitchell, W.R. (1993), *By Gum, Life Were Sparse!: Memories of the Northern Mill Towns*, London: Warner.

Mollo, A. (2000), *The Armed Forces of World War Two*, London: Greenwich Editions.

Morgan, A.E. (1943), *Young Citizen*, Harmodsworth: Penguin.

Mulvagh, J. (1992), *Vogue History of Twentieth Century Fashion*, London: Bloomsbury Books.

Nicholson, M. (1995), *What Did You Do in the War, Mummy?* London: Pimlico.

Ogley, B. (1995), *Doodlebugs and Rockets: The Battle of the Flying Bombs*, Westerham: Froglets Publications.

O'Hara, G. (1989), *The Encyclopaedia of Fashion: From 1840 to the 1980s*, London: Thames and Hudson.

Oliver, P., Davis, I., and Bentley, I. (1981), *Dunroamin: The Suburban Semi and Its Enemies*, London: Barrie and Jenkins.

O'Neil, G. (1999), *My East End: A History of Cockney London*, London: Viking.

Orwell, G. (2000), *Coming Up for Air*, London: Penguin Classics.

Orwell, G. (2000), *Keep the Aspidistra Flying*, London: Penguin Classics.

Orwell, G. (1967), *The Road to Wigan Pier*, Harmondsworth: Penguin.

Osley, A. (1995), *Persuading the People: Government Publicity in the Second World War*, London: HMSO.

Ostick, E. (undated c. 1930s), *What You Should Know about Cloth*, London: Tailor and Cutter.

Panter-Downes, M. (2002), *Good Evening, Mrs Craven: The Wartime Stories of Mollie Panter-Downes*, London: Persephone Books.

Pantin, E. (1943), *Preparing for Motherhood and Training in Infancy and Childhood*, London: Thorson Publishing.

Patten, M. (1995), *The Victory Cookbook*, London: Hamlyn.

Penrose, A. (ed.) (2005), *Lee Miller's War*, Bath: Palazzo Editions Ltd.

Pine, L. (1999), *Nazi Family Policy 1933–1945*, Oxford: Berg.

Pochner, M. (1996), *Christian Dior: The Man Who Made the World Look New*, New York: New Arcade Publishing.

Powell, A. (ed.) (1999), *Shadows of War: British Women's Poetry of the Second World War*, Stroud: Sutton Publishing.

Priestley, J. B. (1942), *Black-Out in Gretley*, London: Heinemann.

Priestley, J. B. (1941), *Britain Under Fire*, London: Country Life Ltd.

Priestley, J. B. (1943), *British Women Go to War*, London: Collins.

Priestley, J. B. (1943), *Daylight on Saturday: A Novel about an Aircraft Factory*, London: Heinemann.

Priestley, J. B. (1994), *English Journey: Being a Rambling but Truthful Account of What One Man Saw and Heard and Felt and Thought during a Journey through England during the Autumn of the Year 1933*, London: Mandarin.

Priestley, J. B. (1939), *Let the People Sing*, London: Heinemann.

Priestley, J. B. (1940), *Postscripts*, London: Heinemann.

Priestley, J. B. (1945), *Three Men in New Suits*, London: Heinemann.

Ransome, A. (2001), *Swallows and Amazons*, London: Red Fox.

Rees, G. (1966), *St. Michael: A History of Marks & Spencer*, London: Weidenfeld and Nicolson.

Reynolds, D. (2000), *Rich Relations: The American Occupation of Britain 1942–1945*, London: Phoenix Press.

Reynolds, F. (1999), 'The Utility Garment: Its Design and Effect on the Mass Market 1942–1945', in J. Attfield (ed.), *Utility Reassessed: The Role of Ethics in the Practice of Design,* Manchester: Manchester University Press.

Reynolds, F. (1999), '"Your Clothes are the Materials of War": The British Government Promotion of Home Sewing during the Second World War', in B. Burman, (ed.), *The Culture of Home Sewing*, Oxford: Berg.

Riley, D. (1983), *War in the Nursery: Theories of the Child and Mother*, London: Virago.

Robins, P. (2004), *Under Fire: Children of the Second World War Tell Their Stories*, London: Scholastic Press.

Robinson, H. (undated c. 1930s), *Behind the Scenes at Moss Bross*, Holborn: A. J. Owen.

Rodger, G. (1990), *The Blitz: The Photography of George Rodger*, London: Penguin.

Roiser, M. (2001), 'Social Psychology and Social Concern in 1930s Britain', in G. C. Bunn, A. D. Lovie, and G. D. Richards, *Psychology in Britain: Historical Essays and Personal Reflections*, Leicester: BPS Books.

Rose, S. O. (2003), *Which People's War?: National Identity and Citizenship in Wartime Britain 1939–1945*, Oxford: Oxford University Press.

Rowntree, B. S. (1941), *Poverty and Progress: A Second Social Survey of York*, London: Longmans, Green and Co.

Samuel, R. (1983, May/June), 'Suburbs under siege: The middle class between the wars', Part III, *New Socialist*, 11.

Samways, R. (1945), *We Think You Ought to Go. An Account of the Evacuation of Children from London during the Second World War Based on the Original Records of the London County Council*, London: Public Relations Office, Corporation of London.

Scott, G. (1998), *Feminism and the Politics of Working Women: The Women's Co-Operative Guild 1880s to the Second World War*, London: UCL Press.

Selwyn, V. (ed.) (1996), *The Voice of War: Poems of the Second World War*, London: Penguin.

Settle, A. (1937), *Clothes Line*, London: Methuen and Company.

Sheridan, D. (1990, Spring), 'Ambivalent Memories: Women and the 1939–1945 War in Britain', in 'Popular Memory', *Oral History*, 18/1, pp. 32–40.

Sheridan, D. (1990), *Wartime Women: A Mass Observation Anthology*, London: Heinemann.

Sheridan, D., and Calder, A. (1984), *Speak for Yourself: A Mass Observation Anthology 1937–1947*, London: Jonathan Cape.

Shipman, D. (1993), *Cinema: The First Hundred Years*, London: QPD.

Sieff, I. (1970), *Memoirs*, London: Weidenfeld and Nicolson.

Sladen, C. (1995), *The Conscription of Fashion: Utility Cloth, Clothing and Footwear 1941–1952*, Aldershot: Scolar Press.

Smith, H. L. (ed.) (1986), *War and Social Change: British Society in the Second World War*, Manchester: Manchester University Press.

Smith, M. (2000), *Britain and 1940: History, Myth and Popular Memory*, London: Routledge.

Spender, H. (1982), *Worktown People: Photographs from Northern England 1937–1938*, Bristol: Falling Wall Press.

Spotts, F. (2003), *Hitler and the Power of Aesthetics*, London: Pimlico.

Spring Rice, M. (1939), *Working Class Wives: Their Health and Conditions*, reprinted 1981 (London: Virago), Harmondsworth: Penguin.

Stack, P. (1984), *Zest for Life*, London: Athlone Press.

Steele, V. (1991), *Women of Fashion: Twentieth Century Designers*, New York: Rizzoli International Publications.

Stevenson, J. (1984), *The Pelican Social History of Britain: British Society 1914–1945*, Harmondsworth: Penguin.

Streatfield, N. (1945), *Saplings*, London: Collins.

Struther, J. (1939), *Mrs Miniver*, London: Chatto and Windus.

Sword, R. (1974), *CC41 Utility Furniture and Fashion 1941–1951*, London: Inner London Education Authority.

Taylor, A.J.P. (1978), *The War Lords*, London: Penguin.

Taylor, L. (2004), *Establishing Dress History*, Manchester: Manchester University Press.

Taylor, L. (1993), 'Paris Couture 1940–1944', in E. Wilson and J. Ash, *Chic Thrills: A Dress History Reader*, London: Pandora.

Taylor, L. (2002), *The Study of Dress History*, Manchester: Manchester University Press.

Taylor, L. (1995), 'The Work and Function of the Paris Couture Industry during the German Occupation of 1940–1944', *Dress: The Annual Journal of the Costume Society of America*, 22.

Tebbutt, M. (1983), *Making Ends Meet: Pawnbroking and Working Class Credit*, Leicester: Leicester University Press.

Thaarup, A., in collaboration with Shackwell, D. (1956), *Heads and Tails*, London: Cassell.

Thesander, M. (1997), *The Feminine Ideal*, London: Reaktion Books Ltd.

Thomas, J. (1955, January), 'A History of the Leeds Clothing Industry', in *Yorkshire Bulletin of Economic and Social Research, Occasional Paper No. 1*, Leeds: Departments of Economics of the Universities of Hull, Leeds and Sheffield.

Thomas, P.A. (1988), *Post-War Hopes and Expectations and Reaction to the Beveridge Report*, Falmer: Mass Observation, University of Sussex.

Train, S. (1991), *Theatre de la Mode*, New York: Rizzoli.

Turner, E.S. (1961), *The Phoney War on the Home Front*, London: Michael Joseph.

Van Caudenberg, A., and Heymen, H. (2004, March), 'The Rational Kitchen in the Interwar Period in Belgium: Discourses in Realities', *Home Cultures,* 1/1.

Veillon, D. (2002), *Fashion under the Occupation*, Oxford: Berg.

Wainwright, D. (1996), *The British Tradition: Simpson—a World of Style*, London: Quiller Press.

Waddell, G. (2004), *How Fashion Works Couture, Ready-to-Wear and Mass Production*, Oxford: Blackwell Science Ltd.

Walford, J. (2008), *The Fashion Forties: From Siren Suit to New Look*, London: Thames and Hudson.

Waller, J. (2006), *Knitting Fashions of the 1940s: Styles, Patterns and History*, Marlborough: Crowood Press.

Waller, J., and Vaughan-Rees, M. (1990), *Women in Wartime: The Role of Women's Magazines 1939–1945*, London: Macdonald and Co. Ltd.

Watson, W. (2009), *Miss Pettigrew Lives for a Day*, London: Persephone Books, first published 1938 (Methuen).

Wells, H. G. (1898), *The War of the Worlds*, London: Heinemann Ltd.

Wilk, C. (ed.) (2006), *Modernism: Designing a New World 1914–1939*, London: Victoria and Albert Publications.

Wilson, E., and Taylor, L. (1989), *Through the Looking Glass: A History of Dress from 1860 to the Present Day*, London: BBC Books.

Worth, R. (2007), *Fashion for the People: A History of Clothing at Marks & Spencer*, Oxford: Berg.

Wray, M. (1957), *The Women's Outerwear Industry*, London: Duckworth and Co. Ltd.

Yoxall, H. A. (1966), *A Fashion of Life*, London: Heinemann.

Ziegler, P. (1998), *London at War 1939–1945*, London: Arrow Books.

Zweiniger-Bargielowska, I. (2000), *Austerity Britain: Rationing, Controls and Consumption 1939–1955*, Oxford: Oxford University Press.

# Index

Numbers in Italics indicate references to photos.